# THE NEW GROVE
# FRENCH BAROQUE

THE NEW GROVE
DICTIONARY OF MUSIC AND MUSICIANS
*Editor: Stanley Sadie*

# The Composer Biography Series

BACH FAMILY
BEETHOVEN
EARLY ROMANTIC MASTERS 1
EARLY ROMANTIC MASTERS 2
FRENCH BAROQUE MASTERS
HANDEL
HAYDN
HIGH RENAISSANCE MASTERS
ITALIAN BAROQUE MASTERS
LATE ROMANTIC MASTERS
MASTERS OF ITALIAN OPERA
MODERN MASTERS
MOZART
NORTH EUROPEAN BAROQUE MASTERS
RUSSIAN MASTERS 1
RUSSIAN MASTERS 2
SCHUBERT
SECOND VIENNESE SCHOOL
TURN OF THE CENTURY MASTERS
TWENTIETH-CENTURY ENGLISH MASTERS
TWENTIETH-CENTURY FRENCH MASTERS
WAGNER

THE NEW GROVE®

# French Baroque Masters

## LULLY CHARPENTIER LALANDE COUPERIN RAMEAU

James R. Anthony
H. Wiley Hitchcock
Edward Higginbottom
Graham Sadler
Albert Cohen

## W. W. NORTON & COMPANY
NEW YORK      LONDON

First published in
The New Grove Dictionary of Music and Musicians ®,
edited by Stanley Sadie, 1980

British Library Cataloguing in Publication Data

French Baroque Masters: Lully, Charpentier, Lalande,
    Couperin, Rameau.—(The Composer biography series)
    1. Composers—France   2. Music—France—
    17th century—History and criticism   3. Music—
    France—18th century—History and criticism
    I. Anthony, James R.   II. The new Grove dictionary
    of music and musicians       III. Series
    780′.92′2      ML270.2

First American edition in book form with additions 1986 by
W. W. NORTON & COMPANY
500 Fifth Avenue, New York NY 10110

ISBN 0-393-30356-x

Printed in the United States of America

1 2 3 4 5 6 7 8 9 0

# Contents

# List of illustrations

## Illustration acknowledgments

We are grateful to the following for permission to reproduce illustrative material: Royal College of Music, London (figs.1, 15); Richard Macnutt, Tunbridge Wells (figs.2, 20, 26); Bärenreiter-Verlag, Kassel (fig.3); Bibliothèque Nationale, Paris (figs.4, 6, 7, 10, 11, 14, 21, 23, 25); Museum of Fine Arts (gift of Elizabeth Paine Cardin), Boston (fig.5); Photographie Bulloz, Paris (fig.8); Österreichische Nationalbibliothek (Fonds Albertina), Vienna (fig.9); Fitzwilliam Museum, Cambridge (fig.13); Mansell Collection, London (fig.16); British Library, London (figs.17, 18); Musée de Beaux-Arts, Dijon (fig.19); Museo Teatrale alla Scala, Milan (fig.22); Lauros Giraudon, Paris (cover).

## A note on the numbering of psalms

The psalms are numbered according to the Revised Standard Version of the Bible (which follows the Hebrew (Masoretic) system). Where, in the title of a work, a composer uses the number that is used in the Latin (Vulgate) bible and where this number differs from that in the RSV, the work-list citation includes the RSV number in brackets.

Symbols for the library sources of works, printed in *italic*, correspond to those used in *Répertoire International des Sources Musicales*, Ser. A.

# General abbreviations

| | | | |
|---|---|---|---|
| A | alto, contralto [voice] | ob | oboe |
| addn | addition | org | organ |
| arr. | arrangement, arranged by/for | orig. | original(ly) |
| | | ov. | overture |
| attrib. | attribution, attributed to | perf. | performance, performed by |
| B | bass [voice] | | |
| b | bass [instrument] | pr. | printed |
| *b* | born | prol | prologue |
| Bar | baritone [voice] | Ps | Psalm |
| bc | basso continuo | pt. | part |
| bn | bassoon | pubd | published |
| BWV | Bach-Werke-Verzeichnis [Schmieder, catalogue of J. S. Bach's works] | *R* | photographic reprint |
| | | rec | recorder |
| | | red. | reduction, reduced for |
| *c* | circa [about] | repr. | reprinted |
| CNRS | Centre National de la Recherche Scientifique | rev. | revision, revised (by/for) |
| collab. | in collaboration with | S | soprano [voice] |
| Ct | countertenor | ser. | series |
| | | str | string(s) |
| *d* | died | suppl. | supplement, supplementary |
| db | double bass | | |
| diss. | dissertation | T | tenor [voice] |
| | | timp | timpani |
| facs. | facsimile | tpt | trumpet |
| fl | flute | Tr | treble [voice] |
| frag. | fragment | tr | treble [instrument] |
| | | trans. | translation, translated by |
| hpd | harpsichord | transcr. | transcription, transcribed by/for |
| inc. | incomplete | | |
| incl. | includes, including | U. | University |
| inst | instrument, instrumental | unperf. | unperformed |
| kbd | keyboard | v, vv | voice, voices |
| lib | libretto | va | viola |
| LWV | H. Schneider, ed.: *Chronologisch-thematisches Verzeichnis sämtlicher Werke von Jean-Baptiste Lully* | vc | cello |
| | | vn | violin |
| | | wint. | winter |
| | | ww | woodwind |
| Mez | mezzo-soprano | | |
| movt | movement | | |

# Bibliographical abbreviations

| | |
|---|---|
| *AcM* | *Acta musicologica* |
| *BSIM* | *Bulletin français de la S[ociété] I[internationale de] M[usique]* [previously *Le Mercure musical*; also other titles] |
| *BurneyH* | C. Burney: *A General History of Music from the Earliest Ages to the Present* (London, 1776–89) |
| *DAM* | *Dansk aarbog for musikforskning* |
| *FAM* | *Fontes artis musicae* |
| *FétisB* | F.-J. Fétis: *Biographie universelle des musiciens* (2/1860–65) (and suppl.) |
| *GerberL* | R. Gerber: *Historisch-biographisches Lexikon der Tonkünstler* |
| *GerberNL* | R. Gerber: *Neues historisch-biographisches Lexikon der Tonkünstler* |
| GMB | *Geschichte der Musik in Beispielen*, ed. A. Schering (Leipzig, 1931) |
| HAM | *Historical Anthology of Music*, ed. A. T. Davison and W. Apel, i (Cambridge, Mass., 1946, rev. 2/1949; ii (Cambridge, Mass., 1950) |
| *HawkinsH* | J. Hawkins: *A General History of the Science and Practice of Music* (London, 1776) |
| *IMSCR* | *International Musicological Society Congress Report* |
| *IRASM* | *International Review of the Aesthetics and Sociology of Music* |
| *JAMS* | *Journal of the American Musicological Society* |
| *JbMP* | *Jahrbuch der Musikbibliothek Peters* |
| *JMT* | *Journal of Music Theory* |
| *JRBM* | *Journal of Renaissance and Baroque Music* |
| *Mf* | *Die Musikforschung* |
| *MGG* | *Die Musik in Geschichte und Gegenwart* |
| *ML* | *Music and letters* |

| | |
|---|---|
| *MMR* | *The Monthly Musical Record* |
| *MQ* | *The Musical Quarterly* |
| *MR* | *The Music Review* |
| *MT* | *The Musical Times* |
| Mw | Das Musikwerk |
| | |
| *NOHM* | *The New Oxford History of Music*, ed. E. Wellesz, J. A. Westrup and G. Abraham (London, 1954–) |
| *NRMI* | *Nuova rivista musicale italiana* |
| | |
| PÄMw | Publikationen älterer praktischer und theoretischer Musikwerke |
| *PRMA* | *Proceedings of the Royal Musical Association* |
| | |
| RBM | Revue belge de musicologie |
| RdM | Revue de musicologie |
| ReM | La revue musicale |
| RHCM | Revue d'histoire et de critique musicales (1901]; *La revue musicale* |
| RISM | [1902–10] |
| RMFC | *Répertoire international des sources musicales* |
| RMI | *Recherches sur la musique française classique* |
| | *Rivista musicale italiana* |
| | |
| *SIMG* | *Sammelbände der Internationalen Musik-Gesellschaft* |
| *SMA* | *Studies in Music* [Australia] |
| | |
| *WaltherMI* | J. G. Walther: *Musicalishes Lexicon oder Musicalische Bibliothec* |
| | |
| *ZIMG* | *Zeitschrift der Internationalen Musik-Gesellschaft* |

# Preface

This volume is one of a series of composer studies derived from *The New Grove Dictionary of Music and Musicians* (London, 1980). In their original form, the texts were written in the mid-1970s, and finalized at the end of that decade. For this reprint, they have been re-read, mostly by their original authors, and in the cases of Lully, Charpentier and Lalande, considerably expanded in the light of recent research; in the case of Rameau, a new essay on his life and music has been supplied by Graham Sadler, who has also provided a new work-list and bibliography.

The fact that the texts of the books in the series originated as dictionary articles inevitably gives them a character somewhat different from that of books conceived as such. They are designed, first of all, to accommodate a very great deal of information in a manner that makes reference quick and easy. Their first concern is with fact rather than opinion, and this leads to a larger than usual proportion of the texts being devoted to biography than to critical discussion. The nature of a reference work gives it a particular obligation to convey received knowledge and to treat of composers' lives and works in an encyclopedic fashion, with proper acknowledgment of sources and due care to reflect different standpoints, rather than to embody imaginative or speculative writing about a composer's character or his music. It is hoped that the comprehensive work-lists and extended bibliographies, indicative of the origins of the books in a reference work, will be valuable to the reader who is eager for full and accurate reference information and who may not have ready access to *The New Grove Dictionary* or who may prefer to have it in this more compact form.

S.S.

# JEAN-BAPTISTE LULLY

James R. Anthony

# CHAPTER ONE

# Life

Giovanni Battista Lulli was born on 28 November 1632 in Florence. Contemporary documents verify that Lully's father, Lorenzo di Maldo Lulli, was a miller by trade and that his mother, Caterina del Sera, was the daughter of a miller. In 1661, both in his letters of naturalization and in his marriage contract, he not only changed the spelling of his name from Lulli to Lully but also eliminated his humble origins by declaring himself to be 'Jean-Baptiste de Lully, escuyer' son of 'Laurent de Lully, gentilhomme Florentin'.

Anecdotes substitute for facts in accounts of Lully's boyhood in Florence. According to Le Cerf de la Viéville a 'good monk . . . first gave him some music lessons and taught him to play the guitar'. He arrived in France in March 1646. He was brought from Florence by Roger de Lorraine, the Chevalier de Guise, at the request of his niece, Mlle de Montpensier, who wished to practise her Italian. Contrary to popular legend he was not employed as a cook but as one of her three *garçons de chambre*, at an annual salary of 150 livres. He remained in her household until he was 20, becoming an accomplished guitarist, dancer and violinist: 'never', reported the *Mercure galant* in March 1687, 'did any man carry so far the art of

1

playing the violin'. It may have been at this time that he studied composition with Nicolas Métru and the harpsichord (and possibly the organ) with Nicolas Gigault and François Roberday, as reported in a document of 1695 pertaining to the long wrangle between the keyboard players and the *ménétriers* of Paris. Lully's own comment – made shortly before his death and cited in the issue of the *Mercure galant* noted above – was that he had 'never learnt more about music than he had known at the age of 17 but that he had worked all his life to perfect this knowledge'.

Mlle de Montpensier's court at the Tuileries gave Lully an excellent opportunity to hear the best in contemporary French music. The *grande bande* (the '24 violons du Roi') often performed for divertissements and festivities, and at balls he heard the most popular French dances of the time, which became models for his own early compositions in this genre. He was also exposed to the court *airs* and dialogues composed by his future father-in-law, Michel Lambert, whose performances with his sister-in-law, Mlle Dupuy, were in great demand. In spite of his patroness's dislike of Cardinal Mazarin and her active involvement in the Fronde, Lully was no stranger to Italian music. In the winter and spring of 1647 he may have heard Luigi Rossi's *Orfeo* at the Louvre and made the acquaintance of his compatriots among the performers in the opera troupe. Through Lambert perhaps, he became a friend, and possibly a pupil, of the Italian violinist Lazzarini, who was *compositeur de la musique instrumentale* at court. After the defeat of the Frondists, Mlle de Montpensier was exiled to her château at St Fargeau. Lully, whose talents as dancer and mime had already attracted the attention of the young Louis XIV, then requested and received release from her service. He returned to Paris in December 1652.

On 23 February 1653 the 20-year-old Lully and the 14-year-old king danced in the same ballet (the *Ballet de la nuit*) for the first time. After Lazzarini's death Lully was appointed *compositeur de la musique instrumentale du Roi* on 16 March 1653. Along with Mazuel, Verpré and Mollier, he was responsible for the instrumental music in court ballets, the vocal music being supplied by Cambefort, J.-B. Boësset and Lambert. From 1655 Lully's fame as dancer, comedian and composer grew rapidly. His was the dominant voice in the *Ballet de l'amour malade* (1657), as is reflected in the dedication 'Pour Baptiste, compositeur de la musique du ballet'. Benserade, who had made his début as a poet of superior literary talents in the *Ballet de Cassandre* (1651), now sought active collaboration with Lully and they continued to work together until 1681. Lully's name (always shortened to 'Baptiste') appears frequently in the journals of the period. After the performance of *L'amour malade*, Jean Loret wrote (in *La muze historique*, 20 January 1657):

Mais pour danse et pour mélodie,
Il faut, toutefois, que je die,
Que Baptiste, en toute façon,
Est un admirable garçon.

Some time before 1656 Lully received permission

to conduct the 'petits violons' (also known as 'petite bande'), which under his discipline soon surpassed its parent organization. The 16 players (later augmented to 21) appeared for the first time under Lully's direction in *La galanterie du temps* in 1656. Lully forbade the group to indulge in the sometimes excessive ornamentation and haphazard improvisation techniques that characterized performances by the '24 violons du Roi': according to Perrault (in *Les hommes illustres*), 'before [Lully] . . . bass and inner parts . . . were often composed on the spot by the performers themselves'. In 1664 he apparently resolved his difficulties with the *grande bande*, and the two groups were combined in court ballet performances.

The years 1661 and 1662 were pivotal in Lully's career. With the death of Mazarin in March 1661 Italian music lost its most powerful champion in France. After the death of Cambefort, Lully was appointed *surintendant de la musique et compositeur de la musique de la chambre* on 16 May 1661; he shared the position with J.-B. Boësset. He received his letters of naturalization from Louis XIV in December 1661. On 16 July 1662 he was appointed *maître de la musique de la famille royale* and eight days later carried his naturalization a step further by marrying Lambert's daughter Madeleine in St Eustache. Among those who signed the marriage contract of 14 July were Louis XIV and his queen, Anne of Austria, and Colbert and his wife; the document is a symbol of his burgeoning power at court.

As in a well-planned scenario, Lully next coupled his name with the most important dramatists in

*1. Jean-Baptiste Lully: engraving by Bonnart*

France. He supplied Corneille with ballet entrées for the revival in August 1664 of his tragedy *Oedipe* at Fontainebleau. With *Le mariage forcé* in January of the same year occurred his first important collaboration with Molière in the writing of *comédies-ballets*; their partnership continued until *Le bourgeois gentilhomme* of 1670. Although the 'deux grands Baptistes' were considered equal partners, Lully had a distinct advantage if only because of the king's interest in dancing. A contemporary source (*Gazette de France,* October, 1670) described *Le bourgeois gentilhomme* as a 'ballet composed of six entrées accompanied by a comedy'.

In 1669 Pierre Perrin received a 12-year privilege to establish Académies d'Opéra anywhere in the realm. According to Brossard (in his *Catalogue des livres de musique . . . escrit en L'Année 1724*, held in the Bibliothèque Nationale, Paris), Lully 'railed against Perrin's academy and affirmed many times that the French language was not proper for . . . large works'. But the great success of Perrin's and Cambert's *Pomone* (1671) was not lost on Lully. When Perrin was victimized by unscrupulous partners (Sourdéac and Champeron) and incarcerated for debts, Lully quickly turned the situation to his own benefit. In 1672 he successfully bought the privilege from Perrin with the support of Colbert and, it was said, the urging of Mme de Montespan, despite the fact that Perrin had on 23 November 1671 sold two-thirds of his privilege to Sablières and his librettist Henri Guichard. Lully gave Perrin a sum sufficient to pay off his creditors and promised him a pension for life.

The royal privilege, dated 13 March 1672, then gave to 'nostre cher et bien amé Jean-Baptiste Lully' and to his heirs the sole right to establish an Académie Royale de Musique and forbade performances, without Lully's written permission, of any work that was sung throughout. Molière attempted, as did Sablières and Guichard in company with Sourdéac and Champeron, to block Lully's privilege. With the power of the throne behind him, however, Lully had little to fear. On 1 April the former Académie d'Opéra located between the rue de Seine and the rue de Mazarine was forced by royal edict to close its doors.

A series of oppressive patents consolidated Lully's absolute control over all aspects of French stage music. A royal ordinance of 14 April 1672 forbade the use of more than six singers and twelve instrumentalists in any stage production. In a royal patent of 20 September 1672, Lully received authorization to have printed each of the *airs de musique* composed by him as well as the texts (prose and poetry), the stage designs and the works themselves for which Lully had supplied the music, 'without any exceptions'. This latter clause posed a particular threat to Molière, who by July 1672 had already begun his collaboration with Marc-Antoine Charpentier. Lully's patents culminated in one of 28 (or 30) April 1673 which reduced to eight (two singers and six instrumentalists) the number of musicians who might appear in productions independent of the Académie Royale de Musique. This patent also stipulated that none of the musicians and dancers hired for such productions could be in the employ of the Académie

Royale de Musique. With the thoroughness that had characterized his earlier moves he next sought a theatre, a machinist and a librettist. For eight months he rented the enclosed tennis court (Jeu de paume de Béquet) in the rue de Vaugirard (today situated between the Théâtre de l'Odéon and the Luxembourg Gardens). He signed an eight year contract with the machinist and architect Carlo Vigarani, whose first task was to make an acceptable theatre out of the former tennis court. For his librettist Lully chose Philippe Quinault, with whom he had already worked in the ballets *La grotte de Versailles* (1668) and *Psyché* (1671).

*Les fêtes de l'Amour et de Bacchus*, a *pastorale-pastiche*, and *Cadmus et Hermione*, the first *tragédie lyrique*, were both performed in Vigarani's theatre. Two months after Molière's death Lully received on 28 April 1673 the king's permission to take over, free of charge, the theatre in the Palais Royal that had formerly served Molière and his troupe. The king, in addition, gave Lully 3000 livres to convert this theatre (in one of the wings of the Palais Royal on the rue Saint-Honoré) into the Académie Royale de Musique.

Philippe Quinault furnished the texts of 11 of Lully's *tragédies lyriques*. Each resulted from a threefold collaboration between poet, composer and the French Académie des Inscriptions et Belles-lettres. The king himself suggested the subject matter for at least *Persée*, *Amadis*, *Roland* and *Armide*. This royal concern may explain the fact that in most of Lully's later operas the dramatic core is the conflict between glory and duty on the one hand and love on the other. Louis XIV certainly approved the political sentiments didactically expressed in the prologues to these works ('Montrons les erreurs où l'amour peut engager un coeur qui néglige la gloire', *Roland*). Evidence suggests that the division of responsibility and labour in the collaboration was far from equitable. Le Cerf related how Lully examined Quinault's verses word by word, making corrections and 'cutting half the scene when necessary'. He sent *Phaëton* back to Quinault 20 times before he was satisfied with the results. He nonetheless insisted that Quinault was the 'only poet with whom he could work and who knew as much about varying metres and rhymes in poetry as he himself knew about varying melody and cadence in music' (*Mercure galant*, 1695).

After *Alceste* (1674) Lully was under considerable pressure from a well-organized cabal to rid himself of Quinault. Perrin, Guichard and even La Fontaine supplied librettos for his approval. La Fontaine, who had asked Racine and Boileau (both of whom hated opera) to advise him about writing a libretto, was particularly distressed at Lully's unequivocal rejection of his vapid text for the pastoral *Daphné* and in 1674 mounted a savage personal attack on him in *Le florentin* ('He is lewd and evil-minded, and he devours all'). Only through the efforts of Benserade were the two men reconciled, and La Fontaine agreed to write dedicatory verses for the printed scores of *Amadis* and *Roland*. Eventually, because of Quinault's disgrace at court, Lully was forced to find a new librettist for the operas composed between *Isis* (1677) and *Proserpine*

# ROLAND,
## *TRAGEDIE*
## MISE
## EN MUSIQUE,

*Par Monsieur de Lully, Escuyer, Conseiller*
*Secretaire du Roy, Maison, Couronne de*
*France & de ses Finances, & Sur-Intendant*
*de la Musique de Sa Majesté.*

A PARIS,
Par CHRISTOPHE BALLARD, seul Imprimeur du Roy pour la Musique,
ruë Saint Jean de Beauvais, au Mont-Parnasse.
ET SE VEND
A la Porte de l'Academie Royale de Musique, ruë Saint Honoré.
_____
M. DC. LXXXV.
AVEC PRIVILEGE DE SA MAJESTE'.

*2. Title-page of Lully's tragédie lyrique 'Roland' (1685)*

(1680). Juno in *Isis* had been interpreted as an unflattering caricature of the jealous Mme de Montespan, the king's mistress. Pierre Corneille, together with Molière and Quinault, had written the text for *Psyché* (1671), a *tragédie-ballet*. Lully asked Thomas Corneille to revise it for performance at the Opéra in 1678; in 1679 he requested another text (*Bellérophon*) from Corneille.

This period of Lully's life held other crises. Many musicians and poets resented the concentration of power in one individual. In an ordinance of 5 February 1677 Lully had even gone so far as to prevent the use of music in marionette theatres. Scarcely veiled criticisms could occasionally be found in the influential *Mercure galant* ('[Paris] should never be reduced to having only one opera every year', June 1683). A serious altercation between Guichard and Lully was the natural by-product of Guichard's privilege of 1674 to establish an Académie Royale des Spectacles. Guichard, a son-in-law of the architect Le Vau, hired Vigarani on 18 February 1675 and offered Lully 10,000 livres for the right to use music in his productions; Lully instead demanded that Guichard cede part of his privilege. Guichard's estranged mistress, Marie Aubry, who was a singer at the Opéra, later told Lully that Guichard had asked her brother to murder him by mixing arsenic with his tobacco. There followed a bitter trial lasting nearly three years. Lully won his suit at first, on 17 September 1676, but then lost after an appeal by Guichard before the Chambre de la Tournelle; Guichard was acquitted on 12 April 1677. Continuing his support of Lully during this difficult time, Louis XIV became the godfather of his eldest son (then aged 13) in an elaborate baptism at Fontainebleau on 9 September 1677. The king, however, also continued to make known his displeasure at Lully's overt homosexual behaviour. In 1685, according to Dangeau's journal (16 Jan), Lully was informed that '[the king] had pardoned him in the past but that in the future he must conduct himself properly' (see Masson, 1961–2).

Lully's greatest personal triumph came in 1681. He had received letters of nobility from Louis XIV some time before this date but had not registered them. He preferred to have his noble rank automatically conferred by his purchase of the office of *secrétaire du Roi*. With the king's full approval and notwithstanding the opposition of the powerful Louvois, this coveted charge was sold to Lully for 63,000 livres by the widow of Joseph Clausel, and he was received as secretary in an impressive ceremony on 29 December 1681. His printed scores henceforward bore – to cite the title-page of *Armide* – the words 'Par Monsieur de Lully, escuyer, conseiller, Secrétaire du Roy, Maison, Couronne de France & de ses Finances, & Sur-Intendant de la Musique de Sa Majesté'.

Between 1673 and 1686 Lully composed 13 *tragédies lyriques*, one a year (except for 1681). After the great success of *Bellérophon* (1679), which enjoyed nine months of performances during its first run, he granted Ballard a contract to print his scores. The contract stated that 750 copies of each score would be printed only after each copy was signed or marked by Lully or one of his secretaries. Hitherto Lully had

sanctioned the sale of manuscript copies at the entrance to the Opéra. Le Cerf left a wealth of information about Lully's compositional practices some
of which information was supplied by the former page
Brunet who had been for a brief period a member of
Lully's household. Le Cerf tells us that Lully, after
receiving the text of a scene from Quinault, would
work at the harpsichord, setting the words to music
and supplying a basso continuo. For the divertissement of each act, however, the situation was reversed:
he outlined the text, composed the music and sent
everything to Quinault, who then fashioned his verses
to fit the music. Lully left the task of filling in many
of the inner voices to his pupils Collasse and Lal-
louette; the latter was in due course dismissed for
boasting that he had composed the best *airs* in *Isis*
(1677). Le Cerf noted that 'Lully himself composed
all the parts of his principal choruses and important
duos, trios and quartets' and that if a chorus were
fugal he 'always marked the entrances'. Le Cerf's
assertion that Lully spent three months in the
composition of his annual opera and did little for the
rest of the year fails to acknowledge his very active
role in preparing the productions of his works. For
the performances at St Germain-en-Laye of *Le
triomphe de l'amour* (21 January to 18 February 1681)
the accounts of the Menus Plaisirs show a minimum
of one daily rehearsal from 16 December to 20
January, involving singers, dancers, 25 'grands
violons', 22 'petits violons' and 21 flutes and oboes.
Le Cerf described Lully's part in the training of
singers and dancers, stating that he 'reformed the

entrées and conceived the expressive steps that related to the subject' and that his *maître de danse*, Pierre Beauchamp, planned the dances of nymphs and shepherds. He exercised strict discipline over all his performers. Le Cerf, writing in the first decade of the 18th century, could only long for the days when Lully would break a violin over the back of an errant musician. He added that 'under Lully's control the female singers did not have colds for six months of the year, and the male performers were not drunk four days a week'.

On 12 April 1684 the eldest of Lully's three daughters, Catherine-Madeleine, married Nicolas Francine, the king's *maître d'hôtel*; it thus became possible for him to hand over many of the administrative details of the Académie Royale de Musique to Francine. (Lully also had three sons, who all became musicians.) In spite of their great popularity his operas incurred the enmity of the clergy and of conservative professors at the Sorbonne, who attacked what Bossuet called the 'corruption reduced to maxims' displayed in such passages as 'Mais rien n'est si charmant qu'une inconstance mutuelle' (*Thésée*, Act 2 scene ii). A similar attitude spread through the court, which after the king's secret marriage to Mme de Maintenon in the autumn of 1683 increasingly took on the 'demeanour of a convent' (Gros). Possibly in response to this situation it was now that Lully composed much of his religious music. On 8 January 1687 at the church of the Feuillants he conducted more than 150 musicians in a performance of his *Te Deum* celebrating the king's recovery from

3. *MS fragment of an unknown work, possibly in Lully's autograph, bound between 'Acis et Galatée and 'Idylle sur la paix'*

15

an operation. 'In the heat of the moment' (Le Cerf) he hit his toe with the sharp point of the cane with which he was beating time. An abscess developed, and gangrene spread rapidly because he refused to let his physician remove the toe. Although in the greatest physical distress, he put his financial affairs in order and made his peace with the church before dying on the morning of 22 March 1687. He was buried in the church of the Petits Pères (now Notre Dame des Victoires). His widow had Michel Cotton build a magnificent mausoleum, which was completed in 1688. The famous bust of him by Coysevox was placed on top. The mausoleum was destroyed during the French Revolution, but sketches survive in the Gaignières Collection (in the Bibliothèque Nationale, Paris, see plate 32 in Benoit: *Versailles et les musiciens du Roi*).

Lully died the possessor of a great personal fortune estimated by Radet to have been 800,000 livres. He owned five houses in Paris. Four of these were in the Palais Royal quarter: rue Royale (now 10 rue des Moulins); rue Neuve des Petits Champs (no.47); rue Ste-Anne (no.43); and the corner of rue Neuve des Petits Champs (no.45) and rue Ste-Anne. The last house, known as the Hôtel Lully (reproduced as plate 28 in Benoit: op cit), was built by Daniel Gittard in 1671 thanks to a 11,000-livre loan to Lully from Molière. Late in 1683 Lully moved his family to a luxurious house surrounded by gardens in the rue de la Madeleine in the suburb of Ville l'Evêque (now ?28 rue Boissy-d'Anglas). He also owned a country house at Puteaux with Lambert, and another at Sèvres.

Most contemporary sources agree that Lully was

'dark complexioned, with small eyes, a large nose and a large, well-formed mouth. He was very near-sighted and was stockier and smaller than represented in engravings' (Boindin). In addition to the bronze bust by Coysevox at Notre Dame des Victoires (see fig.8, p.49) there is a bust by Cotton and a small bronze statue by Garnier, both at Versailles. Among the paintings and engravings of him are those by Bonnart (see fig.1, p.5), Mignard the younger (Chantilly, Castle Museum), Puget (Paris, Louvre), Arlaud (Vienna, Imperial Collection), Desrochers (London, British Library) and Edelinck and Sornique (both in Milan, Civica Raccolta). No authenticated musical autograph is known, although Henry Prunières believed that, because the fragment of an unknown work bound between *Acis et Galathée* and *Idylle sur la paix* (in the private collection of André Meyer, Paris) included text phrases thought to be in Lully's hand, it followed that the musical text was also in his hand (see fig.3, p.15). The lack of autographs and full scores or parts from the period of performance of the court ballets makes the editing of such works particularly difficult. Many of the extant sources date from 20 years after the performance and several were assembled after Lully's death.

# CHAPTER TWO

# Stage music

Lully's stage music may conviently be organized by genre into three distinct categories: the *ballets de cour* and *mascarades* (1654–69); the *comédies-* and *tragédies-ballets* and pastorales (1661–86); and the *tragédies lyriques* (1673–86). Framing the final category are a *pastorale-pastiche*, *Les fêtes de l'Amour et de Bacchus* (1672) and a *pastorale héroïque*, *Acis et Galathée* (1686). Lully had completed only the first act of *Achille et Polyxène*, his final *tragédie lyrique*, when he died.

## I 'Ballets de cour'

The *ballet de cour* afforded Lully a ten-year apprenticeship which helped prepare him for creating the *tragédie lyrique*. It was a valuable proving ground, where the young composer differentiated between the respective styles of his native and adopted countries and could observe at first hand the reactions of the king and Cardinal Mazarin to his efforts. It was as a dancer, comedian and composer of instrumental music for court ballets and Italian opera *intermèdes* that he first attracted attention, and he was known as a violinist as well. In the ballets that he composed before 1661 his vocal music is predominantly Italian in style. His genuine comic gifts became apparent as

early as 1655 in the Italian dialogue and 'récit grotesque' in the *Ballet des bienvenus*. The *Ballet de
l'amour malade* (1657), for which he may have
composed all the music, is really a short Italian *opera
buffa* enclosed within a French ballet. Lully certainly
composed all the instrumental music and some of the
vocal music for the *Ballet d'Alcidiane* (1658). Its
overture, with its dotted rhythms, wide range of
melodies and fugal middle section, displays the
hallmarks of what was to become the classical French
overture. The trumpet-like flourishes and slow
harmonic rhythm of the combat music prefigures the
bellicose divertissements of *Thésée* and *Bellérophon*,
and the final chaconne assumes the proportions and
structural significance of those found in his *tragédies
lyriques*. If the *récit* 'Que votre empire' is by Lully,
as Bénigne de Bacilly claimed, it illustrates how much
at home he already was with the French court *air*. In
fact the bass line, with its downward leaps of two
major 7ths, is a bolder dramatic statement than is
normally found in the *récits* of his French contemporaries (see ex.1).

Ex.1 from 'Que votre empire', *Ballet d'Alcidiane*

mais ____ le mur - mure est dif - fé - rent

Lully's musical naturalization kept pace with the
events of 1661 and 1662 detailed in chapter one. He
composed French *airs* for the *Ballet de l'impatience*

19

(1661), and for the first time, in the *Ballet des saisons* (1661), he included no Italian music. From now on in his ballets he reserved the Italian language for occasional burlesque scenes or for tragic laments. Armide's lament 'Ah, Rinaldo, e dove sei' in the *Ballet des amours déguisez* (1664) served as a model for French *plaintes* in the *Ballet de la naissance de Vénus* (1665) and the *Ballet de Flore* (1669). Through Venus's *plainte* in the latter, however, Lully moved the lament closer to the spirit of the French *air sérieux*, which had become a more personal and expressive genre under the influence of Pierre de Nyert. With its restrained chromaticism, dramatic use of rests, affective melodic intervals and syllabic word-setting, this lament closely resembles *Languir*, an *air sérieux* by Jean Sicard printed in the preceding year: see ex.2*a–b*.

Lully, who had already assimilated the long tradition of French dances, introduced many new *airs de vitesse* into the court ballet. Bourrées and minuets became the most widely used dances; courantes and galliards became rare. This posed problems for the *grands seigneurs*, most of whom were characterized by Lully as being too stupid to master the more rapid steps required in the closing *grand ballet* (see Pure, 1668).

Lully and Benserade gradually transformed the *ballet de cour* from a collection of dances and burlesque scenes for the pleasure of the court into a more unified dramatic spectacle that bordered on opera. Such works as the *Ballet des muses* (1666–7) and the above-mentioned *Ballet de Flore* best illustrate these

Ex.2
(a) from the 'Plainte de Vénus', *Ballet de Flore* (after Philidor copy, *F-Pc*)

(b) from Sicard: *Languir, Airs à boire [et sérieux]*, Book III (Paris, 1668)

basic changes. Brossard wrote of the former in his *Catalogue*: 'according to all appearances this ballet generated the idea of composing operas in French'. The impressive choral finale to its prologue expresses the sentiments found in later operatic prologues: 'Rien n'est si doux que de vivre à la cour de Louis, le plus parfait des rois'. The kind of square, pompous music that Lully wrote for this text consolidated a tradition and was to remain the official gesture of

21

adoration throughout the *grand siècle*. According to Le Cerf, Lully based his recitatives on the intonation and declamatory practices of La Champmeslé at the Hôtel de Bourgogne. Even before her earliest triumphs, however, he had used in the recitative 'Arreste, malheureux' in the *Ballet des muses* both the predominantly anapaestic rhythmic organization and the division of the alexandrine into hemistichs that characterize the recitatives of his *tragédie lyrique*.

The often improvisatory nature of the *ballet de cour* is best illustrated by the performances of the *Ballet des muses*. From the first performance on 2 December 1666 to the final performance on 19 February 1667, this ballet went through six stages of development. Seemingly on a trial and error basis, new material was constantly added to render the ballet 'encore plus agréable'; this in turn necessitated new printings of the libretto. By 14 February it comprehended two of Molière's *comédies-ballets*, *La pastorale comique* and *Le Sicilien*. The lack of autographs or copies approved by the composer did not inhibit the ateliers of André-Danican Philidor (Louis XIV's chief copyist) and Henry Foucault (the Parisian music dealer) from issuing several manuscript copies of the *ballets de cour*. Copies from the Philidor and Foucault ateliers generally reflect two distinct traditions with regard to the number of pieces included, their order and the musical text of the inner voices.

*Le triomphe de l'amour* (1681) and *Le temple de la paix* (1685), which Lully composed after the birth of the *tragédie lyrique*, bear only a structural resemblance to his earlier court ballets. Hard pressed to find a proper category for *Le triomphe de l'amour*, the Parfaicts wrote (in their *Histoire de l'Académie royale de musique*): 'it is properly neither an opera nor a ballet but a collection of entrées mixed with *récits*'. In both these ballets dance is a mere accessory, and *récits* are carefully integrated into the dramatic action. The chorus (including a double chorus in *Le triomphe de l'amour*) plays a prominent part, and *symphonies* often carry precise instructions about instrumentation (see fig.4, p.24) and methods of performance. Even though professional female dancers had been used, albeit rarely, in court entertainments, the performance of *Le triomphe de l'amour* in 1681 marked their first appearance on the stage of the Opéra (female roles there had previously been assigned to professional male dancers).

## II 'Comédies-ballets' and related genres
Lully brought to the composition of both his own and Molière's *comedies-ballets* the skills already tested in his *ballets de cour*. He was presented with an unparalleled opportunity to coordinate his highly developed sense of comic style in music with that of France's greatest comic playwright. The Italian burlesque style was for him a more natural means of expression than the French. His early attempts to create a French *style bouffe* (for example in the bass solos of the magician in *Le mariage forcé*, 1664) are stiff and clumsy in comparison with his later work. No such awkwardness mars the polygamy duet in Act 2 of *Monsieur de Pourceaugnac* (1669).

4. Opening of the 'Prélude pour l'Amour' from Lully's 'Le triomphe de l'amour' (1681), scored for four-part wind ensemble of transverse flutes, tenor recorders, bass recorders and great bass recorders

24

## 'Comédies-ballets', related genres

The *comédies-ballets* form a repository of musical forms and techniques that Lully later used in his *tragédies lyriques*. There are passages in recitative (e.g. ex.3) that clearly presage the 'récitatif simple' of his *tragédies lyriques*, and it is not surprising that Quinault was thought to have modelled his librettos on Molière's verses. With their restricted range, frequent cadences, anapaestic rhythms and syllabic word-setting, the French *airs* of Lully's *comédies-ballets* are deprived of every vestige of Italian influence. A *chanson à boire*, 'Buvons, chers amis, buvons' in Act 4 of *Le bourgeois gentilhomme* was the *air* that, according to Le Cerf, Lully 'loved most throughout his life'.

Ex.3 from *Le bourgeois gentilhomme*

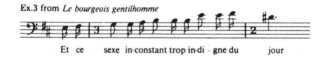

Et ce     sexe in-constant trop in-di - gne du     jour

Besides the titled dances, many *airs de danse* without fixed choreographic intent are found in the *comédies-ballets*. These dances often show considerable freedom in the groupings of phrases and in the counter-rhythms of the inner parts (see, for example, the second *air* in the Turkish ceremony in *Le bourgeois gentilhomme*). Although dominated by the standard five-part string ensemble, the orchestra of the *comédies-ballets* calls at times for a number of supernumeraries. The text of *La princesse d'Elide*, for example, mentions 'several hunting horns and trumpets'.

Lully and Molière introduced the milieu of the

pastorale into their *comédies-ballets*. These pastorales take more from the *ballet de cour* and Italian opera than from the *comédies en musique* of Perrin and Cambert. In contrast to the latter there is no attempt to banish plot. The third *intermède* of *Les amants magnifiques* is a masterpiece that is totally in the bucolic genre; here Molière reduced to one shepherd and one shepherdess the confusing cast of rejected suitors and pairs of lovers typical of the pastorale. The gentle *sommeil* (scene iv) was borrowed from Venetian opera; its *ritournelle* for flutes established a precedent for many such scenes in Lully's later works.

In *George Dandin* and *Les amants magnifiques* the link between music and dramatic action was compromised, and the text was subordinated to music. Molière's text for *Les amants magnifiques* could almost be a substitute for an operatic libretto. The prologue is sung throughout, and the finale, with its brilliant D major passages for trumpets and drums, rises to a climax at the entrance of Apollo. This part was danced by the king; thus *comédie-ballet* and *ballet de cour* were combined.

The fusion of music, dance and verse, best seen in *Le Sicilien* and *Le bourgeois gentilhomme*, foreshadows the *opéra comique*. The *comédie-ballet* has the distinction of being the only combination of poetry and music in France that pleased the partisans of both sung and spoken words. Saint-Evremond recommended it to playwrights as an alternative to opera: 'there you would discover what satisfies both the senses and the mind'.

*Psyché* is called a *tragédie-ballet* in the libretto of 1671, and indeed of all the works discussed in this section it is the nearest to the *tragédie lyrique*. Making minor alterations and adding recitatives, Lully and Thomas Corneille (with the help of Corneille's nephew Bernard Le Bovier de Fontenelle) took just three weeks in 1678 to convert it into a *tragédie lyrique* (according to *Mercure galant*, March 1678). The conception of music and dance as dramatic agents was taken from the *comédie-ballet*. The 'concerts lugubres' and 'pompe funèbre' of Act 1 scene vi prefigure similar scenes in *Alceste*, and Lully never surpassed the spectacular finale that celebrates the marriage of Love and Psyche and that would not be out of place in a genuine opera.

## III  'Tragédies lyriques'

The *tragédies lyriques* (or, more accurately, *tragédies en musique*) of Lully and Quinault are large-scale stage works with continuous music in which the subject matter, drawn from Greek mythology or more rarely from Italian and Spanish chivalric romances, is spread over five acts. They mark the real beginning of French opera. The most innovatory feature of the *tragédie lyrique* was the subordination to overall dramatic unity of every element, whether Lully's music, Quinault's poetry, the staging of Vigarani (and after 1680 Berain) or the dances of Beauchamp and Olivet: it is in essence a 17th-century type of Gesamtkunstwerk, and it was greatly admired. In time-honoured fashion the decorative and panegyric prologues are divorced from the subject of the *tragédie lyrique*; only near the end of their collaboration did Lully and Quinault link them more closely to the drama. In *Amadis* the two main characters of the prologue, Urgande and Alquif, also appear in the tragedy; and in the prologues to *Roland* and *Armide* the Corneille-like theme of the conflict of 'gloire' and 'amour' receives full didactic comment.

The reliance on a *deus ex machina* and the concomitant central position of the *merveilleux* of necessity reduced human involvement in the drama and limited the psychological penetration of character. At the same time, according to aestheticians, poetry was the primary force in the *tragédie lyrique*, no matter how much it was modified to fit its lyric setting ('although the musician may have more talent than the poet, although by the force of his genius he may assure the success of an opera, his art is always regarded in France as secondary to that of poetry', Rochemont: *Réflexions d'un patriot sur l'opéra françois*, 1754). In actuality, as Saint-Evremond complained in *Sur les opéra* (which was published in *Oeuvres meslées*, xi, 1684), 'one thinks 100 times more of Baptiste than of Theseus or Cadmus'. Although composer and librettist were permitted to infringe the classical unities of time and place, unity of action was to be preserved. In *Thésée* the change from a 'frightful desert' to an 'enchanted island' offended no-one, whereas the sub-plot between two minor characters, Arcas and Cleon, whose intrigue parallels the main action between Theseus and Aegle, was considered 'un peu puérile' (Saint-Mard). After *Thésée* Lully's comic muse was silenced, the victim of an inflexible attitude that allowed no mixture of comic and tragic genres such as existed in Venetian and Roman opera. Unfortunately there were to be no more scenes such as that in *Alceste* (Act 4 scene i) between Charon and the shades, paying their tribute to cross the Styx, which is as fine a piece of comic writing and social satire as exists anywhere in French stage music ('Et ce n'est point assez de payer dans la vie; Il faut encore payer au delà du trépas').

The role of the divertissement in the *tragédie lyrique* provides some insight into Lully's musico-dramatic concepts. The divertissement is either a decorative, inessential, dramatically neutral ornament or an integral part of the dramatic action. Dance, chorus, songs and an elaborate *mise-en-scène* are common to both types. Perhaps the finest example of a divertissement combining the functions of spectacle and dramatic agent is the village wedding which encompasses scenes iii–v of Act 4 of *Roland*. This pastoral divertissement of choruses, dances and entrées of joyful shepherds and shepherdesses deepens by contrast the despair of Roland, who inadvertently discovers that his beloved Angélique is the bride of Médor. The bucolic atmosphere is shattered; the end of the divertissement 'Ah fuyons, fuyons tous' elides with Roland's vengeance *air* 'Je suis trahi', which is followed by an accompanied recitative, 'Ah! Je suis descendu dans la nuit du tombeau'. Lully's scheme of tonalities throws this conflict of moods into high relief. The act opens in C and closes in B♭; scene iv, the crucial scene dramatically, shifts the tonality through G minor, the dominant minor. The dram-

5. Grande Salle
of the Palais
Royal during a
performance of
Lully's tragédie
lyrique 'Armide':
watercolour (mid-
18th century) by
Gabriel de
St-Aubin

30

atically integrated divertissement sustains a prevailing mood more often than it contrasts two opposing moods. Typical cases of this sustaining function are the *sommeil* in *Atys*, the funeral cortèges in *Psyché* and *Amadis* and the warlike divertissements exemplified by that in Act 3 of *Thésée* (scenes iv–viii), in which the 'habitants des enfers' are catapulted into the action to underscore the power of Medea. In the 'Pompe funèbre' of *Alceste* (Act 3 scenes v–vi) dramatic *symphonies* take the place of titled dances, and the chorus of 'femmes affligées' and 'hommes désolez' acts out its grief in pantomime.

Lully used the recall of choral or solo fragments as a musico-dramatic device more often than is commonly acknowledged. In Act 1 of *Thésée* a fragment of the chorus 'Il faut périr, il faut vaincre ou mourir', first used in scene i, penetrates Aegle's recitative in scene ii and unifies scenes iii and v. Similarly the choral refrain 'Allons, allons accourez tous' in Act 1 of *Atys* appears as a solo for Atys (scene i), a duo for Atys and Idas (scene ii), a duo for Sangaride and Doris (scene iii) and a quartet for all of these characters. Each scene of the third act of *Alceste* is effectively organized around a few short ensemble or choral fragments, culminating in the often parodied 'Alceste est morte!' of scene iv. Lully also made considerable use of ostinato basses as a purely musical means of organization. In *Persée* dialogue *airs* between Merope and Andromeda are constructed over the same chaconne bass. In his last three operas he gave inner musical unity to entire scenes through a chaconne or *passacaille*. In the divertissement of the final act of *Armide*, for example, a *passacaille* generates three songs, a dance and three choruses; it is dramatically silenced by Renaud's recitative 'Allez, éloignez-vous de moy', which ends the scene.

The main burden of exposing and developing the drama in a *tragédie lyrique* is carried by the recitative. Lully's repeated visits to hear La Champmeslé declaim Racine at the Hôtel de Bourgogne undoubtedly stimulated him to refine and systematize his earlier attempts to create French recitative. In these earlier efforts to translate declamatory passages into music he had often been trapped by a too rigid application of the anapaestic rhythms and the paired symmetrical hexameters of the French alexandrine, as can be seen in ex.4 from *Alceste*. To break this symmetry and to

Ex.4 from *Alceste*

accommodate both a changing speed of delivery and a different number of syllables per line, he used fluctuating metres, the interpretation of which is still in question. In principle, the rhyme of the line and the caesura on the sixth syllable of the line receive metrical accents (see Rosow, 1983). This type of recitative, 'récitatif simple' or 'ordinaire', remained a constant feature of French opera up to Rameau. It was accompanied only by the basso continuo and was apparently performed 'quickly, without appearing bizarre' (Le Cerf) and with little or no ornamentation: 'no embellishments; my recitative is made only for speaking' (Le Cerf again, quoting Lully himself). There is some confusion over the exact metrical relationships to be observed between the constantly shifting metres of the recitative of Lully and his successors. Among the many 17th- and 18th-century sources that deal with the problem (often in a confusing and contradictory manner), Saint-Lambert (*Les principes du clavecin*, 1702) and Etienne Loulié (supplement to *Eléments ou principes de musique*, MS, Bibliothèque Nationale, Paris, Eng. trans., 1965) document most clearly the principle that (to quote Loulié) 'the time-value of a beat in one metre should be equal to that of a beat in the other, even though the note values are not equal', i.e. that a crotchet in C is equivalent to a minim in ¢.

After *Atys* Lully's 'récitatif ordinaire' became more expressive and better able to mirror the text without sacrificing proper declamatory practices. The fragments in ex.5, from four late operas, show greater rhythmic flexibility, an increase in range, the use of affective intervals such as the ascending minor 6th and descending diminished 5th and a more determined attempt to engage in word-painting. Lully's simple recitative is best seen in the famous monologue from *Armide* (Act 2 scene v; in GMB, 318ff) in which Armide's inner conflict is evoked as much by musical means as through standard 17th-century declamation. Rests, for example, are not restricted to caesuras in the text but, more importantly, dramatize her hesitation and confusion. Many 18th-century partisans of

Ex.5
(a) from *Atys* (after Ballard's edition, 1689)

Dieux cru - els, Dieux im-pi -to - yables, n'este vous tout puis-

- sant que pour faire des mi - sé - ra - bles

(b) from *Bellérophon* (after Ballard's edition, 1679)

Ap-pel - lez à grand bruit, et la mort, et la

mort et___ la nuit

(c) from *Proserpine* (after Ballard's edition, 1680)

L'en -fer dé - cou - vre ses gouf - fres té - né - breux

(d) from *Armide* (after Ballard's edition, 1686)

Non rien ne peut changer mon â - me, Non, non

French opera considered this monologue to be, in Titon du Tillet's words, 'the greatest piece in all our opera'; Rameau printed it complete in his *Nouveau système de musique théorique* (1726), used it in *Observations sur notre instinct pour la musique* (1754) to answer Rousseau's criticism of French recitative and gave a detailed harmonic analysis of its opening section in *Code de musique pratique* (1760).

Beginning with *Bellérophon* (1679) Lully turned

more and more to accompanied recitative, in which, though not neglecting the rules of prosody, he subordinated them to heightened musical expression. This type of recitative often includes extended passages that lack the typical fluctuation of metre of simple recitative, thus producing a musical hybrid for which there is no adequate term in French. By Rameau's day it was called 'récitatif mesuré'; perhaps its nearest counterpart is the Italian 'arioso'. In *Amadis* the orchestra is the main protagonist in the accompanied recitatives of the magician Arcalaus and the enchantress Arcabonne. The roles of Amadis and Roland consist almost entirely of accompanied recitative. Scene vii of the third act of *Acis et Galatée* is an accompanied recitative of over 160 bars sung by Galatea. The orchestra plays continuously; there are five 'préludes' that prepare shifts in mood which are then transferred to the voice, with the greatest subtlety. Similarly Act 5 scene i of *Persée* is a long accompanied recitative unified by a motto prelude and Merope's recurring phrase 'O mort venez finir mon destin déplorable'.

The French operatic *air* from Lully to Rameau may be classified into four basic types: dialogue *air*, maxim *air*, monologue *air* and dance song. Most are cast as short binary and rondeau court *airs* with the extended binary form ($A–B–B'$) dominating. Menestrier, writing eight years after Lully's first *tragédie lyrique*, *Cadmus et Hermione*, in *Des représentations en musique anciennes et modernes*, correctly saw the dialogue *airs* by Lambert, Boësset and others as models for what he called 'musique d'action & de théâtre'. In modelling some of his dance-songs and maxim *airs* on *chansons à boire* and brunettes Lully was courting popular favour. Le Cerf related how he was specially pleased when these pieces (sometimes referred to as 'Pont-Neuf tunes') were enjoyed by 'princess and cook alike'.

Lully sometimes used the dialogue *air* in conjunction with 'récitatif simple' to move the drama along. In the first scene of Act 1 of *Amadis*, for example, much of the plot is developed through seven dialogue *airs*, which because they are so short scarcely characterize the protagonists musically. Moreover, purely musical development of these *airs* was inhibited by Lully's use of short-breathed vocal lines, syllabic treatment of the texts (in which few words are repeated) and his frequent use of cadences within each section of each *air*. The strength or passion often inherent in an opening melodic phrase is therefore dissipated in the routine cadence formula that immediately follows (e.g. 'Amants qui vous plaignez' in *Atys*). Most maxim *airs* make general observations and practical comments, usually relating to amorous pursuits. They are normally sung by secondary characters. Because they often draw as much attention to the *galant* mores of the court as to the stage action they may be seen as direct descendants of the *vers* of the *ballet de cour*. Lully reserved accompanied recitatives and monologue *airs* for moments of deep feeling or reflection. Although the accompanied *air* is theoretically more highly organized than the accompanied recitative, this distinction is often more imagined than real. Thus the sharp demarcation between recitative and aria so characteristic of Italian opera was foreign to the French style, in which the recitative was nourished by the restrained melodic patterns of the *air*, and the *air* never completely lost the declamatory bias of the recitative. In the words of Blainville (in *L'esprit de l'art musical*, 1754) 'our recitative sings too much, our airs not enough'. The temporary suspension of stage action in the monologue *air*, however, allowed Lully freedom to exploit long motto preludes, instrumental interludes and a greater melodic amplitude and richer harmony than was possible in the dialogue or maxim *airs* (e.g. 'Bois épais' in *Amadis*). Renaud's monologue *air* 'Plus j'observe ces lieux' from *Armide* illustrates Lully's skill in organizing a large-scale *air* that borders on the through-composed. Unity is achieved by the constantly repeated quaver pairs in the orchestra that represent the gently flowing stream as well as by a brief motif repeated at an ever higher pitch level which transfers from orchestra to voice. At no place, however, is there an exact repetition of any portion of the *air*. Dance-songs in *tragédies lyriques* occur only in the divertissements. They are usually literal transcriptions of the dances that they follow or, less often, precede. There are several examples, however, in which Lully varied the dance in the vocal version either by altering the phrase structure or by changing the melodic or harmonic organization (e.g. the second *air*, and the song of the two old men based on it, in *Thésée*, Act 2 scene vii).

Lully favoured the duo above all other small ensembles in his *tragédies lyriques*. They range from simple duo fragments and strophic dance-songs to a

6. The sommeil
(Act 3 scene iv;
'arrivée des
songes agréables
et funestes') from
Lully's tragédie
lyrique 'Atys':
design by Berain
for a revival,
probably in the
1680s

38

fluid duo–*air*–recitative complex which may dominate a complete scene. Consistent with their being in a style that is responsive to words, most of Lully's duos are homophonic; the points of imitation at the beginning of sections rapidly settle into a note-against-note texture. What P.-M. Masson (in *L'opéra de Rameau*, 1930) has called the 'divergent duo' expresses the opposing sentiments of two people. It is extremely rare in French opera before Rameau. *Proserpine* includes a duo, 'Ma douleur mortelle' (in Act 4 scene iv), which highlights the conflict between Pluto and Proserpine and is as close as Lully ever came to writing an operatic 'divergent duo'. What Rousseau called a 'duo en dialogue' here leads naturally into the formal duo itself, in which there is an attempt to individualize the characters (see ex.6). A trio, 'Dormons, dormons tous', is the heart of the *sommeil* in *Atys* (Act 3 scene iv; see fig.6). It is based on the trio 'Dormez, dormez, beaux yeux' in *Les amants magnifiques* (1670) (a *comédie-ballet*) which in turn was derived from similar trios in Roman opera such as 'Dormite, begli occhi' in Luigi Rossi's *Orfeo* (1647).

Lully's originality may best be observed in the way in which he involved the chorus in the action of a *tragédie lyrique*. Choral fragments of cries of exhortation or supplication are everywhere in evidence. They combine with open-ended sections that defy structural analysis. Act 3 of *Isis* falls just short of being made up exclusively of choruses, some of which employ antiphonal and echo effects. In Act 4 scene iv of *Atys* the chorus watches and comments on the murder of Sangaride in the manner of an ancient

Ex.6 from 'Ma douleur mortelle', *Proserpine* (after Ballard's edition, 1680)

Greek chorus ('Atys, Atys luy même fait périr ce qu'il aime'). Elementary speech-rhythms and repeated notes create impressively bellicose sounds in the great battle choruses of *Thésée* and *Bellérophon*. On the other hand, long, non-functional choruses meant to embellish the divertissements are too often musically static and monotonous; the finale of *Amadis* is an example. They are scored for a *grand* and a *petit choeur*, a division that surely stemmed from such *grands motets* as Lully's own *Miserere* of 1664. The *grand choeur* consists of soprano, countertenor, tenor and bass parts; the most typical vocal distribution in the *petit choeur* is two sopranos and a countertenor. The pervading homophony of these choruses occasionally gives way to brief imitative passages that result from extended melismas on words such as 'volez', 'brillez' and 'coulez'. When doubled by the five-part orchestra this strictly syllabic choral writing produces a massive sound admittedly appropriate to the empty apotheoses to Louis, the 'plus grand des héros', found in the prologues.

Lully's orchestration is conservative, predictable and hierarchical. It exploits strong, somewhat primitive primary colours. There is little attempt to write individually for the various instruments: oboes, flutes, violins and even trumpets share similar material. The more heterogeneous orchestration of the court and comedy ballets is here simplified and standardized. Like the chorus, the opera orchestra was divided into a *grand* and *petit choeur*. Although many details of Lully's instrumentation are not known, it is clear that the five-part string orchestra, usually designated 'tous' or 'violons', formed the core of the *grand choeur*; it called in principle for heavy doubling by the oboes and bassoons, which were the workhorses of Lully's orchestra. The *petit choeur*, composed of about ten of the best instrumentalists (including violins, flutes, theorbos, bass viols and harpsichord), accompanied solo *airs* and alternated with the *grand choeur* in concertato passages.

Lully's writing for strings is extremely conservative when compared with that of his Italian contemporaries. The wide leaps, double stops and rapid arpeggios found in Italian music as early as Biagio Marini (*c*1587–1663) are alien to his style. His dramatic *symphonies* and dances and even his lightly imitative trio *ritournelles* are narrow in range and are usually limited to conjunct motion with little or no crossing of parts. More violent action is often expressed by dotted rhythms and *tirades*, which are obvious by-products of the kinetic vitality of the dance (e.g. the combat music of Act 1 scene iv of *Amadis*). Technique and virtuosity were for Lully less important than rhythmic accuracy and finesse in performance. This dictated his choice of a test piece for instrumentalists aspiring to join his orchestra: the 'Entrée des songes funestes' in *Atys*, an extract from which is shown in ex.7.

Ex.7 from the 'Entrée des songes funestes', *Atys* (after Ballard's edition, 1689)

The *symphonies* of Lully's *tragédies lyriques* may be divided into four main categories: overtures, preludes and *ritournelles*, dramatic *symphonies* and dances. The typical French overture reached opera through the court and comedy ballets. Preludes and *ritournelles*, the latter most often in trio texture, introduce a scene, an act, an *air* or an ensemble, or they carry on the dramatic action. The preludes to 'Amour, que veux-tu de moi' and 'Bois épais', both in *Amadis*, are merely instrumental versions of the *airs* themselves. However, the two preludes in Act 3 scene ii of the same opera are true dramatic *sym*-

7. Set for Lully's tragédie lyrique 'Atys' (Act 5 scene vi) by
Carlo Vigarani, Saint-Germain, 1676: engraving by Lallou-
ette after François Chauveau

*phonies*, in which the stage action is carefully spelt out. Lully achieved his most imaginative orchestration in his dramatic *symphonies*. Two of the most famous nature scenes in French Baroque opera are the *sommeil* in *Atys* (Act 3 scene iv), which calls for strings and flutes (probably recorders), and Act 2 scene iii of *Armide*, in which the strings are instructed to use mutes when playing the introduction to Renaud's monologue *air*, 'Plus j'observe ces lieux' (see ex.8).

It is unfortunately seldom possible to determine the exact scoring of Lully's dances. Prunières (*Oeuvres complètes: Opéras*, ii, p.xxii), after studying collections of partbooks, concluded that 'harpsichord and wind instruments, unless precisely indicated, did not participate in the *airs de danse*'. If true this would allow maximum contrast between the string orchestra and the trio episodes, which were usually scored for two oboes and bassoon, two flutes (or recorders) and viola (a transparent imitation of the two sopranos and countertenor of the *petit choeur* of the chorus), or three solo strings from the *petit choeur*. When Lully used the words 'basse-continue' in his operas he included figures implying the use of a harpsichord realization. Figures are missing, however, from overtures, dances and many independent *symphonies* (see Sadler, 1980).

Minuets and gavottes far outnumber all other titled dances in Lully's operas (see Ellis in *RMFC*, ix, 30); Ellis estimated that 80% of his titled dances are binary. Untitled dances, unfettered by choreographic conventions, permitted him the most freedom in

Ex.8 from 'Plus j'observe ces lieux', *Armide* (after Ballard's edition, 1686)

PRELUDE

lentement

linking dance to action. Although specific information on his innovatory 'danse en action' is
lacking, there is the word of Dubos, who had 'heard
tell of some ballets almost without dance but
composed instead of gesture ... – in a word a pan-

tomime – that Lully had created for the funeral cere-monies in *Psyché* and *Alceste*'. Dubos also singled out the 'shivering chorus' in *Isis* (Act 4 scene i), in which 'not a single step from our ordinary dance was employed'.

# CHAPTER THREE

# Church music, instrumental music

## I  Church music

Though Lully never held an official position at the
royal chapel, he was actively engaged in the composition of *grands* and *petits motets* for 20 years. The
long arm of his influence certainly extended to the
choice of those who sought the coveted position of
*sous-maître* at the royal chapel. According to Tannevot (*Discours sur la vie et les ouvrages de M. De La
Lande*, 1729), Lully suggested in 1683 that the king
hold a competition to fill the positions of four *sous-
maîtres*. Given his attitude towards potential rivals,
especially those from his native land, Lully may well
have played a part in the rejection of one of the candi-
dates, the popular and talented composer Paolo
Lorenzani; and there are those who suggest that the
illness of another candidate, Charpentier, may have
been a diplomatic one in the face of possible opposition from Lully (see Benoit: *Versailles et les musiciens
du Roi*, 105).

Between 1664 and his death Lully composed at
least 25 motets, of which 12 are *grand motets*. The
verses of the psalms used in the *grands motets* are
treated as semi-autonomous sections of *récits*, small
ensembles and choruses. An introductory *symphonie*

prefaces each motet, and larger structural divisions are often, as in the *Te Deum*, defined by *ritournelles*. In the *grands motets* he used a six-part orchestra distributed in a five-part texture of first and second violins, three 'filler' viola parts and continuo. The orchestra normally doubles the choral lines, thus avoiding the independent instrumental counterpoint timorously used by Du Mont and later exploited by Lalande. This distribution of voices in the *grand* and *petit choeur* takes advantage of contrasting sonorities: the *petit choeur* of two sopranos, counter-tenor, tenor and bass emphasizes high voices, whereas the *grand choeur* includes a baritone and no second soprano.

The earliest of Lully's *grands motets*, the *Miserere* (1664), ranks among his best. It was a favourite of Louis XIV, and Mme de Sévigné did not believe 'any other music to exist in heaven'. The sensuous quality of the *récit en duo* 'Amplius lava me', with its parallel 3rds and light polyphony, suggests the duo of Climène and Philis in the fifth *intermède* of *La princesse d'Elide*, composed in the same year. Though conceived primarily as vertical sonorities, the choruses of the *Miserere* occasionally give added dramatic thrust to key words by inserting a few bars of tightly knit polyphony amid sections of *récits*, much in the manner of the exhortatory choral fragments in the *tragédies lyriques* (the settings of the words 'impii' and 'multitudinem miserationum tuarum' are examples). Musically arid moments in the overlong *Te Deum* are compensated for in part by the relentless drive of the large homophonic choruses, in which exciting speech-rhythms are framed by trumpets and drums. This was

*8. Jean-Baptiste Lully: bronze bust by Coysevox at
Notre Dame des Victoires*

the sound of the Versailles motet, which was designed
to glorify the King of France as much as the King of
Heaven, and was undoubtedly the sound that Louis
had in mind when, 'by [his] express order', he had 50
*grands motets* by Lully, Du Mont and Robert printed
by Ballard between 1684 and 1686 for his chapel.

Most of Lully's *petits motets* are probably late

works, according to Philidor all composed for the Dames de l'Assomption at Paris. An important source for ten of them is a collection of *Petits motets et élévations* copied in 1688. Almost half of the 64 motets in this manuscript are by Carissimi and Francesco Foggia and help document the use of Italian music at the royal chapel during Lully's lifetime. Lully, who was aware of the king's liking for the church music of, for example, Lorenzani, may deliberately but discreetly have emulated the Italian style in his *petits motets*. Seven of them are scored for three sopranos and continuo. The extract in ex.9 from *Salve*

Ex.9 from *Salve Regina* (after *F-Pn* Rés. F 1713(1))

*regina* shows how sensitive Lully was to the qualities of dissonance and melody when he was not compelled to adapt heroic postures.

## II  Instrumental music

Recent research (Schneider, 1984) calls attention for the first time to the basic role of Lully in a history of the French chamber trio. Le Cerf wrote that Lully's trios were among his 'earliest works'. Several of them exist in different sources that circulated in the late 17th century; some are in the two volumes of *Trios de différents autheurs* edited by 'Babel' (perhaps William Babell) and E. Roger and published in Amsterdam in

1697 and 1698. The earliest dated trio by Lully is the 'Première pièce à trois', one of the two Lully trios found at the end of the Ballard publication of *Pièces pour le violon à quatre parties* (1665).

The most important source of Lully's chamber trios is a recently identified collection of *Trios de la chambre du roi* (Bibliothèque Nationale, Paris, Rés. 1397; also known as *Trios pour le coucher du roi*), containing 47 pieces, among them several previously unknown Lully chamber trios. These are in the main independent compositions, not arrangements of extracts from Lully's stage music. Although only one piece, an allemande, can be dated (Philidor states that it was composed at Fontainebleau in 1667), the entire source undoubtedly predates the many collections of suites arranged by others from Lully's ballets and operas. There is little influence from the Italian trio sonata. Most of the pieces in the collection are single dance movements in binary form, composed originally for the 'coucher' of Louis XIV. Homophonic texture, with the upper two voices moving in parallel motion, dominates, although two of the minuets are more polyphonically conceived.

We owe to André-Danican Philidor many manuscript copies of Lully's *pièces d'occasion*. The *Airs de trompette, timballes et hautbois* (LWV72) composed 'by order of the king for the carousal of Monseigneur in 1686', is a dance suite consisting of prelude, minuet, gigue and gavotte; the prelude is scored for five trumpets and four oboes. The march composed by Lully in 1672 (LWV48) is one of the rare examples in French ensemble music based on the folía theme and bass line. Clearly, in spite of his pre-eminence among French composers, Lully was expected to contribute such *pièces d'occasion* throughout his career at court. That he may have complained on occasion is suggested by the marginal note by Philidor in his copy of the '4ᵉ Air des hautbois fait par M. de Luly [*sic*]' (LWV75/8). He wrote: 'Philidor composed the inner voices, M de Luly having wished not to have to do it'.

Among Lully's earliest instrumental music are dances collectively titled 'Branles de 1665' or 'Bransles de M de Lully' (LWV31). Although branles dominate the collection of 1665, there are also gavottes, courantes, sarabandes, bourrées and one each of minuet, allemande, *passacaille*, *gaillarde* and boutade. In common with Lully's undated collections of dances, the 1665 collection is generally independent of Lully's stage music; most such dances were surely composed for court balls.

9. Divertisse-
ment in the
garden at
Versailles, the
first day (7 May
1664) of a three-
day 'grand
divertissement'
(Les Plaisirs de
l'Ile Enchantée)
given by Louis
XIV to honour
his mother, Anne
of Austria, and
his queen, Marie-
Thérèse:
engraving by
Israel Silvestre
(1670)

# CHAPTER FOUR

# Influence

At the time of his death in 1687 Lully had already been enshrined in the French Parnassus and was considered by foreigners to be the most representative of French composers. In 1688 *Phaëton* inaugurated the new royal academy at Lyons thanks to an ordinance of 17 August 1684 that gave only Lully permission to 'establish operas in France'. If we may believe the anonymous compiler of the manuscript *Journal* at the Bibliothèque de l'Opéra, *Bellérophon* 'without machines' was performed at the Château d'If in Marseilles in 1680. *Le triomphe de l'amour*, *Phaëton* and *Armide* were performed in Marseilles in 1686. The last two operas (in 1687) and *Bellérophon* (in 1688) were performed in Avignon under the direction of Pierre Gautier with members of the Marseilles opera. The geographical distribution of Lully's music outside France was remarkable: *Cadmus et Hermione* was performed in London (1686) and Amsterdam (1687), *Thésée* in Brussels (1682) and Wolfenbüttel (1687), *Proserpine* in Antwerp (1682) and Wolfenbüttel (1685), *Thésée* in The Hague (1682) followed by *Atys* (1687), *Psyché* in Wolfenbüttel (1686) and Modena (1687), *Persée* in Brussels (1682) and *Amadis* and *Cadmus* in Amsterdam (1687). *Armide* was the first French opera performed in Rome (in 1690) and

*Acis et Galatée* (1689) the first opera by a non-German composer to be heard at the Hamburg opera.

In England, Roger North observed that 'all the compositions of the towne were strained to imitate Baptist's vein' (see Cudworth). Purcell found in *Isis* the model for his famous 'Frost Scene' in Act 3 of *King Arthur* and may have learnt from Lully the technique of organizing an entire scene around a *passacaille* or chaconne. In Germany, in the preface to his *Composition de musique, suivant la méthode françoise contenant six ouvertures de théâtre accompagnées de plusieurs airs* (Stuttgart, 1682), J. S. Kusser acknowledged his debt to Lully, 'whose works at present give pleasure to all the courts of Europe'. Georg Muffat thought himself possibly the first to have introduced the style of Lully's overtures and dances into Austria and Bohemia through 15 orchestral suites contained in his *Florilegium primum* (1695) and *Florilegium secundum* (1698). In Italy the influence of Lully's overtures and *airs de danse* was felt in the concerti grossi of Corelli. According to Titon du Tillet, Theobaldo di Gatti decided to go to France in order to meet the composer whose instrumental music had so delighted him in performances in Florence.

The next generation of composers in France, who were now free to listen to Italian music, still had to deal with an intransigent Lully, who, a legend in his lifetime, had rapidly been canonized after his death as the patron saint of French music. For Le Cerf there was assuredly an aura about him, and Titon du Tillet spoke for many when he described him as the 'father of our beautiful French music'. At the same time some disenchantment with his *tragédies lyriques* became more noticeable as the 18th century progressed. 'How many of the works by these two great masters [Lully and Quinault] have sustained their initial brilliance?', asked the *Mercure galant* for November 1714, adding that '*Bellérophon* nowadays appears too tragic, *Thésée* too listless'. Yet we must not assume a general rejection of the Lullian aesthetic at that time. Box office receipts tell quite a different story: whether or not a latterday Mme de la Fayette could still be moved to tears by the 'prodigious beauties' of *Alceste*, coaches still lined the Faubourg St Honoré on days when Lully's operas were performed. His hold over the French public is clear from the fact that *Thésée*, 'listless' or not, held the stage for 104 years, that *Armide* was performed as late as 1766 and that *Amadis* remained in the Paris Opéra repertory for 87 years.

# WORKS

Editions: *Les chefs d'oeuvres classiques de l'opéra français*, ed. J. B. Weckerlin and others (Paris, 1878–83/*R*) [W]

J.-B. Lully: *Les oeuvres complètes*, ed. H. Prunières, 4 ser., inc. (Paris, 1930–39/*R*) [P]; *Motets iii*, ed. H. Prunières, rev. M. Sanvoisin (New York, 1972) [P, motets iii]

J.-B. Lully: *Complete works*, ed. C. B. Schmidt and others (in preparation) [4 ser., continuation of P and new critical edition]

Catalogue: *Chronologisch-thematisches Verzeichnis sämtlicher Werke von Jean-Baptiste Lully (LWV)*, ed. H. Schneider (Tutzing, 1981) [LWV]

Principal manuscript sources are: *CS-Pnm*; *D-Bd*, *Sl*; *F-B*, *Mc*, *Pa*, *Pc*, *Pmeyer*, *Pn*, *Po*, *TLm*, *V*; *GB-Cfm*, *Lbm*; *US-BE*; for specific sources for each title see Schneider [LWV] (1981), Christout (1967), 257ff and Ellis (1968).

Numbers in the right-hand margin denote references in the text.

### TRAGÉDIES LYRIQUES

*(initial publication dates given are those of first printed full scores, issued Ballard, Paris, unless otherwise stated)*

| LWV | Title (no. of acts) | Libretto | First performances; remarks | Publication | Edition | |
|---|---|---|---|---|---|---|
| 49 | Cadmus et Hermione (prol, 5) | P. Quinault | Paris, Jeu de paume de Béquet, 27 April 1673 | (1719); ov., inst airs pubd separately (Amsterdam, 1682); inst airs pubd separately (Amsterdam, c1687–1700) | P, opéras i | 8, 35, 55 |
| 50 | Alceste, ou Le triomphe d'Alcide (prol, 5) | Quinault | Paris, Opéra, 19 Jan 1674 | (Paris: de Baussen, 1708) [reduced score]; inst airs pubd separately (Amsterdam, c1687–1700) | P, opéras ii, 1 air ed. in HAM, ii | 9, 27, 29, 31, 32, 46, 57, 177 |
| 51 | Thésée (prol, 5) | Quinault | Saint-Germain-en-Laye, 11 Jan 1675; Paris, Opéra, April 1675 | (1688) | W xxvi | 14, 19, 28, 31, 37, 40 55, 57 |
| 53 | Atys (prol, 5) | Quinault | Saint-Germain, 10 Jan 1676; Paris, Opéra, April 1676 | (1689); airs pubd (Amsterdam, 1687); ov., inst airs pubd separately (Amsterdam, 1704) | W xxviii | 31, 33, 38, 39, 43, 44, 55 |
| 54 | Isis (prol, 5) | Quinault | Saint-Germain, 5 Jan 1677; Paris, Opéra, Aug 1677 | (1719); pubd in partbooks (Paris, 1677) | W xvi, 2 choruses ed. H. L. Sarlit (Paris, 1951); 1 monologue ed. in Mw, v (1962) | 9, 11, 13, 39, 46, 56 |
| 56 | Psyché (prol, 5) | Quinault, T. Corneille, B. le Bovier de Fontenelle | Paris, Opéra, 19 April 1678 | (1720); inst airs pubd separately (Amsterdam, c1687–1700), ov., inst airs pubd separately (Amsterdam 1705) | | 31, 46, 55 |
| | | | | | | 18, 19, 22, 27–46, 57, 266 |

| No. | Title | Librettist | Place, date | (Date) | Editions | References |
|---|---|---|---|---|---|---|
| 57 | Bellérophon (prol, 5) | Corneille, Fontenelle, N. Boileau-Despréaux | Paris, Opéra, 31 Jan 1679 | (1679) | W xix | 11, 12, 19, 34, 40, 55, 57, 127 |
| 58 | Proserpine (prol, 5) | Quinault | Saint-Germain, 3 Feb 1680; Paris, Opéra, 15 Dec 1680 | (1680) | W xxiv; 2 airs ed. in R. Petit, *ReM*, vi (1925), suppl. | 9, 39, 55 |
| 60 | Persée (prol, 5) | Quinault | Paris, Opéra, 18 April 1682 | (1682) | W xxii; 1 lament ed. in GMB, 232 | 8, 31, 35, 55, 249 |
| 61 | Phaëton (prol, 5) | Quinault | Versailles, 6 Jan 1683; Paris, Opéra, 27 May 1683 | (1683) | W xxiii | 9, 55 |
| 63 | Amadis (prol, 5) | Quinault | Paris, Opéra, 18 Jan 1684 | (1684) | P, opéras iii | 8, 9, 28, 31, 35, 36, 37, 40, 42, 55, 57 |
| 65 | Roland (prol, 5) | Quinault | Versailles, 8 Jan 1685; Paris, Opéra, 9 March 1685 | (1685) | 1 air ed. in *HawkinsH*, iv, 224; 1 chaconne ed. in GMB, 233; ov. ed. in H. Riemann: *Musikgeschichte in Beispielen* (Leipzig, 1912), 212 | 8, 9, *10*, 28, 29 |
| 71 | Armide (prol, 5) | Quinault | Paris, Opéra, 15 Feb 1686 | (1686) | W xvii; Acts 1, 2 ed. in PÄMw, xiv (1885); ed. F. Martin, with preface by H. Prunières (Geneva, 1924); 1 monologue ed. in GMB, 318; ov. ed. in *Masterpieces of Music before 1750* (New York, 1951), no.36; sommeil (Act 2 scene iii). ed. H. C. Wolff, *The Opera*, i, (Cologne, 1971) | 8, 12, 28, *30*, *31*, 33, 37, 44, 55, 57 |
| 74 | Achille et Polyxène (prol, 5) | J. G. de Campistron | Paris, Opéra, 7 Nov 1687; ov. and Act 1 by Lully, prol, Acts 2–5 by Collasse | (1687) | | 18 |

18–23

BALLETS, MASCARADES, INTERMÈDES

All ballets unless otherwise stated. Many works were written in collaboration with other composers; the number of items composed by Lully is given in square brackets after each title. Printed works were published by Ballard, Paris.

| LWV | Title (genre) | Libretto | First performance | Remarks; publication; edition |
|---|---|---|---|---|
| | | (all or mostly Lully's music) | | |
| 5 | Ballet de la révente des habits [22 nos., incl. 10 entrées] | I. de Benserade | before 1661 [1665 according to Titon du Tillet] | |
| 8 | Ballet de l'amour malade [47 nos., incl. 10 entrées] | F. Buti | Paris, Louvre, 17 Jan 1657 | P, ballets i |
| 9 | Ballet d'Alcidiane [79 nos., incl. 21 entrées] | Benserade | 14 Feb 1658 | P, ballets ii |
| 11 | Ballet de la raillerie [45 nos., incl. 12 entrées] | Benserade | Paris, Louvre, 19 Feb 1659 | |
| 12 | Xerxes (intermèdes) [14 nos., incl. 6 entrées] | N. Minato | Paris, Louvre, 22 Nov 1660 | for P. F. Cavalli: Serse [1st perf. in Paris]; P, ballets ii |
| 14 | Ballet de l'impatience [54 nos., incl. 16 entrées] | Buti [vers by Benserade] | Paris, Louvre, 19 Feb 1661 | |
| 15 | Ballet des saisons [23 nos., incl. 9 entrées] | Benserade | Fontainebleau, 23 July 1661 | |
| 17 | Hercule amoureux [41 nos., incl. 18 entrées] | Buti [vers by Benserade] | for Cavalli: Ercole amante, Paris, Salle des machines des Tuileries, 7 Feb 1662 | |
| 18 | Ballet des arts [29 nos., incl. 7 entrées] | Benserade | Paris, Palais Royal, 8 Jan 1663 | |
| 19 | Les noces de village (mascarade ridicule) [20 nos., incl. 13 entrées] | Benserade | Vincennes, château, 3 Oct 1663 | |
| 21 | Ballet des amours déguisez [38 nos., incl. 14 entrées] | Président de Perigny [vers by Benserade] | Paris, Palais Royal, 13 Feb 1664 | |
| 23 | Entr' actes d'Oedipe (Petit ballet de Fontainebleau) [6 nos.] | P. Corneille | Fontainebleau, 3 Aug 1664 | |
| 27 | Ballet de la naissance de Vénus [45 nos., incl. 12 entrées] | Benserade | Paris, Palais Royal, 26 Jan 1665 | |
| 28 | Ballet des gardes, ou Les delices de la campagne [5 nos.] | anon. | June 1665 | P, ballets ii |

| | |
|---|---|
| | 3,19 |
| | 19 |
| | 19 |
| | 20 |
| | 20 |
| | 20 |

| No. | Title | Librettist | Place, date | Notes | Ref. |
|---|---|---|---|---|---|
| 30 | Ballet de Créquy, ou Le triomphe de Bacchus dans les Indes (mascarade) [8 nos., incl. 5 entrées] | anon. | Paris, Hôtel de Créqui, 9 Jan 1666 | | |
| 32 | Ballet des muses [28 nos., incl. 13 entrées] | Benserade, Molière | Saint-Germain, 2 Dec 1666 | final perfs., Feb 1667, incl. comédies-ballets Lwv33, 34; extracts ed. K. Husa (New York, c1978) | 20, 21 |
| 36 | Le carnaval mascarade, ou Mascarade de Versailles [17 nos., incl. 7 entrées] | Benserade | Paris, Louvre, 18 Jan 1668 | for 2nd version see Lwv52 | |
| 40 | Ballet de Flore [39 nos., incl. 15 entrées] | Benserade | Paris, Tuileries, 13 Feb 1669 | | 20, 21 |
| 46 | Ballet des ballets [81 nos., incl. 7 entrées] | Molière, Quinault | Saint-Germain, 2 Dec 1671 | extracts from Lwv23, 33, 42, 43, 45, perf. between acts of Molière: La comtesse d'Escarbagnas | |
| 52 | Le carnaval mascarade [61 nos., incl. 9 entrées] | Benserade, Molière | Paris, Opéra, 17 Oct 1675 | incl. extracts from Lwv33, 34, 36, 40, 41, 43; for 1st version see Lwv36; (1720) | |
| 59 | Le triomphe de l'amour [72 nos., incl. 20 entrées] | Benserade, Quinault | Saint-Germain, 21 Jan 1681; Paris, Opéra, 10 May 1681 | (1681) | 13, 22, 23, 55 |
| 69 | Le temple de la paix [45 nos., incl. 6 entrées] | Quinault | Fontainebleau, 20 Oct 1685; Paris, Opéra, Nov 1685 | (1685) | 22 |

*(partly Lully's music)*

| No. | Title | Librettist | Place, date | Notes | Ref. |
|---|---|---|---|---|---|
| 1 | Ballet du temps [23 entrées, 1 no.] | Benserade | Paris, Louvre, 30 Nov 1654 | P, ballets i | |
| 2 | Ballet des plaisirs [25 entrées, 6 nos.] | Benserade | Paris, Louvre, 4 Feb 1655 | P, ballets i | |
| 4 | Ballet des bienvenus [16 entrées] | Benserade | Compiègne, 30 May 1655 | for the marriage of Alphonso d'Este and Laura Martinozzi; music lost | 19 |
| 6 | Ballet de Psyché, ou de La puissance de l'amour [27 entrées] | Benserade | Paris, Louvre, 16 Jan 1656 | music lost | |
| 7 | La galanterie du temps (mascarade) [10 entrées] | anon. | 14 Feb 1656 | music lost | |
| 13 | Ballet de Toulouse [ov., 1 gigue] | ?ib lost | Toulouse, April 1660 | 'au mariage du Roy' | 4 |
| 24 | Mascarade du capitaine, ou L'impromptu de Versailles [10 entrées, 1 no.] | anon. | Paris, Palais Royal [Opéra], 1664/Feb 1665 | music lost | |

COMÉDIES-BALLETS, PASTORALES, ETC

(all comédies-ballets unless otherwise stated; printed works published by *Ballard, Paris*)

| LWV | Title (genre; no. of acts, musical items) | Libretto | First performances | Remarks; publication; edition | |
|---|---|---|---|---|---|
| 16 | Les fâcheux | Molière | Vaux-le-Vicomte, 17 Aug 1661 | 3 acts, music mostly by C. L. Beauchamps, Lully only contributed 1 no. | 18, 23–7 |
| 20 | Le mariage forcé (1, 16 nos.) | Molière | Paris, Louvre, 29 Jan 1664 | P, comédies-ballets i | 6, 23 |
| 22 | Les plaisirs de l'île enchantée (divertissement), incl.: 'course de bague' [choreographed tournement] La princesse d'Elide (ballet; 5) Ballet du palais d'Alcine (5 entrées) | Molière | Versailles, 7–12 May 1664 | title is collective term for an extended royal divertissement; P, comédies-ballets ii | 25, 48 |
| 29 | L'amour médecin (prol, 3, 9 nos.) | Molière | Versailles, 14 Sept 1665 | P, comédies-ballets i | 22 |
| 33 | La pastorale comique (pastorale; 1, 13 nos.) | Molière | Saint-Germain, 5 Jan 1667 | see LWV32; P, comédies-ballets ii | 22 |
| 34 | Le Sicilien (1, 8 nos.) | Molière | Saint-Germain, 14 Feb 1667 | see LWV32; P, comédies-ballets ii | 22, 26 |
| 38 | George Dandin (Le grand divertissement royal de Versailles) (comédie-divertissement; 3, 14 nos.) | Molière | Versailles, 18 July 1668 | P, comédies-ballets ii | 26 |
| 39 | La grotte de Versailles (eglogue en musique; 1, 13 nos.) | Quinault | Versailles, April 1668; Paris, Opéra, Nov 1685 [as Eglogue de Versailles] | (1685); P, comédies-ballets ii | 8 |
| 41 | M. de Pourceaugnac (Le divertissement de Chambord) (3, 23 nos.) | Molière, Lully [for It. text] | Chambord, 6 Oct 1669 | P, comédies-ballets iii | 23 |
| 42 | Les amants magnifiques (Le divertissement royal) (5, 35 nos.) | Molière | Saint-Germain, 7 Feb 1670 | P, comédies-ballets iii | 26, 39 |
| 43 | Le bourgeois gentilhomme (22 nos.) [perf. incl. Ballet des nations (19 nos, incl. 5 entrées)] | Molière | Chambord, 14 Oct 1670 | P, comédies-ballets iii | 6, 25, 26 |
| 45 | Psyché (tragédie-ballet; 38 nos.) | Molière, Lully, P. Corneille, Quinault | Paris, Tuileries, 17 Jan 1671 | | 8, 27 |
| 47 | Les fêtes de l'Amour et de Bacchus (pastorale-pastiche; prol, 3, 48 nos.) | Molière, Quinault, Président de Périgny | Paris, Jeu de paume de Béquet, 13/15 Nov 1672 | incl. extracts from LWV33, 38, 40, 42, 43; (1717) | 8, 18 |
| 68 | Idylle sur la paix (idylle; 16 nos.) | J. Racine | Sceaux, 16 July 1685; Paris, Opéra, Nov 1685 | (1685) | 17 |
| 73 | Acis et Galatée (pastorale-héroïque; prol, 3, 54 nos.) | J. G. de Campistron | Anet, 6 Sept 1686; Paris, Opéra, 17 Sept 1686 | (1686) | 17, 18, 35, 56, |

# LWV

*(dates are those of first performance)*

For additional sources, see: *Catalogue thématique des sources du grand motet français, 1663–1792* (Paris, 1984), 170–78

## MOTETS

[6] Motets à deux choeurs pour la chapelle du Roy (Paris, 1684):

47–51

25 — Miserere, wint 1664; P, motets i  *(40, 48)*

37 — Plaude laetare (P. Perrin), 7 April 1668; P, motets ii; ed. G. Roussel (Paris, 1954)

55 — Te Deum, Fontainebleau, 9 Sept 1677; P, motets ii; ed. F. Raugel (Paris, 1949); vocal score ed. W. K. Stanton (London, 1955)  *(14, 48)*

62 — De profundis, May 1683; P, motets iii

64/1 — Dies irae; P, motets ii; ed. H. L. Sarlit (Paris, 1952); vocal score ed. G. Roussel (Paris, 1955)

64/2 — Benedictus

6 grands motets, 2 choirs, orch, unpubd:

26 — O lachrymae (Perrin), Versailles, wint 1664

67 — Quare fremerunt, Versailles, 19 April 1685

77/14 — Domine salvum; P, motets iii

77/15 — Exaudiat te Dominus, 'authore Jo. Baptiste de Lully. an 1687' (Brossard, Pn Rés.Vma.MS 574)

77/16 — Jubilate Deo

77/17 — Notus in Judaea

77/1–13 — 13 petits motets, 3vv (unless otherwise stated): Anima Christi, P. motets iii; Ave coeli manus (Perrin), P. motet iii; Dixit Dominus; Domine salvum; Exaudi Deus. Iste sanctus; Laudate pueri; Magnificat, 2vv; O dulcissime Domine; Omnes gentes, P. motets iii; O sapientia; Regina coeli; Salve regina, ed. J. Chailley (Paris, 1954)  *(50–51)*

## SECULAR VOCAL

3 — Un charmant dialogue de la guerre avecque la Paix, dialogue, 2 May 1655, music lost

76 — [26 airs, 14 text only]

Numerous airs and parodies from the operas, ballets and comédies-ballets (see above) printed in over 65 collections, incl. many reprints; for titles of collections see *RISM*, B/II (1964). Many in MSS: Airs ajoutés à l'opéra d'Atys, F-Pn; Airs de Phaéton, Roland, Thésée, Alceste and Atys, 1700, Pn; Airs tirées des opéras, comédies-ballets, pastorales et ballets de Lully, Pc [incl. some copies from printed collections and operas]

## INSTRUMENTAL

*(dates are those of composition)*

51–3

10 — Première marche des Mousquetaires, 1658

31 — 27 dances, 1664/5: 10 branles, 3 gavottes, 4 courantes, 1 passacaille, 3 sarabandes, 3 bourées, 1 allemande, 1 boutade, 1 gaillarde  *(53)*

35 — [47] Trios de la chambre du Roi, i, ['premiers ouvrages' (Le Cerf)]: 9 menuets, 5 gavottes, 4 sarabandes, 4 chaconnes, 2 allemandes [no.1 'composed 1667' (Philidor)], 5 parodies, 14 symphonies, 1 rondeau, 1 passacaille, 1 boutade, 1 descriptive movt; 9 trios pubd separately in Trios de différents auteurs (Amsterdam, 1698)  *(52)*

44/1 — Batteries de tambour, 1670

44/2 — Marche du Régiment du Roy, 'faite par M. de Lully l'an 1670' (Philidor)  *(51)*

48 — Marche (Air des hautbois des folies d'Espagne), 1672

66 — 5 Marches (de Savoye)

70 — Plusieurs pièces de symphonie, noce de village, airs, pour Mme la Dauphine: 2 menuets, 2 passepieds, 1 gigue, 1 chaconne; pubd in *La grotte de Versailles* (Paris, 1685)  *(52)*

72 — Airs pour le carrousel de Monseigneur, 28 May 1686: prelude, menuet, gigue, gavotte  *(52)*

75 — 15 marches; 40 dances: 8 airs, 3 allemandes, 14 courantes, 4 sarabandes, 2 bourées, 4 chaconnes, 1 menuet, 1 gigue, 2 descriptive movts, 1 trio  *(53)*

78 — 16 pieces ['probably by Lully' (Schneider)]: 1 overture, 1 march, 4 sarabandes, 2 gigues, 1 entrée, 1 air, 2 menuets, 1 chaconne, 1 parody, 2 descriptive movts  *(53)*

Over 40 sources containing suites arranged from Lully's opera and ballet scores are listed in Schneider [LWV] (1981), pp. 8–12. See also *RISM*, B/II (1964); several branles, F-Pn Cassel MS, ed. in J. Ecorcheville: *Vingt suites d'orchestre du XVIIe siècle français*, ii (Paris, 1906/R1970), 125

BIBLIOGRAPHY

M. de Pure: *Idée des spectacles anciens et nouveaux* (Paris, 1668/*R*1972)

H. Guichard: *Requête servant de factums contre B. Lully* (Paris, 1673)

C. Perrault: *Critique de l'opéra, ou Examen de la tragédie intitulée 'Alceste ou Le triomphe d'Alcide'* (Paris, 1674)

H. Guichard: *Mémoires de Guichard contre Lully et de Lully contre Guichard* (Paris, 1675)

Nodot: *Le triomphe de Lulli aux Champs-Elysées* (MS, F-Pa, 1687; repr. in *ReM*, vi/2 (1925), 89)

A. Bauderon de Sénecé: *Lettre de Clément Marot . . . à l'arrivée de J.-B. de Lulli aux Champs-Elysées* (Cologne, 1688; repr. in *Echo musical*, 1913, 5 Feb, 4; 5 March, 4; 5 April, 4)

C. Perrault: 'Eloge de J.-B. Lully', *Les hommes illustres qui ont paru en France*, i (Paris, 1696), 85.

*Recueil général des opéra* (Paris, 1703–46/*R*1971)

J. L. Le Cerf de la Viéville: *Comparaison de la musique italienne et de la musique françoise* (Brussels, 1704–6/*R*1972)

N. Boindin: *Lettres historiques sur tous les spectacles de Paris* (Paris, 1719)

J.-B. Dubos: *Réflexions critiques sur la poésie et sur la peinture* (Paris, 1719, 7/1770/*R*1972; Eng. trans. of 5/1746 as *Critical reflections on poetry, painting and music,* London, 1748/*R*[1978])

E. Titon du Tillet: *Le Parnasse françois* (Paris, 1732–43/*R*1971)

C. and F. Parfaict: *Histoire de l'Académie royale de musique* (MS, 1741, *Pn* nouv. acq. fr.6532) [1835 copy with annotations by Beffara, *Pn* fr.12.355]

R. de Saint-Mard: *Réflexions sur l'opéra* (The Hague, 1741/*R*1972)

C. and F. Parfaict: *Dictionnaire des théâtres de Paris* (Paris, 1756/ *R*1967, 2/1767, with G. d'Auguerbe)

J.-B. Durey de Noinville: *Histoire du théâtre de l'Académie royale de musique en France* (Paris, 1757/1969)

L.-F. Beffara: *Dictionnaire de l'Académie royale de musique* (autograph MS, 1783–4, *Po* Rés.602)

P. Lacombe: 'Lully, professeur de violon', *Chronique musicale*, viii (1875), 167

T. Lajarte: *Lully* (Paris, 1878)

——: 'Bellérophon de Lully', *Le ménestrel*, xlvi (1880), 153

C. Nuitter and E. Thoinan: *Les origines de l'opéra français* (Paris, 1886/*R*1972)

E. de Bricqueville: *Le livret d'opéra français de Lully à Gluck* (Brussels, 1888)

E. Radet: *Lully, homme d'affaires, propriétaire et musicien* (Paris, 1891)

# Bibliography

A. Pougin: 'Les origines de l'opéra français: Cambert et Lully', *Revue d'art dramatique*, xxi (1891), 129

C. Malherbe: 'Un autographe de Lulli', *Le ménestrel*, 1 (1898), 365

J. Ecorcheville: *De Lulli à Rameau, 1690–1730* (Paris, 1906/R1970)

H. Prunières: *Lully* (Paris, 1909, 2/1927)

——: 'La jeunesse de Lully (1632–62)', *BSIM*, v (1909), 234–42, 329–53

——: 'Recherches sur les années de jeunesse de J.-B. Lully', *RMI*, xvii (1910), 646

L. de La Laurencie: *Lully* (Paris, 1911, 2/1919/R1977)

P.-M. Masson: 'Lullistes et Ramistes 1733–1752', *Année musicale*, i (1911), 187

H. Prunières: 'Lettres et autographes de Lully', *BSIM*, viii/3 (1912), 19

——: 'Lully, fils de meunier', *BSIM*, viii/6 (1912), 57

J. Tiersot: 'Les origines de Lully', *Le ménestrel*, lxxviii (1912), 193

G. Lote: 'La déclamation du vers français à la fin du XVII$^e$ siècle', *Revue de phonétique*, ii (1912), 313

M. Denizard: 'La famille française de Lully', *BSIM*, viii/5 (1912), 1

M. Pellisson: *Les comédies-ballets de Molière* (Paris, 1914)

H. Prunières: 'La vie scandaleuse de Jean-Baptiste Lully', *Mercure de France*, cxv (1916), 75

L. de La Laurencie: 'Une convention commerciale entre Lully, Quinault et Ballard en 1680', *RdM*, ii (1920–21), 176

T. Gérold: *L'art du chant en France aux XVII$^e$ siècle* (Strasbourg, 1921/R1971)

L. de La Laurencie: *Les créateurs de l'opéra français* (Paris, 1921, 2/1930)

H. Prunières: 'La Fontaine et Lully', *ReM*, ii/10 (1921), 98

A. Tessier: 'Un document sur les répétitions du "Triomphe de l'Amour" à Saint-Germain-en-Laye (1681)', *Congrès d'histoire de l'art: Paris 1921*, 874

J. Tiersot: *La musique dans la comédie de Molière* (Paris, 1922)

X. de Courville: 'Quinault, poète d'opéra', *ReM*, vi/3 (1925), 74

A. Levinson: 'Notes sur le ballet au XVII$^e$ siècle: les danseurs de Lully', *ReM*, vi/5 (1925), 44

H. Prunières: 'Lully and the Académie de Musique et de Danse', *MQ*, xi (1925), 528

E. Gros: *Philippe Quinault* (Paris, 1926)

M. E. Sainte-Beuve: 'Le tombeau de Lully', *Gazette des beaux arts*, xiv (1926), 198

E. Benham: 'A Musical Monopolist', *ML*, ix (1928), 249

H. Prunières: 'Notes musicologiques sur un autographe musical de Lully', *ReM*, x (1928), 47

W. Storz: *Der Aufbau der Tänze in den Opern und Balletts Lullys vom musikalischen Standpunkte ausbetrachtet* (Göttingen, 1928)

E. Borrel: 'L'interprétation de Lully d'après Rameau', *RdM*, x (1929), 17

H. Prunières: *La vie illustre et libertine de Jean-Baptiste Lully* (Paris, 1929)

F. Noack: 'Die Musik zu der molièreschen Komödie *Monsieur de Pourceaugnac* von Jean Baptiste de Lully', *Musikwissenschaftliche Beiträge: Festschrift für Johannes Wolf* (Berlin, 1929), 139

F. Torrefranca: 'La prima opera francese in Italia?: *l'Armida* di Lulli, Roma 1690', *Musikwissenschaftliche Beiträge: Festschrift für Johannes Wolf* (Berlin, 1929), 191

H. Prunières: 'La première tragédie en musique de Lully: Cadmus et Hermione', *ReM*, xi (1930), 385

——: 'Les comédies-ballets de Molière et de Lully', *Revue de France*, xi/5 (1931), 297

——: 'Le Mariage forcé et l'Amour médecin de Molière et Lully', *ReM*, xii (1931), 289

——: 'Les premiers ballets de Lully', *ReM*, xii (1931), 1

E. Borrel: 'L'interprétation de l'ancien récitatif français', *RdM*, xii (1931), 13

P. Jarry: 'Lully à la Ville-l'Evêque: le no 30 de la rue Boissy-d'Anglas', *Société de l'histoire de Paris et de l'Ile-de-France: Bulletin*, lxi (1934), 103

P. Mélèse: *Le théâtre et le public à Paris sous Louis XIV, 1659–1715* (Paris, 1934)

——: *Répertoire analytique des documents contemporains . . . concernant les théâtres à Paris sous Louis XIV* (Paris, 1934)

P. H. Lang: *The Literary Aspects of the History of Opera in France* (diss., Cornell U., 1935)

D. J. Grout: 'Seventeenth Century Parodies of French Opera', *MQ*, xxvii (1941), 211, 514

B. Champigneulle: 'L'influence de Lully hors de France', *ReM*, xxii (1946), 26

E. Borrel: *Jean-Baptiste Lully* (Paris, 1949)

T. Valensi: *Louis XIV et Lully* (Nice, 1952)

J. Chailley: 'Notes sur la famille de Lully', *RdM*, xxxiv (1952), 101

N. Slonimsky: 'L'acte de naissance de Lully', *Guide du concert* (1 Feb 1952)

M. Pincherle: 'L'interpretazione orchestrale di Lulli', *L'orchestra* (1954), 139

J. Cordey: 'Lully d'après l'inventaire de ses biens', *RdM*, xxxvii (1955), 78

# Bibliography

C. L. Cudworth: '"Baptist's Vein"—French Orchestral Music and its Influence from 1650 to 1750', *PRMA*, lxxxiii (1956–7), 29

A. M. Nagler: 'Lully's Opernbühne', *Kleine Schriften der Gesellschaft für Theatergeschichte*, xvii (1960), 9

A. Ducrot: *Recherches sur Jean-Baptiste Lully (1632–1687) et sur les débuts de l'Académie royale de musique* (diss., Ecole de Chartes, 1961)

J. Eppelsheim: *Das Orchester in den Werken Jean-Baptiste Lullys* (Tutzing, 1961)

C. Masson: 'Journal du Marquis de Dangeau 1684–1720', *RMFC*, ii (1961–2), 193

J. Chailley: 'La déclamation théâtrale aux XVIIᵉ et XVIIIᵉ siècles d'après les récitatifs', *Saggi e ricerche in memoria di Ettore Li Gotti*, bulletin 6 (Palermo, 1962), 355

F. H. Neumann: *Die Aesthetik des Rezitativs: zur Theorie des Rezitativs im 17. und 18. Jahrhundert* (Strasbourg, 1962)

N. Demuth: *French Opera: its Development to the Revolution* (Horsham, Sussex, 1963)

L. Maurice-Amour: 'Comment Lully et ses poètes humanisent dieux et héros', *Cahiers de l'Association internationale des théâtres françaises*, xvii (1965), 59

M.-F. Christout: *Le ballet de cour de Louis XIV, 1643–1672* (Paris, 1967)

W. P. Cole: *The Motets of Jean Baptiste Lully* (diss., U. of Michigan, 1967)

K. Cooper and J. Zsako: 'Georg Muffat's Observations on the Lully Style of Performance', *MQ*, liii (1967), 220

H. M. Ellis: *The Dances of J. B. Lully (1632–1687)* (diss., Stanford U., 1967)

L. A. Auld: *The Unity of Molière's Comedy-ballets* (diss., Bryn Mawr College, 1968)

L. Hibberd: 'Mme de Sévigné and the Operas of Lully', *Essays in Musicology: a Birthday Offering for Willi Apel* (Bloomington, Ind., 1968), 153

H. M. Ellis: 'The Sources of Jean-Baptiste Lully's Secular Music', *RMFC*, viii (1968), 89–130

——: 'Inventory of the Dances of Jean-Baptiste Lully', *RMFC*, ix (1969), 21

R. M. Isherwood: 'The Centralization of Music in the Reign of Louis XIV', *French Historical Studies*, vi (1969–70), 156

Y. de Brossard: 'La vie musicale en France d'après Loret et ses continuateurs, 1650–1688', *RMFC*, x (1970), 117

A. Ducrot: 'Les représentations de l'Académie Royale de Musique à Paris au temps de Louis XIV, 1617–1715', *RMFC*, x (1970), 19

*Lully*

M. Benoit: *Musiques de cour: chapelle, chambre, écurie, recueil de documents, 1661–1733* (Paris, 1971)

——: *Versailles et les musiciens du Roi: étude institutionnelle et sociale, 1661–1733* (Paris, 1971)

C. Girdlestone: *La tragédie lyrique en musique, 1673–1750, considérée comme un genre littéraire* (Geneva, 1972)

F. Lesure, ed.: *L'opéra classique français: XVII<sup>e</sup> et XVIII<sup>e</sup> siècles* (Geneva, 1972)

J. R. Anthony: *French Baroque Music from Beaujoyeulx to Rameau* (London, 1973, rev. 2/1978, rev. Fr. trans., 1981 as *La musique en France à l'époque baroque*)

A. Ducrot: 'Lully créateur de troupe', *XVII<sup>e</sup> siècle*, no.98–9 (1973), 91

N. Dufourcq: 'Les fêtes de Versailles: la musique', *XVII<sup>e</sup> siècle*, no. 98–9 (1973), 67

——: 'Lully: l'oeuvre, à la diffusion, l'héritage', *XVII<sup>e</sup> siècle*, no.98–9 (1973), 109

S. Harris: 'Lully, Corelli, Muffat and the 18th Century Orchestral String Body', *ML*, liv (1973), 197

P. Howard: 'Lully's Alceste,' *MT*, cxiv (1973), 21

R. M. Isherwood: *Music in the Service of the King: France in the Seventeeth Century* (Ithaca, NY, and London, 1973)

G. Mongrédien: 'Molière et Lully', *XVII<sup>e</sup> siècle*, no.98–9 (1973), 3

R. Scott: *J.-B. Lully: The Founder of French Opera* (London, 1973)

A. I. Borowitz: 'Lully and the Death of Cambert', *MR*, xxxv (1974), 231

P. Howard: *The Operas of Lully* (diss., U. of Surrey, 1974)

E. Lance: 'Molière the Musician: a Tercentenary View', *MR*, xxxv (1974), 120

M. Seares: 'Aspects of Performance Practice in the Recitatives of Jean-Baptiste Lully', *SMA*, viii (1974), 8

P. Howard: 'The Académie Royale and the Performances of Lully's Operas', *Consort*, xxxi (1975), 109

P.-M. Masson: 'French Opera from Lully to Rameau', *NOHM*, v (London, 1975), 206

H. Schneider: *Der Rezeption der Lully-Oper im 17. und 18. Jahrhundert in Frankreich* (diss., U. of Mainz, 1976)

R. Fajon: 'Propositions pour une analyse rationalisée du récitatif de l'opéra lullyste', *RdM*, lxiv (1978), 55

J. de La Gorce: *L'Opéra sous le règne de Louis XIV: Le merveilleux ou les puissances surnaturelles, 1671–1715* (thesis, Sorbonne, 1978)

R. P. Wolf: 'Metrical Relationships in French Recitative of the Seventeenth and Eighteenth Centuries', *RMFC*, xviii (1978), 29

68

# Bibliography

J. E. W. Newman: *Jean-Baptiste de Lully and his Tragédies lyriques* (Ann Arbor, 1979)

L. E. Brown: 'Oratorical thought and the *Tragédie-lyrique*: a consideration of Musical-Rhetorical Figures', *Symposium*, xx (1980), 99

W. Hilton: *Dance and Music of Court and Theatre: the French noble style, 1690–1725* (Princeton, 1980)

D. Muller: 'Aspects de la déclamation dans le récitatif de Jean-Baptiste Lully', *Basler Studien zur Interpretation der alten Musik*, ed. H. Oesch, ii (Winterthur, 1980), 231

G. Sadler: 'The role of the keyboard continuo in French opera, 1673–1776', *Early Music*, viii (1980), 148

H. Schneider: 'Zur Rezeption von Molières und Lullys 'Psyché', *Stimmen der Romania, Festschrift T. W. Elwert*, ed. G. Schmidt and M. Tietz (Wiesbaden, 1980), 389

D. Barnett: 'La rhétorique de l'opéra', *XVII$^e$ siècle*, no.132 (1981), 336

J. de La Gorce: 'L'Opéra et son public au temps de Louis XIV', *Bulletin de la Société de l'histoire de Paris et de l'Ile-de-France*, cviii (1981), 27

L. Rosow: *Lully's Armide at the Paris Opéra: a performance history, 1686–1766* (diss., Brandeis U., 1981)

H. Schneider: 'Die Uberlieferung der Frühen Bühnenwerke von Jean-Baptiste Lully', *Mf*, xxxiv (1981), 284

C. Wood: *Jean-Baptiste Lully and his successors: Music and Drama in the 'tragédie en musique', 1673–1715* (diss., U. of Hull, 1981)

——: 'Orchestra and spectacle in the *tragédie en musique*, 1673–1715: oracle, *sommeil* and *tempête*', *PRMA*, cviii (1981–2), 25

H. Schneider: *Die Rezeption der Opern Lullys im Frankreich des Ancien Regime* (Tutzing, 1982)

——: 'Tragédie et tragédie en musique: querelles autour de l'autonomie d'un nouveau genre', *Komparatistische Hefte*, nos.5–6 (Bayreuth, 1982), 43

T. M. Turnbull: *A Critical Edition of Psyché: an Opera with Words by Thomas Corneille and Philippe Quinault, and Music by Jean-Baptiste Lully* (diss., U. of Oxford, 1982)

L. Rosow: 'French Baroque recitative as an expression of tragic declamation', *Early Music*, xi (1983), 468

R. P. Wolf, ed.: 'The Sources of the Lully Ballets: a status report', *French Baroque Music: a Newsletter*, no.1 (1983), 22

R. Fajon: *L'opéra à Paris du Roi-Soleil à Louis le Bien-aimé* (Geneva, 1984)

J. Hajdu: 'Recent Findings in the Sources of Lully's Motets: the Traditions of Philidor and Foucault', *Le grand motet français (1663–1792): CNRS Paris 1984*, 77

M. Little: 'A forgotten early printed source for Lully's music', *French Baroque Music; a Newsletter*, no.2 (1984), 27

——: 'The sources of Lully's Ballets: some procedures for preparing editions', *French Baroque Music: a Newsletter*, no.2 (1984), 28

H. Schneider: 'Die französische Kammersuite zwischen 1670 und 1720', *Jacob Stainer und seine Zeit*, ed. W. Salmen (Innsbruck, 1984), 163

——: 'La parodie spirituelle de chansons et d'airs profane chez Lully et chez ses contemporains', *La Pensée religieuses: Bamberg 1984*, 69

——: 'Lullys Beitrag zur Entstehung des Grand Motet', *Le grand motet français (1663–1792): CNRS Paris 1984*, 67

D. Tunley, 'The union of words and music in seventeenth-century French song: the long and the short of it', *Australian Journal of French Studies*, xxi/3 (1984), 281

W. Weber: '*La musique ancienne* in the waning of the Ancien Regime', *Journal of Modern History*, lvi (March, 1984), 58

W. Hilton: 'Dances to music by Jean-Baptiste Lully', *Early Music*, xiv (1986), 51

J. R. Anthony: 'Towards a principal source for Lully's court ballets: Foucault vs Philidor', *RMFC*, xxv (1987)

J. Hajdu, ed.: *Studies on Jean-Baptiste Lully and the Music of the French Baroque: Essays in Honor of James R. Anthony* (Cambridge, in preparation)

# MARC-ANTOINE CHARPENTIER

H. Wiley Hitchcock

CHAPTER ONE

# Life

Although Marc-Antoine Charpentier never held a position in the musical establishment of Louis XIV, his ability, productiveness and versatility won him several important posts in Paris and considerable renown. He was viewed by many, both during his life and afterwards, as the musical equal, if not the superior, of his more strategically placed contemporary, Lully.

The precise date of Charpentier's birth is unknown. The one most often given, 1634, goes back to Titon du Tillet, who, in his *Description du Parnasse françois* (1727), said that he died in 1702 at the age of 68. But for stylistic and other reasons 1634 seems too early. Circumstantial evidence suggests a time between 1662 and 1667 for the years of study with Carissimi in Rome; if, as Titon du Tillet said, Charpentier was 'in his youth' at the time (confirming Dassoucy, who spoke of him as a 'garçon' in 1672), it is perhaps close to the mark to suggest that he was born c1645–50. The frequently repeated claims that he came from a family of artists and that he went to Rome initially to study painting, not music, are undocumented. Recent research has disclosed the existence in Paris, around the mid-17th century, of several musicians with the surname Charpentier; perhaps he was related to one or another of these. His period of study with Carissimi lasted several years – three according to the *Mercure galant* (February 1681). His earliest music offers ample evidence of his absorption of mid-century Italian styles and forms. Among his extant autographs are copies of Carissimi's *Jephte* in the Bibliothèque Nationale, Paris (Vm[1] 1477) and of the unpublished *Missa mirabiles elationes maris* for four choirs by Francesco Beretta, to which he appended his own *Remarques sur les messes à 16 parties d'Italie*. Sébastien de Brossard, one of the most trustworthy early commentators on his life and music, remarked that he introduced into France copies of various Italian motets and several oratorios by Carissimi. It is probable that Charpentier's own Italianate music was first received favourably only outside court circles, within enclaves of partisans of Italian music such as Claude Nicaise (a canon from Dijon), René Ouvrard (*maître de musique* of the Sainte-Chapelle du Palais) and the Abbé Mathieu (*curé* of St André-des-Arts).

Charpentier's first musical post is uncertain. There is no documentary or contemporary evidence that he was employed immediately on his return from Rome (as a number of later accounts have it) by Marie de Lorraine, the Duchess of Guise. This pious noblewoman boasted one of the largest private musical establishments in France, at least after she inherited her family's fortune in 1675 and moved into the Hôtel de Guise in the Marais district. According to the *Mercure galant* of March 1688, the quality of the music produced in her *hôtel* exceeded that of many of the greatest monarchs. All of Charpentier's extant manuscript scores for the duchess belong to the period *c*1683–8; he also served her (from the early 1680s if not before) as an *haute-contre* and, ultimately, *maître de musique* (a post he seems to have retained until her death in 1688). For her establishment he wrote *La descente d'Orphée aux enfers* and at least seven other secular dramatic works; several dramatic motets ('oratorios'), other motets and psalm settings; and *Idyle sur le retour de la santé du roi* (1686–7). Perhaps because of the duchess's interest in various convents he wrote a number of sacred works for female voices; among them are motets, hymns, a *Magnificat* setting and a mass which were composed specifically for Port Royal.

Probably well before his employment by the Duchess of Guise, Charpentier began a long association with the troupe of Molière, later (in 1680) to become the Comédie Française. The fruitful collaboration between Molière and Lully had dissolved in 1672, when Lully embarked (with monopolistic royal privileges) on his career as opera composer, and it was then that Molière approached Charpentier. When *La comtesse d'Escarbagnas*, given at court on 2 December 1671, was first played before the Parisian public, on 8 July 1672, it had an overture by Charpentier, and instead of preceding the *Ballet des ballets*, with music by Lully (as it had the previous December), it preceded a revival of *Le mariage forcé* with new entr'acte *intermèdes* by Charpentier. Charpentier must have had a hand in a brief revival, early in autumn 1672, of *Les fâcheux* (1661), though no music survives. In that same year rehearsals began on *Le malade imaginaire*, for which extensive music was commissioned from Charpentier. On the assumption that the première would take place before the king, Molière wrote an elaborate prologue, larded with praise for Louis XIV; Charpentier set it as a substantial *pastorale* for six soloists, chorus and orchestra *à 4*. However, since no royal invitation came, the *grand prologue* was put aside and another substituted for the Paris run, which began on 10 February 1673. Charpentier also composed music for three *intermèdes* within the play which he was later to revise twice (and he adapted the original prologue to the text of *La couronne de fleurs* for a performance in 1685 at the Hôtel de Guise). After Molière's death in February 1673 Charpentier continued to work with the company until about 1686: he was commissioned to replace earlier music for plays by Molière and others with new settings that observed the restrictive terms of several royal ordinances (obtained by Lully) limiting the players' use of musicians; he also composed original music for the first runs of seven other stage works. Much of this music can be dated quite precisely from the company's account books preserved in the archives of the Comédie Française. Charpentier's skill as a composer of dramatic music was sought by others, among them M. Rians, the king's prosecutor for the old Châtelet, at whose Parisian *hôtel* (according to the *Mercure galant*, November 1678) *Les amours d'Acis et de Galatée* (now lost) was performed on several occasions during Carnival earlier that year.

In the meantime, Charpentier had been building a reputation as a composer of church music, receiving commissions from a number of churches and parishes, among them St Hippolyte (for the feast of St Louis, 25 August 1679) and the Abbaye-aux-Bois (Holy Week, 1680). By the early 1680s Charpentier was in the employ of the *grand* Dauphin, for a time as his musical director; in that capacity Charpentier was charged with providing music for special masses, which the king sometimes attended when not at Versailles. Other sacred works composed for the dauphin include two large-scale motets on the death of Queen Marie-Thérèse (nos.189 and 409) in the summer of 1683. It was probably for the dauphin that Charpentier composed two dramatic works on courtly subjects, *Les plaisirs de Versailles* and *La fête de Rueil* (nos.480 and 485), and possibly the cantata in praise of the Elector of Bavaria on the occasion of his wedding in the spring of 1685 (no.473).

Meanwhile, in 1683 he presented himself as a candidate for one of four newly created positions of *sous-maître* of the royal chapel, but illness prevented him from appearing for the second of two eliminations. Two months later Louis XIV granted him a pension, officially in gratitude for his service to the dauphin. This was as close as he came to royal patronage, although he again approached the edge of the court circle when he was made music teacher to Philippe, Duke of Chartres, later to become Duke of Orleans (in 1701) and Regent of France (from 1715 to 1723). For him Charpentier wrote a brief treatise on composition and a summary of the principles of

MOTETS

MELÉZ DE SYMPHONIE,
COMPOSEZ
PAR MONSIEUR CHARPENTIER

Maître de Musique de la Sainte Chapelle de Paris.

Dédiez à Son Altesse Royale,

MONSEIGNEUR LE DUC D'ORLEANS.

Partition in-4° gravée 3. l. broché.

A PARIS,
Chez Jacques Edouard, ruë Neuve N. Dame,

AVEC PRIVILEGE DV ROY.
M. D CC. IX.

10. Title-page
of Charpentier's
'Motets meléz de
symphonie',
published by
Jacques Edouard
in 1709

thoroughbass. Early sources claim that the two collaborated on an opera, *Philomèle*, which was played three times in the duke's apartments in the Palais Royal.

Perhaps also in the 1680s Charpentier became attached as composer and *maître de musique* to the principal church of the Jesuits in Paris (St Louis, later named St Paul–St Louis) in rue St-Antoine. Brossard spoke of the post as being 'among the most brilliant' in French musical life; Le Cerf de la Viéville called the Jesuit church 'l'église de l'opéra' (in fact some of Charpentier's manuscripts of sacred music from this period mention singers at the Opéra – the Académie Royale de Musique – such as the baritone Dun). Besides composing an immense number of religious works for the Jesuit church Charpentier also contributed *tragédies en musique* as *intermèdes* to the sacred dramas of Jesuit colleges such as the Collège d'Harcourt (no.498) and the Collège Louis-le-grand (*Celse Martyr*, 1687; *David et Jonathas*, 1688).

His only *tragédie lyrique* for the Opéra was *Médée*, to a libretto by Thomas Corneille, first performed on 4 December 1693 and perhaps restaged at Lille on 17 November 1700. The *Mercure galant*, always well disposed towards Charpentier, defended the opera in its issue of December 1693, noting that His Majesty, on receipt of the published score (dedicated to him), had been complimentary and that 'Monsieur' (the king's brother) and the dauphin had each attended several performances. Despite the Lullian cast of the opera, there were those, led by Le Cerf de la Viéville, who described the opera as an abomination; Brossard blamed the opera's relatively poor reception on 'cabals of the envious and ignorant', believing himself that the work was 'without a doubt the most expert and refined of all those that have been printed, at least since the death of Lully'.

On 20 May 1698 the post of *maître de musique* of the Sainte-Chapelle fell vacant with the death of François Chaperon, and on 28 June Charpentier was named his successor. The position, which he held until his death, was second in French sacred music only to the directorship of the royal chapel at Versailles. He composed some of his richest and most impressive works for the Sainte-Chapelle: the *Motet pour une longue offrande* and the dramatic motet *Judicium Salomonis* (1702), both written for the annual 'Messe rouge' of the Parlement, which was celebrated in the Sainte-Chapelle; three massive psalm settings (nos.228–30) for Tenebrae services; and the master-piece among his masses, '*Assumpta est Maria*'. He remained in the Sainte-Chapelle post until his death, recorded by Brossard as 7 a.m. on 24 February 1704, at his home in the rue Dauphine.

Just over five years later, the *Journal de Trévoux* reflected that in spite of his reputation primarily as a composer of 'la musique latine', Charpentier was one of France's finest and most original composers. Brossard praised his prodigious memory; Titon du Tillet described him as one of the wisest and most industrious musicians of his time. Very little of Charpentier's music was published during his lifetime, however: some *airs* from *Circé* (Paris, 1676), a few *airs sérieux et à boire* (in various issues of the *Mercure galant* and elsewhere) and *Médée* (Paris, 1694). A few years after his death 12 of his smaller motets were published by his nephew and inheritor, Jacques Edouard (in 1709), and other slight works appeared occasionally in the annual volumes of *Meslanges* issued by the firm of Ballard. By far the greatest number of his works are to be found in unique autograph copies. Fortunately, the bulk of these manuscripts was kept intact and sold in 1727 to the king's library; this collection of autographs is now in the Bibliothèque Nationale (Rés.Vm$^1$259; 28 vols.).

CHAPTER TWO

# Works

As a reflection of both the nature of his career and the musical posts he occupied, Charpentier's extant music consists primarily of sacred works, both vocal and instrumental, for churches, private chapels and convents. Second in importance are his theatre compositions: *intermèdes* and incidental music for plays; pastorals and chamber operas; and two full-scale lyric tragedies. Finally there is a relatively small number of independent secular works: *airs sérieux et à boire*, cantatas and pieces for instrumental ensembles.

Charpentier's vocal music for the church consists of 11 mass settings and other liturgically functional works (4 sequences, 37 antiphons, 19 hymns, 10 *Magnificat* settings, 9 settings of the Litany of Loreto, 54 lessons and responsories for Tenebrae services and 4 *Te Deum* settings); 84 psalm settings; and 207 motets of various types, including the dramatic motets that are generally termed oratorios or (by the French) 'histoires sacrées'. His instrumental music for the church, much less extensive than the vocal, consists exclusively of ensemble music: versets for a mass (lacking the Agnus Dei); several antiphons and offertories; sets of pieces for bishops' consecrations and for street-altar (*reposoir*) ceremonies on the feast of Corpus Christi; carol settings (noëls); and miscellaneous overtures, preludes and brief one-movement *symphonies*.

In almost every category of the sacred music there is great diversity among the individual works in length, forces required, compositional techniques and forms. Their common ground is Charpentier's personal style. This was based initially on mid-century Italian models, especially the *motetti concertati*, oratorios and polychoral works of Romans such as Carissimi, Luigi Rossi, Domenico and Virgilio Mazzocchi, Francesco Foggia, Benevoli and Francesco Beretta. Quite quickly, however, Charpentier incorporated French modes of expression as well – the 'official' grandeur, even ponderosity, of the *grand motet* of Du Mont and Lalande; the shapely, heightened declamatory manner, midway between recitative and aria styles, of the court *air* of Antoine Boësset and Lambert and the *récit* in the motets and operas of Lully; the 'popular' simplicity of nöels; and, particularly in the Tenebrae pieces, an often elaborately ornamented, arabesque-like melodic line. His rich harmonic style was specially remarked upon by his contemporaries, some with admiration ('Neuvièmes et tritons brillèrent sous sa main'), some with distaste ('Quels tristes accords écorchent nos oreilles'). Particularly in the early works his harmonic practice is marked by audacious false relations both simultaneous and successive, Corelli clashes, and single and double suspensions that create an extraordinary harmonic tension. Charpentier deserves a place along with Lalande and Couperin as one of the few French composers of his time to be at home in a contrapuntal style of choral writing; an outstanding example is the final chorus of the oratorio *Le Reniement de St Pierre*. Although he almost never attempted to write in the *stile antico*, some works for unaccompanied equal voices (e.g. nos.28 and 71) evoke the spirit of 16th-century polyphony. Word-painting was a basic resource for him, as was a tendency to dwell on monosyllabic expletives such as 'Oh' and 'Ah' that seems to reveal a delight in and sensitivity to sheer sonority.

Depending on the resources available to him Charpentier was clearly interested in colour contrasts of all kinds. His manuscript annotations are uncommonly detailed and illuminating, even regarding the *parties de remplissage*. More than any of his French contemporaries he exploited the kaleidoscopic possibilities of the concertato style of opposed voices and instruments and the concerto style of opposed *petits* and *grands choeurs* (vocal, instrumental and combined). For even greater contrast, he often scored the *grand choeur* in four or more parts, the *petit choeur* in three. He seized every opportunity afforded by the texts of his sacred works to dramatize, characterize and personalize them. This is true not only of the dramatic motet-oratorios but of many other works such as the *Messe pour plusieurs instruments au lieu des orgues* (early 1670s) in which ten different ensembles are employed, and the ceremonial music for Corpus Christi street-altar rites (nos.508, 515, 523). In these works, often organized according to symmetrical plans, the element of contrast is the basic principle of structural organization, and that of diversity, which Charpentier claimed to be 'the very essence of music', is the ultimate goal.

Underlying Charpentier's rich orchestration is a stable sense of tonality, governed by the relationship between what he called the 'énergie des modes' and the affect of the chosen text. Charpentier is perhaps the first composer-theorist to have drawn up a systematic table of the expressive character of each of the major and minor keys in his vocabulary, which he included in the brief *Règles de composition*.

Charpentier's music for approximately 30 theatre pieces shares some of the characteristics outlined above. However, on the whole it is less Italianate in character and more indebted to French models. Thus we find French overtures and many orchestral ballet *airs*, the former properly pompous, the latter light in texture, buoyant and full of delicate nuances of chromaticism and rhythmic interplay between the parts. The pastorals for the Duchess of Guise are like short *ballets de cour*, diverting song-and-dance spectacles with no particular dramatic tension. *La fête de Rueil* and *Les plaisirs de Versailles* are similar, though they are bigger works (Charpentier timed the latter at an hour and a half). To his compositions of prologues, *intermèdes* and incidental music (largely songs and dances) for the Comédie Française, Charpentier brought considerable élan and wit: one might point to the very funny 'laughing trio' of musicians in *Les fous divertissants* or the apothecaries' mortars, scored like drums, in the 'Cérémonie des médecins' of *Le malade imaginaire*. *Médée* and *David et Jonathas*, both

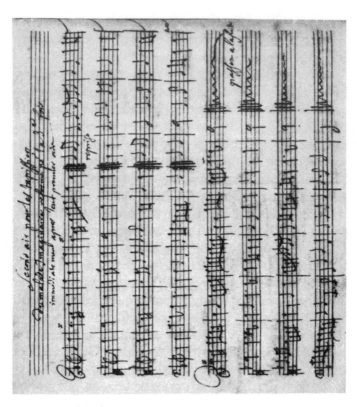

11. Autograph MS of the 'Second air pour les tapissiers' from Charpentier's 'Le malade imaginaire rajusté autrement pour la 3ème fois', composed 1685

*tragédies lyriques* on the Lullian model, are technically skilful major works that transcend in various ways the conventions of the genre. Revivals of both in the 1980s illuminated their subtleties; *Médée* especially has a dramatic integrity and nuances of characterization (particularly that of the heroine) exceptional in French Baroque opera, and its pastoral prologue and fantastic mid-act *divertissements* reveal a composer of unusual theatrical bent and striking wit.

Charpentier was also an important contributor to the related (but little studied) genres of the *air sérieux* and the *air à boire*. Some 30 airs by him are extant, for the most part brief *airs sérieux* for solo voice and continuo, including a fine triptych on stanzas from Corneille's *Le Cid*. Two unaccompanied trios, *Veux-tu, compère Grégoire* and (if it is his) the satirical *Beaux petits yeux d'écarlate*, are notable among his *airs à boire*. The noël *Un flambeau, Jeanette-Isabelle*, sung to Charpentier's music for the *air à boire* 'Qu'ils sont doux, bouteille jolie' in *Le médecin malgré lui* (Act 1 scene v), is known in English-speaking countries as the carol *Bring a torch, Jeanette Isabella*. A decade in advance of any other Frenchman, Charpentier composed cantatas bordering on secular oratorios in the Italian manner, among them *Orphée descendant aux enfers* (1683), the *Epithalamio* for the Elector of Bavaria (1685) and the amusing *Epitaphium Carpentarij* (the composer's ghost is a principal character), in which he indulges in musical puns to mock his predecessor at the Sainte-Chapelle, Chaperon.

All of Charpentier's instrumental music is written

for ensemble or orchestra; the majority are preludes. Of his instrumental pieces for the theatre, there are 110 dances. Compared to those of Lully, Charpentier's seem somewhat artless, even naive, but their surface simplicity is belied by the carefully led inner parts and the balanced spacing of voices; they are light in texture, buoyant, and full of delicate nuances of chromaticism and rhythmic interplay between the parts. The most notable secular instrumental works are a suite of dances for strings (no.545), two triumphal rondeaux for orchestra with trumpets and drums (no.547) and a chamber sonata for eight instruments (no.548).

# WORKS

The numbering system is that used in Hitchcock's catalogue (1982). Titles given are Charpentier's own, followed by text incipits where different. For untitled works the text incipit is given either alone or with an editorial title in square brackets. Generic scoring (e.g. ww, str) indicates that although parts were written out specific instruments are not stipulated. Roman numerals in the *Source* column refer to volumes of Charpentier's autographs (*F-Pn* Rés. Vm¹259; 28 vols.).

Recueil d'airs sérieux et à boire (Paris, 1695–1704) [Recueil (date)]   80–81
Motets melez de symphonie (Paris, 1709) [Motets (1709)]   78, 81
Meslanges de musique latine, françoise et italienne (Paris, 1726–9) [Meslanges (date)]   81

Numbers in the right-hand margin denote references in the text.   82, 83–5

## SACRED VOCAL

| No. | Title | Scoring | Date | Source | First published | |
|---|---|---|---|---|---|---|
| | | **MASSES** | | | | |
| 1 | [Mass] [see also no.281] | 6/4vv, 2 tr str, bc | ?c1670 | xiv | Colorado Springs, 1958 | 82 |
| 2 | Messe pour les trépassés [see also no.234] | 4/8vv, 2 fl, str, bc | ?early 1670s | i | | |
| 3 | Messe à 8 voix et 8 violons et flûtes [see also nos.236, 283] | 6/8vv, 2 fl, str, bc | ?early 1670s | xv | London, 1971 (in part) | |
| 4 | Messe à 4 choeurs [see also no.285] | 20/16vv, str, bc | ?early 1670s | xvi | | |
| 5 | Messe pour le Port Royal | 3/1v, bc | ?late 1680s | xxii | | 75 |
| 6 | Messe pour Mr Mauroy [see also no.299] | 8/4vv, 2 fl, 2 ob, str, bc | ?early 1690s | x | | |
| 7 | Messe des morts à 4 voix [see also nos.2 3, 263] | 8/4vv, bc | ?early 1690s | xxiv | | |
| 7a | Agnus Dei (inc.) | 4vv, bc | 1690s | xxvii | | |
| 8 | Messe pour le samedi de Pâques à 4 voix | 8/4vv, bc | ?early 1690s | v | Paris, 1949 | |
| 9 | Messe de minuit pour Noël | 6/4vv, 2 fl, str, bc | ?early 1690s | xxv | St Louis, 1962 | |
| 10 | Messe des morts à 4 voix et symphonie [see also no.269] | 8/4vv, ww, str, bc | ?mid-1690s | xxvi | | |
| 11 | Assumpta est Maria: Missa 6 vocibus cum simphonia [see also no.303] | 8/6vv, 2 fl, str, bc | ?1699 | xxvii, *F-Pn* Vm¹942 | | 80 |
| | | **SEQUENCES** | | | | |
| 12 | Prose des morts ('Dies irae') | 8/8vv, str, bc | ?early 1670s | i | Paris, 1984 | |
| 13 | Prose pour le jour de Pâques ('Victimae paschali laudes') | 2 Ct, B, bc | ? early 1670s | xv | | |
| 14 | Prose du saint sacrement ('Lauda Sion') | Tr, S, B, 2 tr str, bc | ?late 1670s | iii | | |
| 15 | Stabat mater pour des religieuses ('Stabat mater dolorosa') | 1/1v, bc | | xiii | Cologne, 1960 | |

| No. | Title | Scoring | Date | Source | First published |
|---|---|---|---|---|---|
| | | ANTIPHONS | | | |
| 16 | 'Regina coeli laetare' | Tr, S, bc | ?early 1670s | i | |
| 17 | Autre [antienne] ('Veni sponsa Christi') | Tr, S, fl, bc | ?early 1670s | i | |
| 18 | Salve regina | Tr, S, Mez, bc | ?early 1670s | i | |
| 19 | Ave regina coelorum | Tr, S, Mez, bc | ?early 1670s | i | Paris, 1955 |
| 20 | Sub tuum praesidium | Ct, T, B, bc | ?early 1670s | i | |
| 21 | Alma Redemptoris mater | 2 Tr, bc | ?mid-1670s | ii | Dubuque, Iowa, 1973 |
| 22 | Ave regina | 2 Tr, bc | ?mid-1670s | ii | Motets (1709) |
| 23 | Salve regina à 3 voix pareilles | Ct, T, B, bc | ?mid-1670s | ii, iii | Paris, 1952 |
| 24 | Salve regina à 3 choeurs | 3/8vv, bc | ?mid-1670s | iii | |
| 25 | Antiphona in honorem beatae virginis a redemptione captivorum ('Beata es Maria') | Ct, T, 2 tr str, bc | ?late 1670s | iii | |
| 26 | 'Inviolata, integra et casta' | 2 S, B, bc | ?late 1670s | iv | Paris, 1949 |
| 27 | Salve regina des Jésuites | T, bc | ?late 1670s | iv | Paris, 1952 |
| 28 | Antiphona sine organo ad virginem ('Sub tuum praesidium') | 2 Tr, Mez | 1681–2 | xxviii | |
| 29 | Antiphona in honorem beatae Genovefae voce sola ('Gloriosam Christi sponsam') | S, bc | 1685 | vii | |
| 30 | 'Regina coeli laetare' | Ct, T, B, bc | ?late 1680s | viii | Paris, 1953 (kbd red.) |
| 31 | Regina coeli voce sola cum [?flauti] | Ct, 2 fl, bc | ?late 1680s | viii | Paris, 1951 |
| 32 | Antienne à la vierge à 2 dessus ('Regina coeli laetare') | 2 Tr, bc | ?late 1680s | xxiii | |
| 33–5 | [Antiphon cycle for a confessor not pontiff]: 1ère antienne ('Domine quinque talenta') 3ème antienne ('Fidelis servus') 5ème antienne ('Serve bone') | 2 Tr, S, bc<br>Ct, T, 2 vn, bc<br>2 Tr, bc | ?early 1690s | xxv | |
| 36–43 | Salut de la veille des O et les 7 O suivant le romain: | Ct, T, B, bc | ?early 1690s | v | Paris, 1963 |
| | 1er O ('O Sapientia') | Ct, T, B, bc | | | |
| | 2nd O ('O Adonai') | Ct, T, B, bc | | | |
| | 3ème O ('O radix Jesse') | Ct, T, B, bc | | | |
| | 4ème O ('O clavis David') | 3/4vv, str, bc | | | |
| | 5ème O ('O Oriens') | 3/4vv, str, bc | | | |
| | 6ème O ('O Rex gentium') | Ct, 2 vn, bc | | | |
| | 7ème O ('O Emmanuel Rex') | Ct, T, B, bc | | | |

| | | | | | |
|---|---|---|---|---|---|
| 44–7 | [Marian antiphon cycle for the church year]: | 3/4vv, 2 vn, bc | ?early 1690s | v | Sèvres, 1951 (kbd red.) |
| | 'Alma Redemptoris mater' | | | | |
| | 'Ave regina coelorum' | | | | Paris, 1955 (choral pt.) |
| | 'Regina coeli laetare' | | | | |
| | 'Salve regina' | | | | |
| 48 | Antienne à la vierge pour toutes les saisons de l'année ('Inviolata, integra et casta') | Ct, T, B, bc | ?early 1690s | v | |
| 49 | Antienne à 3 voix pareilles pour la veille des O ('O admirabile commercium') | Ct, T, B, bc | ?mid-1690s | xxvi | |
| 50–52 | Antiennes pour les Vêpres de l'Assomption de la vierge: | | ?late 1690s | xxviii | Paris, 1953 (kbd red.) |
| | Après Dixit Dominus ('Assumpta est Maria') | Mez, 2 vn, bc | | | |
| | Après Laetatus sum ('In odorem unguentor um') | Tr, 2 fl, bc | | | |
| | Après Lauda Jerusalem Dominum ('Fulchra es et decora') | 2 Tr, Mez, bc | | | |
| | HYMNS | | | | |
| 53 | Jesu corona virginum | 2 S, fl, bc | ?early 1670s | i | |
| 54 | Hymne du Saint Esprit ('Veni Creator Spiritus') | Ct, T, B, 2 vn, bc | ?early 1670s | xv | |
| 55–7 | In Sanctum Nicasium Rothomagensem archiepiscopum et martyrem: | 1v | ?early 1670s | xv | |
| | Hymnus ad Vesperas ('Claram Nicasii martyrio') | T | | | |
| | Hymnus in eundem ad Matutinem ('Quo vos terror') | B | | | |
| | In eundem ad Laudes ('Clare martyr sancte praesul') | T | | | |
| 58 | Pange lingua | Ct, T, B, 2 tr str, bc | ?mid-1670s | ii | |
| 59 | Gaudia virginis Mariae ('Gaude virgo mater Christi') | 3 S, bc | ?mid-1670s | ii | Paris, 1955 |
| 60 | Hymne pour toutes les fêtes de la vierge ('Ave maris stella') | Tr, S, B, 2 tr str, bc | ?mid-1670s | iii | |
| 61 | Pour un reposoir: Pange lingua | Tr, S, B, 2 tr str, bc | 1680–81 | xviii | |
| 62 | Pange lingua pour des religieuses, pour le Port Royal | 1/1v, bc | 1681 | vxiii | |
| 63 | 'Ave maris stella' | 2 S, bc | early 1680s | iv | Cologne, 1960 |
| 64 | Hymne du saint sacrement ('Pange lingua') | 5/4vv, 2 fl, str, bc | ?late 1680s | xxii | |
| 65 | Ave maris stella | 4/4vv, str, bc | ?late 1680s | xxii | |
| 66 | Hymne du Saint Esprit: Veni Creator (inc.) | 6/4vv, 2 fl, str, bc | ?late 1680s | xxiii | |
| 67 | Ave maris stella | Tr, Ct, 3 B, bc | ?late 1680s | ix | |

75

| No. | Title | Scoring | Date | Source | First published | |
|---|---|---|---|---|---|---|
| 68 | Pange lingua à 4 pour le Jeudi Saint ('Nobis datus, nobis natus') | Tr; Ct, B, bc | ?late 1680s | xxiii | Paris, 1948 | |
| 69 | Veni Creator pour 1 dessus seul au catéchisme | Tr, bc | ?late 1680s | xxiii | Paris, 1731 | |
| 70 | Veni Creator Spiritus pour 1 dessus seul pour le catéchisme | Tr, bc | ?late 1680s | xxiii | Paris, 1951 (transcr. 4vv) | 84 |
| 71 | Iste confessor | 2 S | ?early 1690s | xxiv | | 82 |
| MAGNIFICAT SETTINGS | | | | | | |
| 72 | [Magnificat] | 8/4vv, 2 tr str, bc | ?1670 | xiv | | |
| 73 | [Magnificat] | Ct, T, B, 2 tr str, bc | ?early 1670s | xv | | |
| 74 | Magnificat à 8 voix et 8 instruments | 8/8vv, ww, str, bc | early 1680s | xi | Lausanne, 1949 | |
| 75 | Magnificat à 3 dessus | Tr, S, Mez, bc | 1683–5 | vi | | |
| 76 | Canticum B.V.M. | 4/4vv, bc | ?late 1680s | viii, v | | |
| 77 | [Magnificat] | 5/4vv, 2 fl, str, bc | ?late 1680s | ix | | |
| 78 | Magnificat | 4/4vv, 2 fl, str, bc | ?late 1680s | ix | | |
| 79 | 3ème Magnificat à 4 voix avec instruments | 8/4vv, 2 fl, str, bc | ?early 1690s | xxiv | St Louis, 1960 | |
| 80 | [Magnificat] | 4/4vv, 2 fl, str, bc | 1690s | xxiv | | 75 |
| 81 | Magnificat pour le Port Royal | 3/3vv, bc | ?late 1690s | xxviii | | 82 |
| LITANY OF LORETO SETTINGS | | | | | | |
| 82 | Litanies de la vierge à 3 voix pareilles | Ct, T, B, bc | early 1680s | xi | | |
| 83 | Litanies de la vierge à 6 voix et 2 dessus de violes | 6/6vv, 2 tr viols, bc | 1683–5 | vi | | |
| 84 | Litanies de la vierge à 3 voix pareilles avec instruments | Ct, T, B, 2 tr str, bc | ?late 1680s | xxii | | |
| 85 | Litanies de la vierge | 6/6vv, 2 fl, str, bc | ?late 1680s | xxiii | | |
| 86 | Litanies de la vierge à 2 dessus et 1 basse chantante | 2 Tr, B, bc | ?early 1690s | xxv | | |
| 87 | Litanies de la vierge à 4 voix | 8/4vv, bc | ?early 1690s | xxiv | | |
| 88 | Litanies de la vierge à 4 voix | 8/4vv, bc | ?early 1690s | xxiv | | |
| 89 | Litanies de la vierge | 8/4vv, bc | ?early 1690s | xxv | | |
| 90 | Courtes litanies de la vierge à 4 voix | 4/4vv, bc | ?early 1690s | v | | |
| TENEBRAE LESSONS AND RESPONSORIES | | | | | | |
| 91 | Leçon de ténèbres ('De lamentatione Jeremiae') | Tr, S, Ct, 2 fl, bc | ?early 1670s | i | | |
| 92 | Autre leçon de ténèbres ('JOD. Manum suam') | Tr, S, bc | ?early 1670s | i | | |
| 93 | Autre leçon de ténèbres ('ALEPH. Ego vir videns') | Tr, S, bc | ?early 1670s | i | | |
| 94 | Autre Jerusalem pour les leçons de ténèbres à 2 voix | Tr, S, bc | ?early 1670s | i | | |

| No. | | Scoring | Date | | Publisher |
|---|---|---|---|---|---|
| 95 | 'Incipit oratio Jeremiae' | Tr, S, 2 tr str, bc | ?early 1670s | i | |
| 96–110 | Les neuf leçons de ténèbres: | | ?late 1670s | iv | Paris, 1952 |
| | 1ère leçon du mercredi ('Incipit lamentatio Jeremiae') | S, bc | | | |
| | 2de leçon du mercredi ('VAU. Et egressus est') | S, bc | | | |
| | 3ème leçon du mercredi ('JOD. Manum suam') | Tr, S, bc | | | |
| | Lettres hébraïques de la 1ère leçon du vendredi | S, S, A, bc | | | |
| | Ritornelles pour la 1ère leçon du mercredi | 2 vn, bc ard 2 viols, bc in alternation | | | |
| | Prélude pour la 1ère leçon du jeudi ('De lamentatione Jeremiae') | 2 tr str, bc | | | |
| | 1ère leçon du jeudi ('De lamentatione Jeremiae') | S, bc | | | |
| | 2de leçon du jeudi ('LAMED. Matribus suis') | Tr, S, bc | | | |
| | 3ème leçon du jeudi ('ALEPH. Ego vir videns') | S, bc | | | |
| | 1ère leçon du vendredi ('De lamentatione Jeremiae') | S, tr viol, bc | | | |
| | 2de leçon du vendredi ('ALEPH. Quomodo obscuratum est') | Tr, bc | | | |
| | 2de leçon du jeudi ('LAMED. Matribus suis') | S, bc | | | |
| | 3ème leçon du mercredi ('JOD. Manum suam') | 2 Tr, A, bc | | | |
| | 3ème leçon du jeudi ('ALEPH. Ego vir videns') | 2 Tr, A, bc | | | |
| | 3ème leçon du vendredi ('Incipit oratio Jeremiae') | 2 Tr, A, bc | | | |
| 111–19 | Les neuf répons de chaque jour: les neuf répons du Mercredi Saint: | | 1680 | iv | |
| | 'In monte Oliveti' | 2 Tr, A, bc | | | |
| | 'Tristis est anima mea' | 2 Tr, bc | | | |
| | 'Amicus meus' | A, bc | | | Paris, 1949 |
| | 'Unus ex discipulis meis' | Tr, A, bc | | | |
| | 'Eram quasi agnus' | Tr, bc | | | |
| | 'Una hora non potuistis' | 2 Tr, A, bc | | | |
| | 'Seniores populi' | A, bc | | | Paris, 1952 |
| | 'Revelabunt coeli' | 2 Tr, A, bc | | | |
| | 'O Juda' | 2 Tr, bc | | | |

| No. | Title | Scoring | Date | Source | First published |
|---|---|---|---|---|---|
| 120–22 | [Three Tenebrae lessons]: 1ère leçon du mercredi ('Incipit lamentatio Jeremiae') / 1ère leçon du jeudi ('De lamentatione Jeremiae') / 1ère leçon du vendredi ('Misericordiae Domini') | B, ww, str, bc | ?late 1680s | xxiii | |
| 123–5 | [Three Tenebrae lessons]: 3ème leçon du mercredi ('JOD. Manum suam') / 3ème leçon du jeudi ('ALEPH. Ego vir videns') / 3ème leçon du vendredi ('Incipit oratio Jeremiae') | Bar, 2 fl, 2 vn, bc | ?late 1680s | xxiii | |
| 126–34 | [Nine Tenebrae responsories]: 'Tristis est anima mea' / 'Amicus meus' / 'Velum templi' / 'Tenebrae factae sunt' / 'Jerusalem surge' / 'Ecce quomodo' / 'Unus ex discipulis meis' / 'Tanquam ad latronem' / 'O vos omnes' | 2 T, bc / T, 2 fl, bc / 3/4vv, fl, str, bc / B, fl, str, bc / 2 T, 2 fl, bc / Ct, str, bc / B, 2 vn, bc / B, 2 fl, 2 vn, bc / Tr, 2 fl, bc | ?early 1690s | x | |
| 135–7 | [Three Tenebrae lessons]: 3ème leçon du mercredi ('JOD. Manum suam') / 3ème leçon du jeudi ('ALEPH. Ego vir videns') / 3ème leçon du vendredi ('Incipit oratio Jeremiae') | 3/6vv, fl, str, bc | ?early 1690s | xxiii | |
| 138–40 | [Three Tenebrae lessons]: 2de leçon du mercredi ('VAU. Et egressus est') / 2de leçon du jeudi ('LAMED. Matribus suis') / 2de leçon du vendredi ('ALEPH. Quomodo obscuratum est') | Ct, bc | ?early 1690s | v | |

82

| | | | | | |
|---|---|---|---|---|---|
| 141–3 | [Three Tenebrae lessons]:<br>3ème leçon du mercredi ('JOD. Manum suam')<br>3ème leçon du jeudi ('ALEPH. Ego vir videns')<br>3ème leçon du vendredi ('Incipit oratio Jeremiae') | B, 2 tr str, bc | ?early 1690s | xxv | |
| 144 | Répons après la 1ère leçon du jeudi ('Omnes amici mei') | T, 2 fl, bc | ?mid-1690s | xxvi | |
| | | TE DEUM SETTINGS | | | |
| 145 | Te Deum à 8 voix avec flûtes et violons | 8,8vv, ww, str, bc | ?early 1670s | xv, xvii | Paris, 1969 |
| 146 | Te Deum | 8/4vv, ww, tpt, timp, str, bc | ?early 1690s | x | Vienna, 1957 |
| 147 | Te Deum à 4 voix | 8/4vv, str, bc | ?early 1690s | v | |
| 148 | Te Deum à 4 voix | 8/4vv, bc | 1698–9 | xii | |
| | | PSALMS | | | |
| 149 | [Ps cxiii] ('Laudate pueri') | 5/4vv, 2 tr str, bc | ?c1670 | xiv | |
| 150 | [Ps cxxvii] ('Nisi Dominus') | 4/4vv, 2 tr str, bc | ?c1670 | xiv | |
| 151 | Confitebor tibi [Ps cxi] à 4 voix et 2 violons | 8/4vv, 2 vn, bc | ?c1670 | xiv | |
| 152 | [Ps cxvii] ('Laudate Dominum') | 4/4vv, 2 tr str, bc | ?c1670 | xiv | |
| 153 | [Ps cx] ('Dixit Dominus') | 7/4vv, 2 tr str, bc | ?c1670 | xiv | |
| 154 | [Ps cxii] ('Beatus vir') | 8/4vv, 2 tr str, bc | ?c1670 | xiv | |
| 155 | [Ps cxxxii] ('Memento, Domine') | 6/4vv, 2 tr str, bc | ?c1670 | xiv | |
| 156 | De profundis [Ps cxxx] (and 'Requiem aeternam') | 8/4vv, bc | ?early 1670s | i | Paris, 1930 |
| 157 | Miserere [Ps ii] | Tr, S, 2 fl, bc | ?early 1670s | xv | |
| 158 | Psalmus David 147 [Ps cxlvii.12–20] ('Lauda Jerusalem') | 8/4vv, 2 vn bc | ?early 1670s | xv | |
| 159 | [Ps cxvii] ('Laudate Dominum') | Ct, T, B, 2 tr str, bc | ?early 1670s | i | Paris, 1948 (kbd red.) |
| 160 | Psalmus 126us [Ps cxxvii] ('Nisi Dominus') à 4 voix | 7/4vv, bc | ?early 1670s | xv, v | |
| 161 | Psalmus David 121us [Ps cxxii] ('Laetatus sum') | 7/4vv, 2 fl, str, bc | ?early 1670s | xv | St Louis, 1965 |
| 162 | Exaudiat [Ps xx] à 8 voix, flûtes et violons | 7/8vv, fl, str, bc | ?early 1670s | xv | |
| 163 | Psalmus David 8us ('Domine, Dominus noster') | Tr, S, B, 2 tr str, bc | ?mid-1670s | ii | |
| 164 | Prière pour le roi [Ps xxi] ('Domine, in virtute tua') | Tr, S, B, 2 tr str, bc | ?mid-1670s | ii | |
| 165 | Precatio pro rege [Ps xx] ('Exaudiat te Dominus') | Tr, S, B, 2 tr str, bc | ?mid-1670s | ii | |

| No. | Title | Scoring | Date | Source | First published |
|---|---|---|---|---|---|
| 166 | Precatio pro filio regis (Ps lxxii.1–17, 'Deus judicium tuum') | Tr, S, B, 2 tr str, bc | ?mid-1670s | ii | |
| 167 | Quam dilecta: Psalmus David 83us [Ps lxxxiv] | 8/8vv, fl, str, bc | 1675 | xviii | |
| 168 | Psalmus David 5us [recte 2us] in tempore belli pro rege ('Quare fremuerunt gentes') | 8/8vv, str, bc | ?mid-1670s | iii, xvii | |
| 169 | Psalmus David 125us [Ps cxxvi] ('In converten-do Dominus') | 8/8vv, str, bc | ?late 1670s | iii | |
| 170 | Psalmus David 136us [Ps cxxxvij: Super flumina Babylonis | Tr, S, B, 2 fl, bc | ?late 1670s | iii | |
| 171 | Super flumina: Psalmus 136us [Ps cxxxvij] 8 vocibus cum instrumentis | 6/8vv, str, bc | ?late 1670s | iii, xvii | |
| 172 | Psalmus 3us ('Domine quid multiplicati?') | Tr, S, B, 2 tr str, bc | ?late 1670s | iii | |
| 173 | Miserere [Ps li] | 2 Tr, Ct, bc | ?late 1670s | iv | |
| 174 | [Ps xlij] ('Quemadmodum desiderat cervus') | Tr, S, B, 2 tr str, bc | 1679–80 | xix | |
| 175 | [Ps i] ('Beatus vir, qui non abiit') | Tr, S, B, 2 tr str, bc | 1679–80 | xix | |
| 176 | [Ps xcviii] ('Cantate Domino') | Tr, S, B, 2 tr str, bc | 1679–80 | xix | |
| 177 | [Ps cxlviii] ('Laudate Dominum de coelis') | Tr, S, B, 2 tr str, bc | 1679–80 | xix | |
| 178 | Psalmus David 127us [Ps cxxviii] ('Beati omnes') | Tr, S, B, 2 tr str, bc | 1680–81 | xviii | |
| 179 | Psalmus David 75us [Ps lxxvj] ('Notus in Judea') [see also no.206] | Tr, S, B, 2 tr str, bc | 1681 | xviii | |
| 180 | Exaudiat [Ps xx] pour le roi | 8/4vv, bc | early 1680s | xi, v | |
| 181 | Psalmus David 84us [Ps lxxxv] ('Benedixisti, Domine') | Tr, S, B, 2 tr str, bc | 1681–2 | xxviii | |
| 182 | Psalmus David 116us [Ps cxvij] sine organo ('Laudate Dominum omnes') | 2 Tr, S, Mez | 1681–2 | xxviii | Paris, 1955 |
| 183 | Psalmus David 107us [Ps cviii] ('Paratum cor meum Deus'; verses 1–5) | Ct, T, B, bc | early 1680s | xi | |
| 184 | Psalmus David 5us [recte 2dus] ('Quare fremuerunt gentes') | Tr, S, B, 2 tr str, bc | 1682–3 | xx | |
| 185 | Psalmus David 91us [Ps cxii] ('Bonum est confiteri Domino') | Tr, S, B, 2 tr str, bc | early 1680s | xi | |
| 186 | Psalmus David 83us [Ps lxxxiv] ('Quam dilecta') | Tr, S, B, 2 tr str, bc | early 1680s | xi | |
| 187 | Psalmus 86 [Ps lxxxvj] ('Fundamenta ejus') | 2 S, B, bc | early 1680s | xi | |
| 188 | Psalmus 62 [Ps lxiij] ('Deus, Deus meus') | Tr, S, B, 2 tr str, bc | 1683 | xx | |
| 189 | De profundis [Ps cxxx] (and 'Requiem aeternam') | 9/8vv, fl, str, bc | 1683 | xx | |
| 190 | Psalmus 109us [Ps cxl]: Dixit Dominus 8 vocibus et totidem instrumentis | 8/8vv, ww, str, bc | 1683–5 | vi | |

| No. | Title | Scoring | Date | Ref. | Pub. |
|---|---|---|---|---|---|
| 191 | Psalmus 147 [Ps cxlvii.12–20] ('Lauda Jerusalem') | 8/8vv, str, bc | 1683–5 | vi | |
| 192 | [Ps xlvij] ('Omnes gentes plaudite') | Tr, S, B, 2 tr str, bc | 1683–5 | vi | |
| 193 | Psalmus David 50us [Ps lij]: Miserere des Jésuites | 6/6vv, 2 vn, bc | 1683–5 | vii, xxiii | Paris, 1984 |
| 194 | Psalmus David 99us [Ps c] ('Jubilate Deo omnis terra') | Tr, S, B, 2 tr str, bc | 1685 | xxi | |
| 195 | Bonum est confiteri Domino: Psalmus David 91us [Ps xcij] | 6/6vv, 2 tr str, bc | 1687–8 | xxii | |
| 196 | Psalmus David 12us [Ps xiij] ('Usquequo Domine') | Tr, S, Bar, B, tr rec, fl, b rec, bc | ?late 1680s | xxii | |
| 197 | Psalmus David 109us [Ps cx] ('Dixit Dominus') | 4/4vv, bc | ?late 1680s | viii, v | |
| 198 | Psalmus David 4us ('Cum invocarem') | 5/4vv, fl, str, bc | ?late 1680s | viii | |
| 199 | Psalmus David 111us [Ps cxij] ('Beatus vir') | 4/4vv, bc | ?late 1680s | viii, v | |
| 200 | Psaume 110ème [Ps cxi] Confitebor tibi | 6/4vv, bc | ?late 1680s | viii, v | |
| 201 | Psalmus David 34us [Ps xxxv] ('Judica Domine nocentes me') | Tr, S, 2 B, 2 tr str, bc | ?late 1680s | ix | |
| 202 | Dixit Dominus: Psalmus David 109us [Ps cx] | 5/4vv, ww, str, bc | ?late 1680s | ix | |
| 203 | Psalmus 112us [Ps cxiij] ('Laudate pueri') | 6/4vv, bc | ?late 1680s | ix, v | |
| 204 | Psaume 109 [Ps cx] ('Dixit Dominus') | 5/4vv, fl, str, bc | ?late 1680s | ix | |
| 205 | Gloria Patri pour le De profundis en C sol ut bémol à 4 voix, 4 violons, et flûtes | 3/4vv, fl, str, bc | ?late 1680s | ix | |
| 206 | Psalmus David 75us [Ps lxxvj] ('Notus in Judea') [a revision of no.179] | 4/4vv, fl, str, bc | ?early 1690s | x | |
| 207 | Psalmus David 87us [Ps lxxxviij] ('Domine Deus salutis meae') | 6/4vv, fl, str, bc | ?early 1690s | x | |
| 208 | Psalmus David 111us [Ps cxij]: Beatus vir qui timet Dominum 4 vocibus cum symphonia | 3/4vv, ww, str, bc | ?early 1690s | x | |
| 209 | Psalmus David 115us [Ps cxvi.10–16] ('Credidi propter quod') | 5/4vv, bc | ?early 1690s | xxv, v | |
| 210 | Lauda Jerusalem: Psalmus David 147us [Ps cxlvii.12–20] | 4/4vv, str, bc | ?early 1690s | xxv | |
| 211 | Psalmus David 129us [Ps cxxx]: De profundis (and 'Requiem aeternam') à 4 voix | 7/4vv, bc | ?early 1690s | xxiv | |
| 212 | Psalmus David 129us [Ps cxxx] 4 vocibus ('De profundis' and 'Requiem aeternam') | 7/4vv, bc | ?early 1690s | xxiv | |
| 213 | De profundis [Ps cxxx] (and 'Requiem aeternam') [composed as part of no.7; ?model for no.213a] | 8/4vv, bc | ?early 1690s | xxiv | |
| 213a | De profundis [Ps cxxx] (and 'Requiem aeternam') (inc.) [?derived from no.213] | 8/4vv, bc | 1690s | xxvii | |

| No. | Title | Scoring | Date | Source | First published |
|---|---|---|---|---|---|
| 214 | Psalmus David 116us [Ps cxvij] ('Laudate Dominum omnes') | 6/4vv, bc | ?early 1690s | xxiv | Paris, 1954 |
| 215 | Psalmus David 67us [Ps lxviij] ('Exsurgat Deus'; verses 1–3, variants of verses 35, 34, 18) | 3/4vv, 2 tr str, bc | ?early 1690s | xxv | |
| 216 | Psalmus David 121us [Ps cxxij] ('Laetatus sum') | 5/4vv, 2 tr str, bc | ?early 1690s | xxv | |
| 217 | Psalmus David 123us [Ps cxxiv] ('Nisi quia Dominus') | 4/4vv, 2 tr str, bc | ?early 1690s | xxv | |
| 218 | Psalmus David 45us [Ps xlvj] ('Deus noster refugium') | 3/4vv, 2 tr str, bc | ?early 1690s | xxv | |
| 219 | Miserere: [Psalmus] 50 [Ps lj] à 4 voix et 4 instruments | 8/4vv, fl, str, bc | ?early 1690s | xxv | |
| 220 | Psalmus David 110us [Ps cxj] ('Confitebor tibi') à 4 voix | 5/4vv, bc | ?early 1690s | v | |
| 221 | Psalmus David 111us [Ps cxij] ('Beatus vir') à 4 voix | 5/4vv, bc | ?early 1690s | v | |
| 222 | Court De profundis à 4 voix [Ps cxxx] (and 'Requiem aeternam') | 3/4vv, bc | ?early 1690s | v | |
| 223 | Laudate Dominum omnes gentes [Ps cxvij] 8 vocibus et totidem instrumentis | 8/8vv, fl, str, bc | ?mid-1690s | xxvi | Vienna, 1973 |
| 224 | Beatus vir qui timet Dominum [Ps cxij] 8 vocibus e totidem instrumentis | 8/8vv, fl, str, bc | ?mid-1690s | xxvi | |
| 225 | Confitebor [Ps cxi] à 4 voix et instruments | 6/4vv, fl, str, bc | ?mid-1690s | xxvi | |
| 226 | Dixit Dominus [Ps cx] pour le Port Royal | 3/2vv, bc | ?late 1690s | xxviii | |
| 227 | Laudate Dominum omnes gentes [Ps cxvij] pour le Port Royal | 3/2vv, bc | ?late 1690s | xxviii | |
| 228 | Psalmus David 70us [Ps lxxj] ('In te Domine speravi'): 3ème psaume du 1er nocturne du Mercredi Saint | 7/5vv, str, bc | 1699 | xii | 80 |
| 229 | Psalmus David 26us [Ps xxvij] ('Dominus illuminatio mea'): 3ème psaume du 1er nocturne du Jeudi Saint | 8/5vv, str, bc | 1699 | xii | 80 |
| 230 | Psalmus David 15us [Ps xvj] ('Conserva me, Domine'): 3ème psaume du 1er nocturne du Vendredi Saint | 6/5vv, str, bc | 1699 | xii | 80 |
| 231 | [Ps cxxvij] ('Nisi Dominus') | Tr, S, B, 2 tr str, bc | | Pn Rés.Vmc.28 | |
| 232 | De profundis [Ps cxxx] (and 'Requiem aeternam') | Tr, S, B, 2 tr str, bc | | Pn Rés.Vmc.28 | |

| No. | Title | Scoring | Date | Index | Source | Publication |
|---|---|---|---|---|---|---|
| 233 | 'Ave verum corpus' | Tr, S, 2 tr str, bc | ?early 1670s | i | | |
| 234 | 'Pie Jesu' [composed as part of no.2] | 3/8vv, bc | ?early 1670s | i | | |
| 235 | O sacrum convivium à 3 dessus | Tr, S, Mez, bc | ?early 1670s | i | | |
| 236 | Elévation ('O salutaris hostia') [composed as part of no.3] | B, 2 fl, bc | ?early 1670s | xv | | London, 1971 |
| 237 | Elévation pour la paix ('O bone Jesu dulcis') | Ct, T, B, 2 tr str, bc | ?mid-1670s | ii, iii | | |
| 238 | Elévation ('Gaudete dilectissimi') | B, 2 tr str, bc | ?mid-1670s | ii | | |
| 239 | O sacrum à 3 ('O sacrum convivium') | 2 Tr, A, bc | ?mid-1670s | iii, | Pn Vm¹ 1693 (inc.) | |
| 240 | O sacrum pour trois religieuses ('O sacrum convivium') | 2 Tr, A, bc | ?mid-1670s | iii | | |
| 241 | Elevatio ('Venite fideles ad convivium') | B, 2 tr str, bc | ?late 1670s | iii | | |
| 242 | Ecce panis voce sola: Elévation ('Ecce panis angelorum') | S, bc | ?late 1670s | iii | | |
| 243 | Panis angelicus voce sola: Elévation | Tr, bc | ?late 1670s | iii | | Motets (1709) |
| 244 | Elévation à 2 dessus et 1 basse chantante ('O bone Jesu') | Tr, S, B, bc | ?late 1670s | iii | | |
| 245 | Elévation ('O pretiosum') | Tr, 2 vn, bc | ?late 1670s | iii | | |
| 246 | Elévation ('Caro mea vere est cibus') | Tr, S, B, bc | ?late 1670s | iii | | |
| 247 | 'O pretiosum et admirabile convivium' | Tr, bc | ?late 1670s | iii | | |
| 248 | Elévation ('O salutaris hostia') | B, 2 tr str, bc | 1679–80 | xix | | |
| 249 | 'O salutaris hostia' | Tr, bc | 1681 | xviii | | |
| 250 | Elevatio ('Ascendat ad te Domine') | Bar, 2 tr str, bc | early 1680s | iv | | |
| 251 | Elévation à 5 sans dessus de violon ('Transfige dulcissime Jesu') | 2 S, Ct, T, B, bc | 1683 | xx | | |
| 252 | Elévation ('O coelestis Jerusalem') | Ct, T, B, bc | 1683–5 | vi | | Paris, c1900 |
| 253 | O Amor: Elévation à 2 dessus et 1 basse chantante | Tr, S, B, bc | 1683–5 | vi, xxiii | | |
| 254 | 'O pretiosum et admirabile convivium' | 2 S, bc | 1683–5 | vi | | |
| 255 | 'O pretiosum et admirandum convivium' | Tr, S, B, 2 tr str, bc | 1683–5 | vi | | |
| 256 | Elévation à 3 dessus ('O clementissime Domine Jesu') | 3 Tr, bc | 1683–5 | xxi | | |
| 257 | Elevatio ('Gustate et videte quam suavis') | Tr, bc | 1683–5 | xxi | | |
| 258 | Elevatio ('Nonne Deo subjecta erit') | S, bc | 1686–7 | viii | | |
| 259 | Elévation ('Transfige amabilis Jesu') | Tr, S, B, bc | 1687–8 | xxii | | |
| 260 | Elevatio ('O sacramentum pietatis') | 2 T, B, 2 fl, 2 vn, bc | ?late 1680s | ix | | |
| 261 | O salutaris à 3 dessus ('O salutaris hostia') | 2 Tr, S, bc | ?early 1690s | xxiii | | |
| 262 | O salutaris hostia | Tr, 2 ob, bc | ?early 1690s | xxv | | |
| 263 | Elévation ('Pie Jesu') [composed as part cf no.7] | 2 Tr, bc | ?early 1690s | xxiv | | |
| 264 | Elévation au saint sacrement ('O amantissime salvator noster') | Ct, T, B, bc | ?early 1690s | xxiv | | |

| No. | Title | Scoring | Date | Source | First published |
|---|---|---|---|---|---|
| 264a | Elévation à 3 voix pareilles [variant of no.264] | Ct, T, B, bc | 1690s | xxvii | |
| 265 | Elévation ('Bone pastor') | Ct, T, B, bc | ?early 1690s | xxiv | Paris, 1948 |
| 266 | 'Ave verum corpus' | Ct, 2 fl, bc | ?early 1690s | x | |
| 267 | Elévation ('Verbum caro, panem verum') | Ct, T, B, bc | ?early 1690s | v | |
| 268 | Elévation à voix seule pour 1 taille ('Lauda Sion') | T, bc | ?early 1690s | xxv | Motets (1709) (variant) |
| 269 | A l'élévation de la sainte hostie ('Pie Jesu') [composed as part of no.10] | 2 Tr, bc | ?mid-1690s | xxvi | |
| 270 | Pour le saint sacrement à 3 voix pareilles ('O dulce, o ineffabile') | Ct, T, B, bc | ?mid-1690s | xxvi | |
| 271 | Pour le saint sacrement à 3 voix pareilles ('Amate Jesum omnes') | Ct, T, B, bc | ?mid-1690s | xxvi | |
| 272 | Elévation à 2 dessus et 1 basse ('Quare tristis est anima mea') | 2 Tr, B, bc | ?mid-1690s | xxvi | |
| 273 | Elévation ('O vere, o bone') | Ct, bc | 1698–9 | xii | Cologne, 1960 |
| 274 | Elévation ('O sacramentum pietatis') | Mez, 2 fl, 2 vn, bc | ?late 1690s | xxviii | |
| 275 | 'Panis quem ego dabo' | Tr, S, Ct, T, B, 2 fl, bc | | $Pn$ Rés.Vmc.27 | |
| 276 | 'Adoramus te Christe' | Tr, S, B, 2 fl, bc | | $Pn$ Rés.Vmc.27 | |
| 277 | 'Cantemus Domino' | Tr, S, bc | | $Pn$ Rés.Vmc.27 | |
| 278 | Motet du saint sacrement à 4 ('O sacrum convivium') | Tr, Ct, T, B, bc | | $Pn$ Vm¹1175bis | |
| 279 | Motet à voix seule pour une élevation ('O amor, o bonitas') | Tr, bc | | Motets (1709) | |
| 280 | Motet de saint sacrement ('Egredimini filiae Sion') | Tr, 2 tr str, bc | | Motets (1709) | |
| | | DOMINE SALVUM MOTETS | | | |
| 281 | Domine salvum [composed as part of no.1] | Tr, Ct, T, B, 2 tr str, bc | ?c1670 | xiv | |
| 282 | 'Domine salvum fac regem' | Tr, S, bc | ?early 1670s | i | |
| 283 | Domine salvum de la messe à 8 [composed as part of no.3] | 5/8vv, fl, str, bc | ?early 1670s | xv | Colorado Springs, 1958 |
| 284 | Domine salvum à 3 voix pareilles avec orgue | 2 Ct, B, bc | ?early 1670s | xv | |
| 285 | 'Domine salvum fac regem' [composed as part of no.4] | 6/16vv, str, bc | ?early 1670s | xvi | |
| 286 | Domine salvum | Tr, S, B, 2 tr str, bc | ?mid-1670s | ii | |
| 287 | Domine salvum: trio | Ct, T, B, 2 tr str, bc | ?mid-1670s | iii | |
| 288 | Domine salvum pour trois religieuses | 2 Tr, A, bc | ?mid-1670s | iii | |
| 289 | 'Domine salvum fac regem' (unfinished) | Tr, S, B, 2 tr str, bc | 1679–80 | xix | |
| 290 | Domine salvum sine organo en C sol ut | 2 Tr, S, Mez | 1681–2 | xxviii | |

| No. | Title | Scoring | Date | Source |
|---|---|---|---|---|
| 291 | 'Domine salvum fac regem' | 8vv, str, bc | early 1680s | xi |
| 292 | 'Domine salvum fac regem' | 3/4vv, bc | 1682–3 | xx |
| 293 | 'Domine salvum fac regem' | Tr, S, B, 2 tr str, bc | 1683–5 | vi |
| 294 | Autre Domine [salvum] | Tr, S, B, 2 tr str, bc | 1683–5 | vi |
| 295 | 'Domine salvum fac regem' | Tr, S, B, 2 tr str, bc | 1686–7 | xxii |
| 296 | 'Domine salvum fac regem' | 2 T, B, bc | ?late 1680s | viii |
| 297 | 'Domine salvum fac regem' | Tr, S, bc | ?late 1680s | ix |
| 298 | Domine salvum pour 1 haut et 1 bas dessus | Ct, T, B, bc | ?early 1690s | xxiii |
| 299 | Domine salvum [composed as part of no.6] | 2/4vv, fl, str, bc | ?early 1690s | x |
| 300 | Domine salvum à 3 dessus | 2 Tr, S, bc | ?early 1690s | x |
| 301 | Domine salvum à 3 voix pareilles | Ct, T, B, bc | ?early 1690s | xxiv |
| 302 | Domine salvum à 3 voix pareilles | Ct, T, B, bc | ?early 1690s | xxiv |
| 303 | Dominum salvum [composed as part of no.11] | 6vv, fl, str, bc | 1698–1702 | xxvii |
| 304 | 'Domine salvum fac regem' | Tr, Ct, T, str, bc | | *Pn* Rés.Vmc.27  Paris, 1730 |
| 305 | Motet ('Domine salvum fac regem') | | | Motets (1709) |

OCCASIONAL MOTETS

| No. | Title | Scoring | Date | Source |
|---|---|---|---|---|
| 306 | [Motet for St Bernard] ('Gaudete fideles') | Tr, S, 2 fl, bc | ?early 1670s | i |
| 307 | [Motet for St Augustine] ('O doctor optimae') | Tr, S, bc | ?early 1670s | i |
| 308 | [Motet for Easter] ('Haec dies') | Tr, S, 2 fl, bc | ?early 1670s | i |
| 309 | Nativité de la vierge ('Sicut spina') | Tr, S, bc | ?early 1670s | i |
| 310 | St François ('Jubilate Deo fideles') | Tr, S, 2 tr str, bc | ?early 1670s | i |
| 311 | Motet pour les trépassés à 8: Plainte des âmes du purgatoire ('Miseremini mei') | 5/8vv, str, bc | ?early 1670s | i |
| 312 | O filii à 3 voix pareilles ('Alleluia O filii et filiae') | 2 Ct, B, 2 fl, bc | ?early 1670s | xv |
| 313 | Pour la conception de la vierge ('Conceptio tuo Dei genitrix virgo') | Tr, A, bc | ?early 1670s | xv |
| 314 | In nativitatem Domini canticum ('Quem vidistis pastores') | S, Ct, T, B, 2 fl, 2 vn, bc | ?early 1670s | xv |
| 315 | Pour Ste Anne ('Gaude felix Anna') | 2 Tr, bc | ?early 1670s | ii |
| 316 | In circumcisione Domini ('Postquam consummati sunt') | Tr, S, B, 2 tr str, bc | ?mid-1670s | ii |
| 317 | Pour le jour de Ste Geneviève ('Gaudia festivae percurrant') | Tr, S, B, 2 tr str, bc | ?mid-1670s | ii |
| 318 | In festo purificationis ('Erat senex in Jerusalem') | Tr, S, B, 2 tr str, bc | ?mid-1670s | ii |
| 319 | Motet pour la Trinité ('O altitudo divitiarum') | S, Ct, B, bc | ?mid-1670s | ii |
| 320 | Motet de St Louis ('In tympanis et organis') (inc.) | Ct, 2 tr str, bc | ?mid-1670s | iii |
| 321 | Motet de St Laurent ('Beatus Laurentius') | Ct, 2 tr str, bc | ?mid-1670s | iii |

101

| No. | Title | Scoring | Date | Source | First published |
|---|---|---|---|---|---|
| 322 | Motet de la vierge pour toutes ses fêtes ('Quam pulchra es') | 2 Tr, A, 2 fl, bc | ?mid-1670s | iii | Paris, 1954 (org red.) |
| 323 | In honorem S Ludovici Regis Galliae canticum tribus vocibus cum symphonia ('In tympanis et organis') | Tr, S, B, 2 tr str, bc | ?late 1670s | iii | |
| 324 | In nomine Jesu ('O nomen Jesu') (inc.) | Ct, T, B, bc | ?late 1670s | iv | |
| 325 | Canticum Annae ('Exultavit cor meum in Domine') | Tr, S, B, 2 tr str, bc | early 1680s | iv | |
| 326 | Gratiarum actiones ex sacris codicibus excerptae pro restituta serenissimi galliarum delphini salute ('Circumdederunt me dolores') | Tr, S, B, 2 fl, b fl, bc | early 1680s | iv | |
| 327 | Motet pour toutes les fêtes de la vierge ('Corde et animo Christo canamus gloriam') | Tr, S, B, 2 tr str, bc | 1681–2 | xviii | Paris, 1954 (partial) |
| 328 | Supplicatio pro defunctis ad beatam virginem ('Languentibus in purgatorio') | Tr, S, B, 2 fl, b fl, bc | 1681–2 | xviii | Paris, 1953 |
| 329 | Pour un reposoir ('Ave verum corpus') [see also no.523] | Tr, S, B, 2 fl, str, bc | 1682–3 | xx | |
| 330 | Gaudia Beatae Virginis Mariae ('Gaude virgo mater Christi') | Tr, S, B, 2 tr str, bc | early 1680s | xi | |
| 331 | Luctus de morte augustissimae Mariae Theresiae Reginae Galliae ('Laeta sileant organa') | Ct, T, B, 2 tr str, bc | 1683 | vi | |
| 332 | In honorem S Ludovici Regis Galliae ('In tympanis et organis') | Ct, T, B, 2 tr str, bc | 1683 | vi | |
| 333 | Pro omnibus festis B.V.M. ('Annuntiate superi, narrate coeli') | 6/6vv, str, bc | 1683–5 | vi | |
| 334 | Motet pour la vierge ('Alma Dei creatoris') | S, bc | 1683–5 | xxi | Paris, 1952 |
| 335–8 | Quatuor anni tempestatis Ver ('Surge, propera, amica mea') Aestas ('Nolite me considerare') Autumnus ('Osculetur me osculo oris sui') Hyems ('Surge aquilo et veni auster') | 2 Tr, bc | 1685 | xxi, xxiii | |
| 339 | Chant joyeux du temps de Pâques ('O filii et filiae') | 6/5vv, 2 tr viols, bc | early 1685 | vii | |
| 340 | Ad beatam virginem canticum ('Hodie salus') | Ct, T, B, 2 fl, 2 vn, bc | 1686 | vii | Pn Vm¹1269, Vm¹1264 |
| 341 | Gratiarum actiones pro restituta regis christianissimi sanitate anno 1686 ('Circumdederunt me dolores') | 2 Tr, 2 fl, 2 vn, bc | 1686 | vii | |
| 342 | Pour Ste Thérèse ('Flores o gallia') | 2 Tr, S, bc | 1686–7 | viii, Pn Vm¹1269 | |

| | | | | | |
|---|---|---|---|---|---|
| 343 | Magdalena lugens voce sola cum symphonia ('Sola vivebat in antris') | Tr, 2 tr str, bc | 1686–7 | viii | |
| 344 | In festo corporis Christi canticum ('Venite ad me') | 5/5vv, 2 tr str, bc | 1686–7 | xxii | New York, 1966 |
| 345 | Canticum Zachariae ('Benedictus Dominus Deus') | 5/6vv, 2 tr str, bc | 1686–7 | viii | |
| 346 | Pour le saint sacrement au reposoir ('Oculi omnium in te sperant') | 5/5vv, 2 fl, bc | ?late 1680s | xxii | Sèvres, 1951 (kbd red.) |
| 347 | In honorem S Benedicti ('Exultet omnium turba fidelium') | Tr, S, bc | ?late 1680s | xxii | |
| 348 | Motet du saint sacrement pour un reposoir ('Ecce panis angelorum') | T, Bar, B, 2 tr str, bc | ?late 1680s | xxii | Paris, 1957 |
| 349–50 | Pour la passion de notre Seigneur 1ère pause ('O crux ave spes unica') 2de pause ('Popule meus quid feci tibi') | Ct, T, bc | ?late 1680s | xxiii | |
| 351 | Pour le jour de la passion de notre Seigneur Jésus Christ ('O crux ave spes unica') | Ct, T, B, bc | ?late 1680s | xxiii | Paris, 1957 |
| 352 | Second motet pour le catéchisme à la pause du milieu: à la vierge ('Sub tuum praesidium') | Tr, bc | ?late 1680s | xxiii | Paris, 1948 |
| 353 | In Assumptione Beatae Mariae Virginis ('Suspirabat Maria') | 5/4vv, fl, str, bc | ?late 1680s | ix | |
| 354 | Motet pour St François de Borgia ('Beatus vir qui inventus est') | Ct, 2 tr str, bc | ?late 1680s | ix | |
| 355 | In honorem S Xaverij canticum ('Vidi angelum volantem') | 5/4vv, fl, str, bc | ?late 1680s | ix | |
| 355a | Canticum de S Xaverio ('Vidi angelum volantem') [abbreviated variant of no.355] | 5/4vv, ww, str, bc | ?early 1690s | x | |
| 356 | O filii pour les voix, violons, flûtes et orgue ('Alleluia. O filii et filiae') | 1/4vv, str, bc | ?late 1680s | xxiii | |
| 357 | In purificationem B.V.M. canticum ('Psallite coelites') | 2 Tr, B, 2 fl, 2 vn, bc | ?late 1680s | xxiii | |
| 358 | In festo corporis Christi canticum ('Pandite portas populi') | 2 Tr, B, 2 tr str, bc | ?late 1680s | xxiii | |
| 359 | Motet pour la vierge à 2 voix ('Omne die dic Maria') | Ct, T, bc | ?early 1690s | x | |
| 360 | Pour la vierge ('Felix namque es') | T, B, bc | ?early 1690s | x | |
| 361 | Pour plusieurs martyrs: motet à voix seule sans accompagnement ('Sancti Dei per fidem') | B | ?early 1690s | x | |
| 362 | Pour le Saint Esprit ('Veni Creator Spiritus') | Ct, T, B, bc | ?early 1690s | xxv | |
| 363 | Motet pendant la guerre ('Quare fremuerunt gentes') | 4/4vv, 2 vn, bc | ?early 1690s | xxv | |
| 364 | Pour le Saint Esprit ('Veni Sancte Spiritus') | Ct, T, B, bc | ?early 1690s | xxiv, xxvii | |

| No. | Title | Scoring | Date | Source | First published |
|---|---|---|---|---|---|
| 365 | In honorem S Ludovici Regis Galliae canticum ('Dies tubae et clangoris') | 5/4vv, ww, str, bc | ?early 1690s | xxiv | |
| 365a | In honorem S Ludovici Regis Galliae canticum ('Dies tubae et clangoris') [abbreviated variant of no.365] | 5/4vv, ww, str, bc | 1690s | xxvii | |
| 366 | Pour le Saint Esprit ('Veni Sancte Spiritus') | Ct, T, B, bc | ?early 1690s | v | |
| 367 | La prière à la vierge du Père Bernard ('Memorare, o piissima virgo') | 3/4vv, 2 tr str, bc | ?early 1690s | xxv | |
| 368 | Motet de St Joseph ('Justus germinabit') | 4/4vv, bc | ?early 1690s | xxv | |
| 369 | Pro virgine non martyre ('Ante torum hujus virginis') | Ct, T, B, bc | ?early 1690s | xxv | |
| 370 | Pour le catéchisme ('Gloria in excelsis Deo') | Tr, bc | ?early 1690s | xxv | Cologne, 1960 |
| 371 | A la vierge à 4 voix pareilles ('Ego mater agnitionis') | Ct, 2 T, B, bc | ?early 1690s | v | |
| 372 | Pour la 2de fois que le saint sacrement vient au même reposoir ('O Deus, o salvator noster') | 5/4vv, str, bc | ?mid-1690s | xii | |
| 373 | [Motet for Mary Magdalene] ('Sola vivebat in antris') | Tr, S, 2 fl, bc | | Pn Rés.Vmc.27 | |
| 374 | [Motet for St Teresa] ('Flores o Gallia') | Tr, S, 2 fl, bc | | Pn Rés.Vmc.27 | Paris, 1729 |
| 375 | Pour un confesseur non pontife ('Euge serve bone') | Ct, T, bc | | Motets (1709) | |
| 376 | Pour un confesseur ('Beatus vir qui inventus est') | Ct, bc | | Motets (1709) | |
| 377 | Pour tous les saints ('O vos amici Dei') | T, bc | | Motets (1709) | |
| 378 | Pour le Carême ('Peccavi Domine') | 2 S, B, bc | | Pn Vm¹1269 | Motets (1709) |
| 379 | Pour plusieurs fêtes ('Cur mundus militat') | Ct, T, B, bc | | Motets (1709) | |
| 380–89 | Méditations pour le Carême<br>1ère ('Desolatione desolata est')<br>2de ('Sicut pullus hirundinis')<br>3ème ('Tristis est anima mea')<br>4ème ('Ecce Judas')<br>5ème ('Cum cenasset Jesus')<br>6ème ('Quarebat Pilatus dimittere Jesum')<br>7ème ('Tenebrae factae sunt')<br>8ème ('Stabat mater dolorosa')<br>9ème ('Sola vivebat in antris')<br>10ème ('Tentavit Deus Abraham') | Ct, T, B, bc | | Pn Vm¹1175bis | Paris, 1954 |
| 390 | Motet de la vierge à 4 ('Omne die dic Maria') | 4/4vv, bc | | Pn Vm¹1175bis | |

DRAMATIC MOTETS (ORATORIOS)

| No. | Title | Scoring | Date | Vol. | Edition |
|---|---|---|---|---|---|
| 391 | Judith sive Bethulia liberata ('Stabat Holofernes super montes') | 8/4vv, fl, str, bc | ?mid-1670s | ii | |
| 392 | Canticum pro pace ('Totus orbis personet tubarum clangore') | 8/8vv, str, bc | ?mid-1670s | ii | |
| 393 | Canticum in nativitatem Domini ('Frigidae noctis umbra') | Tr, S, B, 2 tr str, bc | ?mid-1670s | ii | |
| 394 | In honorem Caeciliae, Valeriani et Tiburtij canticum ('Est secretum, Valeriane') | Tr, S, B, 2 tr str, bc | ?mid-1670s | ii | |
| 395 | Pour la fête de l'Epiphanie ('Cum natum esset Jesus in Bethlehem') | Tr, S, B, 2 tr str, bc | ?mid-1670s | ii | |
| 396 | Historia Esther ('Assuerus anno tertio regni sui') | 7/8vv, 2 fl, 2vn, bc | ?mid-1670s | iii | |
| 397 | Caecilia virgo et martyr octo vocibus ('Est secretum, Valeriane') | 6/8vv, str bc | ?mid-1670s | iii | |
| 398 | Pestis Mediolanensis ('Horrenda pestis Mediolanum vastabat') | 8/8vv, fl, str, bc | ?late 1670s | iii, xvii | Paris, c1905 (in part); Chapel Hill, N. Carolina, 1979 |
| 399 | Filius prodigus ('Homo quidam duos habebat filios') | 4/4vv, 2 tr str, bc | 1680 | iv; $Pn$ Vm¹1480, $V$ 58 | |
| 400 | Canticum in honorem Beatae Virginis Mariae inter homines et angelos ('Annuntiate superi, narrate coeli') | 2 S, Ct, T, B, bc | c1680 | iv | Paris, 1954 (in part) |
| 401 | Extremum Dei judicium ('Audite coeli quae loquor') | 9/4vv, 2 tpt, 2 tr str, bc | early 1680s | iv | |
| 402 | Sacrificium Abrahae ('Cum centum esset annorum Abraham') | 8/4vv, str, bc | 1680–81 | xviii; $Pn$ Vm¹1479 | |
| 402a | Symphonies ajustées au Sacrifice d'Abraham | 2 tr str, bc | — | xvi | |
| 403 | Mors Saülis et Jonathae ('Cum essent congregata ad praelium') | 8/4vv, 2 tr str, bc | early 1680s | iv | |
| 404 | Josue ('Cum audisset Adonisedec rex Jerusalem') | 6/4vv, str, bc | early 1680s | xi, xvii | |
| 405 | In resurrectione Domini nostri Jesu Christi canticum ('Hei mihi dilecta Maria') | Tr, S, B, 2 tr str, bc | 1681–2 | xxviii | |
| 406 | In circumcisione Domini: Dialogus inter angelum et pastores ('Xenia, xenia pastores') | Ct, T, B, 2 tr str, bc | 1682–3 | xx | |
| 407 | Dialogus inter esurientem, sitientem et Christum ('Famem meam quis replebit') | 2 S, B, bc | 1682–3 | xi | |
| 408 | Elévation ('Famem meam quis replebit') | Tr, S, B, str, bc | 1683 | xx | |
| 409 | In obitum augustissimae nec non piissimae gallorum reginae lamentum ('Heu, heu me miserum') | 9/vv, fl, str, bc | 1683 | xx | |

| No. | Title | Scoring | Date | Source | First published | |
|---|---|---|---|---|---|---|
| 410 | Praelium Michaelis archangeli factum in coelo cum dracone ('Audita est vox angelorum multorum') (inc.) | 6/8vv, 2 tr str, bc | 1683 | xx | | |
| 411 | Caedes sanctorum innocentium ('Surge Joseph e somno') | 6/6vv, 2 tr str, bc | 1683–5 | xxi | | |
| 412 | Nuptiae sacrae ('Incipite Domino in tympanis') | 6/6vv, 2 tr str, bc | 1683–5 | xxi | | |
| 413 | Caecilia virgo et martyr ('Est secretum, Valeriane') | 6/6vv, 2 tr str, bc | 1683–5 | vi | | |
| 414 | In nativitatem Domini nostri J[esu] C[hristi] canticum ('Frigidae noctis umbra') | 6/6vv, 2 tr str, bc | 1683–5 | vi | St Louis, 1959 | |
| 415 | Caecilia virgo et martyr ('Est secretum, Valeriane') | 6/6vv, 2 tr str, bc | 1686 | vii, xxii | | |
| 416 | In nativitatem Domini canticum ('Usquequo avertis faciem tuam Domine') | 8/4vv, fl, str, bc | ?late 1680s | ix | | |
| 417 | Dialogus inter Christum et homines ('Homo deus fecit coenam magnam') | Ct, T, Bar, 2 fl, 2 vn, bc | ?early 1690s | xxiii | | |
| 418 | In honorem S Ludovici Regis Galliae ('Languebat Ludovicus inter suorum cadavera') | 3/4vv, 2 fl, 2 vn, bc | ?early 1690s | v | | |
| 419 | Pour St Augustin mourant ('Bonum certamen certavit Augustinus') | 2 Tr, bc | ?late 1690s | xxviii | Motets (1709) | |
| 420 | Dialogus inter angelos et pastores Judeae in nativitatem Domini ('Usquequo avertis faciem tuam Domine') | 8/4vv, fl, str, bc | ?late 1690s | xxviii | | |
| 421 | In nativitate Domini nostri Jesu Christi canticum ('Frigidae noctis umbra') | 2 Tr, S, bc | 1698–9 | xii | | |
| 422 | Judicium Salomonis ('Confortatum est regnum Israel') | 8/4vv, ww, str, bc | 1702 | xxvii; *Pn* Vm¹1481 *Pn* Vm¹1478 | New Haven, 1964 | 80 |
| 423 | Dialogus inter Magdalenam et Jesum ('Hei mihi infelix Magdalena') | S, A, bc | | xi | Paris, c1905 | |
| 424 | Le reniement de St Pierre ('Cum caenasset Jesus') | 5/5vv, bc | | *Pn* Vm¹1269 | Paris, c1905 | 84 |
| 425 | Dialogus inter Christum et peccatores ('Mementote peccatores') | 2 Tr, Bar, bc | | xvii; *Pn* Vm¹ 1269 | Paris, 1725 | |
| | MISCELLANEOUS MOTETS | | | | | |
| 426 | 'Quae est ista quae ascendit de deserto' | Tr, S, bc | ?early 1670s | i | | |
| 427 | Pie Jesu | Tr, S, B, 2 tr str, bc | ?mid-1670s | ii | | |
| 428 | '... et invocate sanctum nomen ejus' (inc.) | Tr, Ct, T, B, bc | early 1680s | xi | | |
| 429 | 'Eamus, volamus o chare sodales' | Tr, S, B, 2 tr str, bc | 1682–3 | xx | Lausanne, 1949 | |

| No. | Text incipit (title) | Scoring | Date | Source | |
|---|---|---|---|---|---|
| 430 | '... gaudium meum qui es pax' (inc) | 5vv, bc | 1686–7 | viii | |
| 431 | Gratitudinis erga Deum canticum ('Os meum cur taces') | Tr, S, B, 2 tr str, bc | 1686–7 | viii | |
| 432 | Offertoire pour le sacre d'un évêque à 4 parties de voix et d'instruments ('Ecce sacerdos magnus') | 6/4vv, str, bc | ?early 1690s | v | 80 |
| 433 | Domine non secundum pour 1 basse tail e avec 2 violons ('Domine non secundum') | Bar, 2 vn, bc | ?mid-1690s | xxvi | |
| 434 | Motet pour une longue offrande ('Paravit Dominus in judicio thronum suum') | 8/4vv, ww, str, bc | 1698–9 | xii | |
| 435 | 'O coelestis Jerusalem' | Tr, S, B, bc | | Pn Vm¹1175ter | |
| 436 | 'Dilecte mi, dilecte votorum' | Ct, T, B, bc | | Pn Vm¹1269   Paris, c1905 | |
| 437 | 'Ferte coronas coelites' | 2 Tr, B, bc | | Pn Vm¹1269 | |
| 438 | 'Venite et audite omnes qui timetis' | 2 Tr, B, bc | | Pn Vm¹1269 | |
| 439 | Bone pastor ('Bone pastor amantissime Jesu') | Tr, S, B, bc | | Pn Vm¹1272 | |

AIRS SÉRIEUX ET À BOIRE
(dates of composition unknown)

| No. | Text incipit (title) | Scoring | Source | |
|---|---|---|---|---|
| | | | | 82, 87 |
| 440 | 'A ta haute valeur' (Air pour le roi) | Tr, bc | xxii (datable 1685) | |
| 441 | 'Ah! laissez-moi rêver' (Air tendre [de] Charpentier) | S, bc | Psg 3175; Phibault Rec.H.P.No.x | |
| 442 | 'Ah! qu'ils sont courts les beaux jours' | S, bc | Mercure galant (June 1680) | |
| 443 | 'Ah! qu'on est malheureux' (Air nouveau) | S, bc | Mercure galant (Nov 1678) | |
| — | Airs on stanzas from Corneille: Le Cid | | see 457–9 | |
| 444 | 'Allons sous ce verd feuillage' (Pastorelle, duo de M. Charpentier) | 2 S, bc | Meslanges (1728) | |
| 445 | 'Amour vous avez beau redoubler mes alarmes' | A, bc | Pn Rés.Vmc.27 | |
| 446 | 'Auprés du feu l'on fait l'amour' (Chansonette, de feu M. Charpentier) | S, bc | Meslanges (1728) | |
| 447 | 'Ayant bu du vin clairet' (Air à boire, de M. Charpentier) | S, B, bc | Recueil (1704) | |
| 448 | 'Beaux petits yeux d'écarlate' (La vieille, de M. Charpentier), doubtful | Tr, S, B, (?bc) | Meslanges (1726); Pn Fol. Y292, Y292(1) | 87 |
| 449 | 'Brillantes fleurs naissez' (Air) | S | Mercure galant (Oct 1689) | |
| 449a | 'Feuillages verds naissez' (variant of no.449) | 2 S | Les duos à la mode (Amsterdam, c1750) | |
| 449b | 'Charmantes fleurs naissez' (variant of no.449) | 2 S, bc | Pn Vm⁷4822 | |
| 449c | 'Printemps, vous renaissez' (Air: Sort de la jeunesse) (variant of no.449) | Tr, bc | Nouvelles poésies spirituelles et morales, ii (Paris, 1731) | |
| 450 | 'Celle qui fait tout mon tourment' (Gavotte) | S, bc | Mercure galant (July 1695); Recueil (1695) | |
| 451 | 'Consolez-vous, chers enfants de Bacchus' (Air nouveau) | Bar | Mercure galant (Oct 1680) | |
| — | 'Deux beaux yeux un teint de jaunisse' | | see 460a | |
| 452 | 'En vain rivaux assidus' (Air) | S, bc | Mercure galant (Feb 1678) | |
| 453 | 'Faites trêve (Musette de M. Charpentier) | S, bc | Les parodies nouvelles (Paris, 1737) | |

107

| No. | Text incipit (title) | Scoring | Source | First published |
|---|---|---|---|---|
| 454 | 'Fenchon, la gentille Fenchon' | 2 S, bc | Pn Y296(1) | 87 |
| — | 'Le beau jour dit une bergère' | | see 460b | |
| 455 | 'Non, non je ne l'aime plus' (A voix seule, de M. Charpentier) | A, bc | Phibault Rec.H.P.No.x | |
| 456 | 'Oiseaux de ces bocages' (Air sérieux, de M. Charpentier) | S, bc | Concerts parodiques, livre 4 (Paris, 1732) | |
| | Airs on stanzas from Le Cid: | | | |
| 457 | 'Percé jusque au fond du coeur' (no.1) | A, bc | Mercure galant (Jan 1681) | |
| 458 | 'Père, maîtresse, honneur, amour' (no.3) | A, bc | Mercure galant (March 1681) | |
| 459 | 'Que je sens de rudes combats' (no.2) | A, bc | Mercure galant (Feb 1681) | |
| 460 | 'Qu'il est doux, charmante Climène' | S | La clef des chansonniers (Paris, 1717) | |
| 460a | 'Deux beaux yeux un teint de jaunisse' (contrafactum) | Tr | Pn Fonds Weckerlin 189C (vol.iii) | |
| 460b | 'Le beau jour dit une bergère' (contrafactum) | S | Pn Rés.Vmc.201(2) | 87 |
| 460c | 'Un flambeau, Jeanette-Isabelle' (contrafactum) | Tr | Noëls français (Paris, [1901]) | |
| 461 | 'Quoi! je ne verrai plus' (Air à voix seule, de M. Charpentier) | A, bc | Phibault Rec.H.P.No.x | |
| 462 | 'Quoi rien ne peut vous arrêter' (Air nouveau) | S, bc | Mercure galant (Jan 1678) | |
| 463 | 'Rendez-moi mes plaisirs' (Air sérieux) | A, bc | Meslanges (1729) | |
| 464 | 'Rentrez trop indiscrets soupirs' (Air à voix seule, de M. Charpentier) | S, bc | Psg 2368, Phibault Rec.H.P.No.x | |
| 465 | 'Retirons-nous, fuyons' (Récit de M. Charpentier) | S, bc | Meslanges (1728) | |
| 466 | 'Ruisseau qui nourris dans ce bois' (Air à voix seule, de M. Charpentier) | S, bc | Psg 3175, Phibault Rec.H.P.No.x | |
| 467 | 'Sans frayeur dans ce bois' (Chaconne) | S, bc | Mercure galant (March 1680) | |
| 468 | 'Tout renait, tout fleurit' (Printemps, duo de M. Charpentier) | 2 S, bc | Meslanges (1728) | |
| 469 | 'Tristes déserts, sombre retraite' (Récit de M. Charpentier) | S, bc | Meslanges (1728) | 87 |
| 470 | 'Veux-tu, compère Grégoire' (Trio: Air à boire) | A, T, B | Recueil (1702); Pn Y292, Y296(1); Airs choisis (Paris, 1738) | 82 |

CANTATAS

| No. | Title | Scoring | Date | Source | First published |
|---|---|---|---|---|---|
| 471 | Orphée descendant aux enfers ('Effroyables enfers où je conduis mes pas') | Ct, T, B, tr rec, fl, 2 vn, bc | 1683 | vi | 87 |
| 472 | Serenata a 3 voci e sinfonia ('Sù, sù, sù, non dormite') | S, A, B, 2 tr str, bc | c1685 | vii | |
| 473 | Epithalamio in lode dell'Altezza Serenissima Elettorale di Massimiliano Emanuel Duca di Baviera concento a 5 voci con stromenti ('O del Bavaro soglio') | 2 Tr, A, T, B, ww, 2 tpt, timp, str, bc | 1685 | vii | 77, 87 |
| 474 | Epitaphium Carpentarij ('Quid audio, quid murmur') | Tr, S, 2 A, T, B, bc | | xiii | |

| No. | Title | Scoring | Date | Source | Edition | Pages |
|---|---|---|---|---|---|---|
| 475 | Beate mie pene, (Duo a 2 canti del Signor Charpentier) | 2 S, bc | | $PnVm^{78}$, $Vm^{753}$ | | 82, 85-6 |
| 476 | 'Superbo amore' | Tr, S, bc | | $Pn Vm^{718}$ | | 76 |
| 477 | 'Il mondo cosi va' | S, bc | | $Pn Vm^{718}$ | | 77, 85 |
| 478 | Cantate françoise de M. Charpentier ('Coulez coulez charmants ruisseux') (extreme y doubtful authenticity) | T, 2 vn, bc | | $AB$ 1182 | | |
| — | Le Roi d'Assyrie mourant | | | lost | | |
| | 'Quand je vous dis que je me meurs d'amour' | | | | | |
| | 'Et comment se garder des ruses de l'Amour' | | | | | |

PASTORALS, DIVERTISSEMENTS AND OPERAS

| No. | Title | Scoring | Date | Source | Edition | Pages |
|---|---|---|---|---|---|---|
| 479 | Petite pastorale (inc.) | Ct, T, B, 2 fl, bc | ?mid-1670s | ii | | |
| — | Les amours d'Acis et de Galatée | 5/4vv, 2 tr rec, b rec, bc | early 1678 | lost | | |
| 480 | Les plaisirs de Versailles | 6/4vv, 2 tr str, bc | early 1680s | xi | | |
| 481 | Actéon: pastorale en musique | 6/5vv, 2 tr str, bc | 1683-5 | xxi | | |
| 481a | Actéon changé en biche [revision of no.481] | 6/5vv, 2 vn, bc | 1683-5 | xxi | | |
| 482 | Sur la naissance de notre Seigneur Jésus Christ: pastorale | | 1683-5 | xxi | | |
| 483 | Pastorale sur la naissance de notre Seigneur Jésus Christ | 6/5vv, 2 fl, 2 vn, bc | 1683-5 | xxi | | |
| 483a | Seconde partie du noël français qui commence par Que nos soupirs [substitute for pt 2, no.483] | 4/5vv, 2 fl, 2 vn, bc | 1685-6 | xxii | | |
| 483b | Seconde partie du noël français qui commence par Que nos soupirs, Seigneur [substitute for pt 2, no.483] | 4/5vv, 2 tr str, bc | 1686-7 | xxii | | |
| 484 | Il faut rire et chanter: dispute de bergers | 5/5vv, 2 tr str, bc | 1684-5 | xxi | | |
| 485 | La fête de Rueil | 7/4vv, ww, str, bc | 1685 | xxii; $Pn Vm^{617}$ | | 77, 85 |
| 486 | La couronne de fleurs: pastorale | 8/5vv, 2 tr viols, bc | 1685 | vii | Paris, 1907 | 76 |
| 487 | Les arts florissants: opéra | 6/5vv, 2 fl, 2 tr viols, bc | 1685-6 | vii, $Pn Vm^{618}$ | | |
| 488 | La descente d'Orphée aux enfers (inc.) | 8/5vv, 2 tr str, 2 viols, bc | ?mid-1680s | xiii | | 75 |
| 489 | Idyle sur le retour de la santé du roi | 5/5vv, 2 tr str, bc | 1686-7 | viii | | 75 |
| — | Celse Martyr, tragédie en musique ('pour servir d'intermède à la tragédie du P[ère] M. Paulu') (P. Bretonneau) | | 1687 | lost | Paris, 1687 (lib only) | 79 |
| 490 | David et Jonathas (Bretonneau) (inc.) | 10/4vv, 2 fl, 2 ob, str, bc | 1688 | Pn Rés.F.924 (Paris, 1694) | Paris, 1981 | 79, 85-6 |
| 491 | Médée, tragédie mise en musique (T. Corneille) | 10/4vv, 2 fl, 2 tr rec, b rec, 2 ob, tpt, timp, str, bc | 1693 | | | 79, 81, 85-6 |

| No. | Title | Scoring | Date | Source | First published | |
|---|---|---|---|---|---|---|
| 492 | Pastorelette del Sgr M. Ant. Charpentier: Amor vince ogni cosa ('All'armi') | 4vv, 2 tr str, bc | | Pn Vm$^7$71 | | |
| 493 | 'Cupido perfido dentr'al mio cor' | 4vv, 2 tr str, bc | | | | |
| — | Le jugement de Pan (?opera) | | | lost | | |
| — | Le retour du printemps (?opera) | | | lost | | |
| — | Philomèle (opera, music partly composed by Duke of Chartres) | | | lost | | 79 |
| | **INTERMÈDES AND INCIDENTAL MUSIC** | | | | | |
| 494 | Ouverture de La comtesse d'Escarbagnas [et] intermèdes nouveaux du Mariage forcé (Molière) | Ct, T, B, str, bc | 1672 | xvi | | 82 |
| — | Les fâcheux (Molière) | | 1672 | lost | | 75 |
| 495 | Le malade imaginaire (Molière) (inc.) | 6/5vv, 2 fl, str, bc | 1672–3 | xvi, xiii | Geneva, 1973 | 76, 85 |
| 495a | Le malade imaginaire avec les défenses [rev. of parts of no.495] | Tr, S, A, str, bc | 1674 | xvi | Geneva, 1973 | 76 |
| 495b | Le malade imaginaire rajusté autrement pour la 3ème fois [rev. of parts of no.495] | str, bc | 1685 | vii, xxii | Geneva, 1973 | 86 |
| 495c | Profitez du Printemps [excerpt from second intermède of 495] | Tr, bc | — | Pn Vm$^7$4822 | | |
| 496 | Circé (T. Corneille, D. de Visé) | 6/5vv, str, bc | early 1675 | xvii | Paris, 1676 (part) | 80 |
| — | L'inconnu (De Visé, T. Corneille) | | 1675 | lost | | |
| — | Le triomphe des dames (T. Corneille) | | 1676 | lost | | |
| 497 | Sérénade pour le sicilien (Molière) | A, B, str, bc | 1679 | xvii | | |
| 498 | Ouverture du prologue de Polieucte pour le Collège d'Harcourt | 2 tpt, timp, str, bc | ?mid-1679 | xvii | | 79 |
| 499 | Ouverture du prologue de l'Inconnu (T. Corneille, De Visé) | ww, str, bc | ?mid-1679 | xvii | | |
| 499a | 'Le bavolet' (De Visé) [air for no.499] | S | 1679 | Mercure galant (Oct 1680) | | |
| 499b | 'Si Claudine ma voisine' (De Visé) [air for no.499] | B | 1679 | Airs de la Comédie françoise (Paris, 1753) | | |
| 500 | Les fous divertissants: comédie (R. Poisson) | S, A, T, B, str, bc | 1680 | xviii | | 85 |
| 501 | La pierre philosophale (T. Corneille, De Visé) | 3/4vv, str, bc | 1681 | xviii | | |
| 502 | Endimion: tragédie mêlée de musique (anon.) | A, T, B, str, bc | 1681 | xviii | | |
| 503 | Air pour des paysans dans la Nopce de village au lieu de l'air du marié (Brécourt) | str, bc | 1681 | xviii | | |

| No. | Title | Scoring | Date | | Publication | |
|---|---|---|---|---|---|---|
| 504 | Andromède: tragédie (P. Corneille) | 4/4vv, 2 fl, str, bc | 1682 | xxviii | | |
| — | Psyché (Corneille, Molière) | | 1684 | lost | | |
| 505 | [Overture and chaconne for] Le rendez-vous des Tuileries (Baron) | str | 1685 | xxi | | |
| 506 | Dialogue d'Angélique et de Médor (Dancourt) | S, T, bc | 1685 | vii | | |
| 507 | Vénus et Adonis (De Visé) | Tr, A, str, bc | 1685 | xxii | | |
| — | Le médecin malgré lui (Molière) 'Qu'ils sont doux, bouteille jolie' [for contrafacta, see 460–460c] | | | lost | | |
| — | Apothéose de Laodamus à la memoire de M le Maréchal Duc de Luxembourg (P. de Longuemare): 1er: 'O ciel, o disgrâce cruelle' 2nd: 'Quel malheur aujourd'hui m'accompagne en tous lieux?' 3ème: 'Que tout répond à nos concerts de joie' | | before 1695 | lost | | |
| **SACRED INSTRUMENTAL** | | | | | | |
| 508 | [Symphonies] pour un reposoir | str | ?early 1670s | i | Paris, 1962 (org transcr.) | 82 |
| 509 | Symphonie devant Regina [coeli] | 2 tr str, bc | ?early 1670s | i | | 84 |
| 510 | [?Prélude] | 2 tr str, bc | ?early 1670s | i | | |
| 511 | [Prélude] pour O filii [et filiae] | 2 tr str, bc | ?early 1670s | i | | |
| 512 | [?Prélude] | 2 tr str, bc | ?early 1670s | i | | |
| 513 | Messe pour plusieurs instruments au lieu des orgues (inc.) | ww, str, bc | ?early 1670s | i | Paris, 1962 (partial; org transcr.) | 84 |
| 514 | Offerte | 2 fl, 2 ob, str, bc | ?early 1670s | xv | | |
| 515 | Symphonies pour un reposoir | str, bc | ?early 1670s | xv | | |
| 516 | Après Confitebor: Antienne [en] d | 2 fl, str, bc | c1675 | xvii | Paris, 1962 (org transcr.) | 84 |
| 517 | Après Beati omnes: Antienne en G | str, bc | c1675 | xvii | | |
| 518 | [Overture and offertory] pour le sacre d'un évèque | str, bc | ?late 1670s | iii | | |
| 519 | Symphonies pour Le jugement de Salomon (inc., for lost dramatic motet) | str, bc | 1679 | xvii | | |
| 520 | Prélude, [menuet, et passepied] . . . devant l'ouverture | 2 fl, 2 ob, bn | 1679 | xvii | | |
| 521 | Prélude pour ce qu'on voudra | str | 1679 | xvii | | |
| 522 | Offerte non encore exécutée | ww, str, bc | 1679 | xviii | | |
| 523 | Pour un reposoir: Ouverture dès que la procession paraît [composed in conjunction with no.329] | 2 fl, b fl, str, bc | 1682–3 | xx | | |
| 524 | Ouverture pour l'église | fl, str | 1683 | xx | | 82–3, 84 |
| 525 | Antienne | 2 fl, str, bc | ?late 1680s | ix | | |

| No. | Title | Scoring | Date | Source | First published | |
|---|---|---|---|---|---|---|
| 526 | Antienne | 2 fl, str, bc | ?late 1680s | ix | | |
| 527 | Prélude pour Sub tuum praesidium | 2 vn, bc | ?late 1680s | xxiii | | |
| 528 | Prélude en g | fl, str, bc | ?late 1680s | xxiii | | |
| 529 | Symphonie en g | 2 vn/fl, bc | ?late 1680s | xxiii | | |
| 530 | Prélude en C | fl, str, bc | ?late 1680s | xxiii | | |
| 531 | [Three noëls] | 2 fl, str, bc | ?late 1680s | ix | | |
| 532 | Antienne pour les violons, flûtes, et hautbois à 4 parties | 2 fl, str, bc | ?early 1690s | x | Vienna, 1973 | |
| 533 | Prélude pour le 2nd [lost] Magnificat | 2 tr str, bc | ?early 1690s | v | | |
| 534 | Noëls sur les instruments | 2 fl, str, bc | ?early 1690s | v | Vienna, 1973 | |
| 535 | Prélude pour le Domine salvum en F | 2 tr str, bc | ?early 1690s | xxv | | 82 |
| 536 | Ouverture pour le sacre d'un évêque | fls, obs, str, bc | ?early 1690s | v | | |
| 537 | Ouverture pour le sacre d'un évêque | fls, obs, str, bc | ?early 1690s | xxv | Vienna, 1962 | |
| 538 | Prélude | 2 tr str, bc | 1690s | xxiv | | |
| 539 | Prélude pour le 2nd Dixit Dominus [en] F | 2 tr str, bc | 1690s | xxiv | | 88 |
| | | SECULAR INSTRUMENTAL | | | | |
| 540 | Ouverture pour quelque belle entreprise | str | 1679 | xvii | | |
| 541 | [Two minuets]: Menuet pour les flûtes allemandes Autre menuet pour les mêmes flûtes | 2 fl, bc | 1679 | xvii | | |
| 542 | Caprice | 2 vn, bc | 1679 | xvii | | |
| 543 | [inc., conclusion of dance-movement] | b viol | 1679–80 | iv | | |
| 544 | [inc., conclusion of an overture] | 2 tr str, bc | 1679–80 | iv | | |
| 545 | Concert | 4 viols | 1680–81 | xviii | Paris, 1952 | 88 |
| 546 | Commencement d'ouverture pour ce qu'on voudra, en la rectifiant un peu (unfinished) | str | ?early 1690s | x | | |
| 547 | [Two triumphal airs]: Marche de triomphe 2nd air de trompettes | ww, tpt, timp, str, bc | ?early 1690s | x | Vienna, 1973 | 88 |
| 548 | Sonate | 2 fl, 2 vn, b viol, b vn, hpd, theorbo | | Pn Vm⁷4813 | ed. in Vertrees, 1978 | 88 |
| — | Symphonies … de Charpentier (Collection Philidor, vol.xxv) | | | lost | | |
| | | WRITINGS | | | | |
| 549 | Remarques sur les messes à 16 parties d'Italie | | ?c1670 | Pn Rés.Vm¹260 | | 74 |
| 550 | Règles de composition par Mʳ Charpentier | | ?c1692 | Pn nouv.acq. fr.6355,6356 | facs. in Ruff, 1967 | 85 |
| 551 | Abrégé des règles de l'accompagnement de Mʳ Charpentier | | ?c1692 | Pn nouv.acq. fr.6355,6356 | | |

# BIBLIOGRAPHY

### CATALOGUES AND BIBLIOGRAPHICAL ITEMS

J. Ecorcheville: *Catalogue du fonds de musique ancienne de la Bibliothèque nationale* (Paris, 1910–14), iv, 2–74

A. Gastoué: 'Notes sur les manuscrits et sur quelques oeuvres de M.-A. Charpentier', *Mélanges de musicologie offerts à M. Lionel de La Laurencie* (Paris, 1933), 153

H. W. Hitchcock: 'Deux "nouveaux" manuscrits de Marc-Antoine Charpentier', *RdM*, lviii (1972), 253

——: *Les oeuvres de Marc-Antoine Charpentier: Catalogue raisonné* (Paris, 1982)

——: 'Marc-Antoine Charpentier: Mémoire [I. Jacques Edouard's "Mémoire des ouvrages de . . . Mr Charpentier" (1726) and the "mélanges autographes"] and Index [index to *Les oeuvres de M.-A. Charpentier*]', *RMFC*, xxiii (1986), 5

### SOURCE MATERIAL

A. du Pradel: *Le livre commode contenant les adresses de la ville de Paris* (Paris, 1692, 2/1878), ed. E. Fournier as *Le livre commode des adresses de Paris*)

H. Omont, ed.: 'La bibliothèque du roi au début du règne de Louis XV (1718–1736): journal de l'abbé Jourdain, secrétaire de la Bibliothèque', *Mémoires de la Société de l'histoire de Paris*, xx (1893), 207–94

J. Guiffrey: 'Testament et inventaire de Mademoiselle de Guise, 1688', *Nouvelles archives de l'Art français*, 3rd ser., xii (1896), 200–33

M. Brenet: *Les musiciens de la Sainte-Chapelle du Palais* (Paris, 1910/*R*1973), 260

P. Soccanne: 'Marc-Antoine Charpentier et la "Couronne des Fleurs" à l'hôtel de Guise (1680)', *Guide du concert*, xvii/10 (12 Dec 1930), 295 [transcription of an imaginary document]

P. Mélèse: *Répertoire analytique des documents contemporains . . . concernant le théâtre à Paris sous Louis XIV, 1659–1715* (Paris, 1934)

### BIOGRAPHY AND CRITICISM

C. Dassoucy: *Les rimes redoublées* (Paris, 1672); ed. E. Colombey as *Aventures burlesques de Dassoucy* (Paris, 1858)

[Journal de Trévoux]: *Mémoires pour l'histoire des sciences et des beaux-arts* (Nov 1704), 1895f; (Aug 1709), 1488

J. L. Le Cerf de la Viéville: *Comparaison de la musique italienne et de la musique française* (Brussels, 1704–6/*R*1972)

[S. de Brossard]: *Catalogue des livres de musique* (MS, *F-Pn* Rés.Vm⁸21)

E. Titon du Tillet: *Description du Parnasse françois* (Paris, 1727), 144ff

——: *Le Parnasse françois* (Paris, 1732/*R*1971), 490f

M. Brenet: 'Marc-Antoine Charpentier', *Tribune de Saint-Gervais*, vi (1900), 65

H. Quittard: 'Note sur un ouvrage inédit de Marc-Antoine Charpentier [no.473]', *SIMG*, vi (1904–5), 323

——: '*La Couronne de fleurs* de Marc-Antoine Charpentier sur des vers inconnus de Molière (réédition par M. H. Busser)'. *Revue musicale* [*RHCM*], viii (1908), 482

M. Brenet: 'Note sur le "Jugement de Salomon" et son auteur M.-A. Charpentier', *Tribune de Saint-Gervais*, xx (1914), 128

J. Tiersot: *La musique dans la comédie de Molière* (Paris, 1922)

J. de Froberville: '*L'Actéon* de Marc-Antoine Charpentier', *RdM*, xxvi (1928), 75

L. de La Laurencie: 'Un opéra inédit de M.-A. Charpentier: La descente d'Orphée aux enfers', *RdM*, x (1929), 184

K. Nef: 'Das Petrus-Oratorium von Marc-Antoine Charpentier und die Passion', *JbMP 1930*, 24

R. Dumesnil: 'Un ouvrage inédit de Marc-Antoine Charpentier ... *Le Jugement de Salomon*', *Mercure de France* (Sept 1939), 703

C. Crussard: 'Marc-Antoine Charpentier, théoricien', *RdM*, xxiv (1945), 49

——: *Un musicien français oublié: Marc-Antoine Charpentier, 1634–1704* (Paris, 1945)

Y. Rokseth: 'Un *Magnificat* de Marc-Antoine Charpentier', *JRBM*, i (1946–7), 192

M. F. Bukofzer: *Music in the Baroque Era* (New York, 1947)

A. R. Oliver: 'Molière's Contribution to the Lyric Stage', *MQ*, xxxiii (1947), 350

D. Launay: 'Charpentier, Marc-Antoine', *MGG*

M. Barthélemy: 'Notes sur M. A. Charpentier à propos d'un article du M.G.G.', *RBM*, vii (1953), 51

E. Borrel: 'La vie musicale de M.-A. Charpentier d'après le Mercure galant (1678–1704)', *XVIIᵉ siècle*, no.21–2 (1954), 433

H. W. Hitchcock: *The Latin Oratorios of Marc-Antoine Charpentier* (diss., U. of Michigan, 1954)

S. Spycket: 'Thomas Corneille et la musique', *XVIIᵉ siècle*, no.21–2 (1954), 442–55

C. Barber: *The Liturgical Music of Marc-Antoine Charpentier (1634–1704): the Masses, Motets, Leçons de Ténèbres* (diss., Harvard U., 1955)

# Bibliography

H. W. Hitchcock: 'The Latin Oratorios of Marc-Antoine Charpentier', *MQ*, xli (1955), 41

D. Loskant: *Untersuchungen über die Oratorien M.-A. Charpentiers* (diss., U. of Mainz, 1957)

H. W. Hitchcock: 'The Instrumental Music of Marc-Antoine Charpentier', *MQ*, xlvii (1961), 58

J. P. Dunn: *The 'Grands motets' of Marc-Antoine Charpentier (1634–1704)* (diss., Iowa State U., 1962)

F. Raugel: 'Marc-Antoine Charpentier', *Festschrift Karl Gustav Fellerer*, ed., H. Hüschen (Regensburg, 1962), 417

C. Barber: 'Les oratorios de Marc-Antoine Charpentier', *RMFC*, iii (1963), 91–130

N. Dufourcq: 'Le disque et l'histoire de la musique: un exemple, Marc-Antoine Charpentier', *RMFC*, iii (1963), 207

H. W. Hitchcock, ed.: Preface to *Marc-Antoine Charpentier: Judicium Salomonis* (New Haven, 1964)

R. Lowe: 'Marc-Antoine Charpentier, compositeur chez Molière', *Les études classiques*, xxxiii (1965), 34

T. Käser: *Die Leçon de Ténèbres im 17. und 18. Jahrhundert* (Berne, 1966)

W. Kolneder: 'Die *Règles de composition* von Marc-Antoine Charpentier', *Zum 70. Geburtstag von Joseph Müller-Blattau* (Kassel, 1966), 152

R. Lowe: *Marc-Antoine Charpentier et l'opéra de collège* (Paris, 1966)

G. Massenkeil: 'Marc-Antoine Charpentier als Messenkomponist', *Colloquium amicorum: Joseph Schmidt-Görg zum 70. Geburtstag* (Bonn, 1967), 228

B. Nielsen: 'Les grands oratorios bibliques de Marc-Antoine Charpentier', *DAM*, v (1966–7), 29–61

L. M. Ruff: 'Marc-Antoine Charpentier's *Règles de composition*', *Consort*, xxiv (1967), 233–70

H. W. Hitchcock: 'Marc-Antoine Charpentier and the Comédie-Française', *JAMS*, xxiv (1971), 255

——: 'Problèmes d'édition de la musique de Marc-Antoine Charpentier pour *Le malade imaginaire*', *RdM*, lviii (1972), 3

R. B. Petty: 'Charpentier's Mass *Assumpta est Maria*', *Music Analysis*, i (1972), 39

S. Rialland-Barbarin: *Une source d'information musicale: Le Mercure galant, 1679–1683* (diss., Conservatoire national supérieur de musique, Paris, 1972)

J. R. Anthony: *French Baroque Music from Beaujoyeulx to Rameau* (London, 1973, rev. 2/1978, rev. Fr. trans., 1981 as *La musique en France à l'époque baroque*)

H. W. Hitchcock: 'Some Aspects of Notation in an *Alma Re-*

*demptoris Mater* (c. 1670) by Marc-Antoine Charpentier (d. 1704)', *Notations and Editions: a Book in Honor of Louise Cuyler* (Dubuque, Iowa, 1973/*R*1977), 127

D. B. Stein: *The French 'Te Deum' from 1677–1744: its Esthetic, Style and Development* (diss., U. of Illinois, 1974)

D. Tunley: *The Eighteenth Century French Cantata* (London, 1974)

H. E. Smither; 'The Oratorio in the Baroque era; Italy, Vienna, Paris', *A History of the Oratorio*, i (Chapel Hill, N. Carolina, 1977)

J. A. Vertrees: *The Bass Viol in French Baroque Chamber Music* (diss., Cornell U., 1978)

J. A. Sadie: 'Charpentier and the Early French Ensemble Sonata', *Early Music*, vii (1979), 330

J. R. Burke: 'Sacred music at Notre-Dame-des-Victoires under Mazarin and Louis XIV', *RMFC*, xx (1981), 19

J. S. Powell: *Music in the theatre of Molière* (diss., U. of Washington, 1982)

A. Desautels: 'Un manuscrit autographe de M.-A. Charpentier à Québec', *RMFC*, xxi (1983), 118

J. Duron: 'L'année musicale 1688', *XVII$^e$ siècle*, no.139 (1983), 229

——: 'Les deux versions de la messe *Assumpta est Maria* de Marc-Antoine Charpentier', *RdM*, lxx (1984), 83

H. W. Hitchcock: 'Les oeuvres de Marc-Antoine Charpentier: post-scriptum à un catalogue', *RdM*, lxx (1984), 37

——: 'Charpentier's *Médée*', *MT*, cxxv (1984), 563

P. Ranum: 'Mademoiselle de Guise, ou les défis de la quenouille', *XVII$^e$ siècle*, no.144 (1984), 221

A. P. Rose: 'Marc-Antoine Charpentier's *Premier Leçon du Vendredy Saint* – an important source of music for solo treble viol', *Chelys*, xiii (1984), 47

'Marc-Antoine Charpentier: *Médée*', *L'avant-scène opéra*, no.68 (Oct 1984)

J. R. Burke: *Marc-Antoine Charpentier (c1634–1704): sources of style in the liturgical works* (diss., U. of Oxford, 1985)

A. Parmley: *The secular stage works of Marc-Antoine Charpentier* (diss., U. of London, 1985)

# MICHEL-RICHARD DE LALANDE

James R. Anthony

CHAPTER ONE

# Life

Michel-Richard de Lalande, the leading composer of the high Baroque *grand motet*, was born in Paris on 15 December 1657. The spelling of his name is a subject of some controversy (see Sawkins, 1981): he and his family normally used the spelling 'Delalande' for documents, but contemporaries referred to him as 'Lalande', and the *Mercure de France* often used the form 'M. de la Lande'.

Lalande was the 15th child of Michel Lalande, a master tailor, and Claude Dumourtiers. Most information about his early life comes from scattered notarial documents, church registers and the anecdotal *Discours sur la vie et les ouvrages de M. De la Lande* by 'M. T\*\*\*' (presumably Alexandre Tannevot) which served as a preface to the posthumous engraved edition (1729) of 40 *grand motets*. About 1666, Lalande entered the choir of the royal church of St Germain-l'Auxerrois, Paris, where he remained until his voice changed at the age of 15. François Chaperon directed the choir of which Marin Marais was a member. At this time, according to the *Discours*, Lalande left his parents' home to live with one of his brothers-in-law who (like Lalande's father) was a master tailor. To introduce Lalande to the public, his brother-in-law gave weekly concerts at his home

119

where his earliest compositions were performed.

Nothing is known of Lalande's formal musical training. The *Discours* tells that he preferred the violin among the instruments he cultivated in his youth, but when he was rejected by Lully for the opera orchestra he 'renounced the violin forever'. He mastered both harpsichord and organ, perhaps studying the latter with Charles Damour, the organist at St Germain-l'Auxerrois. The Maréchal de Noailles, who had employed him as a harpsichord teacher for his daughter, recommended that Louis XIV should do likewise for his two daughters by Mme de Montespan, Louise-Françoise (Mlle de Nantes) and Françoise-Marie (Mlle de Blois). According to the *Discours*, Lalande played the organ for the king at St Germain-en-Laye but Louis XIV thought him too young to be appointed *organiste du roy*.

His skill as an organist was sufficient to gain him employment in four Paris churches: the Jesuit church of St Louis, the conventual church of Petit St Antoine, St Gervais and St Jean-en-Grève. At St Louis he also composed *intermèdes* and choruses (now lost) for the dramatic productions of the Jesuits. On the death in 1679 of Charles Couperin, Lalande was contracted to remain at St Gervais (for illustration see fig.16, p.168) until Couperin's eldest son, François, was 18 (1686). However, after Lalande's appointment as *sous-maître* at the royal chapel in 1683, the young Couperin (as well as Lalande's older brother, François) must have deputized for Lalande on a regular basis at St Gervais; in 1690 Lalande, in his *approbation*, found François Couperin's two organ masses 'fort belles, et dignes d'estre données au Public'. In 1682 Lalande replaced Pierre Meliton at St Jean-en-Grève. He remained there as organist until the increasing responsibilities of his court positions forced his resignation in 1691.

In 1683, after Du Mont and Robert retired from the royal chapel, the king ordered a competition to be held for the four positions of *sous-maîtres* for his chapel; 35 musicians competed. This number was narrowed to 15 from which four were chosen to share the responsibilities by quarters: Coupillet (January), Collasse (April), Minoret (July) and Lalande (October). According to the *Discours*, Louis XIV himself intervened to assure the quarter for Lalande, initiating his rise as a favoured court composer. In September 1693, after the enforced retirement of Coupillet (for whom Henry Desmarest had 'ghost written' several *grands motets*), Lalande added the quarter of January to that of October. In March 1704, on the retirement of Collasse, the king gave the April quarter to 'nostre bien amé Richard Michel de La Lande'. The Marquis de Dangeau noted in his journal for 29 September 1714: 'There are several changes in the king's music for the chapel. The *maître de musique* for the July quarter . . . the Abbé Minoret, has retired. The king gave him 3500 livres as a pension and joined his quarter to the three others already held by La Lande . . . When [Lalande] is ill and there is no one assigned to his post, [Jean-Baptiste] Matho will conduct [*battra la mesure*] for him'. Thus for the first time the music of the royal chapel was under the control of one man.

*12. Michel-Richard de Lalande: engraving by Simon Henri Thomassin after Santerre*

Although described in the *Discours* as 'shy in public', Lalande does not seem to have been deterred in his accumulation of most of the official positions available to a court musician. In January 1685 he was appointed *compositeur de la musique de la chambre*, sharing half the year with Collasse, the other half being controlled by Pierre Robert. In 1700, after Robert's death, Lalande was given three-quarter control, and following Collasse's death in 1709 all charges of *compositeur de la musique de la chambre* were his. In January 1689 he was appointed *surintendant de la musique de la chambre*, replacing Jean-Louis de Lully and sharing the year with Jean-Baptiste Boësset. In 1695 Boësset sold his charge of *maître de la musique de la chambre* to Lalande for 16,000 livres. Lalande, who could raise only part of the money, turned to the king's music librarian André-Danican Philidor, who lent him 14,400 livres over a two year period.

On 7 July 1684 Lalande married the singer Anne Rebel, daughter of Jean Rebel, *ordinaire de la musique du roy*, and half-sister of Jean-Féry Rebel, the violinist, conductor and director of the Paris Opéra. According to the *Discours*, Louis XIV himself covered all the wedding expenses. The couple had two daughters, Marie-Anne (*b* 1686) and Jeanne (*b* 1687), both of whom became well-known singers; they were rewarded for their industry by Louis XIV, who in 1706 gave each a pension of 1000 livres. Unhappily both succumbed to smallpox in May 1711. The death of the dauphin in the same year forged an even closer bond between the king of France and the son of a

Paris tailor; Louis XIV is quoted as saying to Lalande, a few days after the death of the composer's daughters, 'You have lost two daughters who were deserving of merit. I have lost Monseigneur ... La Lande we must submit [*se soumettre*]'. A few months later (18 April 1712), at the king's request, Lalande conducted 129 musicians of the royal chapel in a memorial service for the dauphin and his wife at St Denis.

Lalande lived comfortably as a result of royal appointments and lucrative pensions which included one of 6000 livres paid to him and his wife from 1713 out of the revenues of the Paris Opéra. He was one of the few composers of his day to own a coach. When in Paris, he lived in a large three-storey house on the rue Ste-Anne which had formerly belonged to his father-in-law. An inventory of 11 May 1722 following the death of Anne Rebel reveals an abundance of material possessions, including much silver, more than 50 paintings, a fine harpsichord (valued at 300 livres), two viols and two violins. In addition to his town house, he had a ground-floor apartment in the Grand Commun at Versailles close to the château and a country house and garden in the Parc-aux-Cerfs.

After the king's death in 1715, Lalande gradually abandoned his heavy responsibilities at Versailles. In doing so he made sure that his best pupils, André-Cardinal Destouches, François Collin de Blamont and Jean-François de La Porte, received good positions. In February 1718 Destouches took over one of the charges of *surintendant*. He was succeeded in the same post by Collin de Blamont in November 1719.

In March 1718, Lalande's brother-in-law, Jean-Féry Rebel, and La Porte succeeded him as *compositeur de la musique de la chambre*.

On 5 May 1722, Lalande's wife died. Soon afterwards Louis XV made the composer a Chevalier of the Order of St Michel. Late the same year, Lalande expressed his desire to remit voluntarily three-quarters of his salary at the royal chapel in order to return to the original situation of four *sous-maîtres*. Touched by his request, Louis XV agreed and in January 1723 granted him an annual life pension of 3000 livres. A new generation of composers, protégés of the regent, Philippe of Orleans, were quickly chosen for the three vacancies (André Campra, Nicolas Bernier and Charles Hubert Gervais).

Lalande remarried in 1723; his bride was Marie-Louise de Cury (1692–1775), a daughter of the surgeon of the Princess of Conti. They had one daughter, Marie-Michelle (1724–81). According to the *Discours*, Lalande died of pneumonia in 1726; he was buried in the church of Notre Dame de Versailles, not far from the château where he had served for 43 years.

# CHAPTER TWO

# Works

## I  Sacred Latin music

The 'Versailles style', initiated by Veillot and Formé and nurtured by Du Mont, Lully and Robert, reached full flower in the 75 authenticated *grands motets* composed by Lalande for the royal chapel over 43 years. During the entire 18th century they were considered to be 'masterpieces of the genre' (Rousseau). As late as 1780 La Borde in his *Essai sur la musique ancienne et moderne* (1780/*R*1972) viewed Lalande the 'creator of a new genre of church music'. Their eloquent message touched both the favoured few who attended the king's Mass in the royal chapel and, after 1725, the crowds who applauded them at the newly established Concert Spirituel in Paris. During the first 45 years of the Concert Spirituel, there were more than 590 performances of 41 different Lalande *grands motets* and throughout the 18th century they were heard at the royal chapel. The volume of the *Livre de motets pour la Chapelle du Roy* printed by Ballard in 1792 gives the titles of 14 motets by Lalande performed between January and June of that year. The durability of Lalande's motets is also attested by the many manuscript copies found in provincial libraries throughout France. The Bibliothèque Méjanes in Aix-en-Provence, for example, even has several *parties* bearing the date of 1819. The popularity of these works in the 18th century is further documented by the number of *récits* in manuscript collections which were extracted from the *grands motets*, to provide a solo repertory for church or convent. One such collection of *Tous les récits du Basse Taille des Motets de M<sup>r</sup> De La Lande* (held in the Bibliothèque Méjanes, Aix-en-Provence) was made for the Duc de Noailles by Le Noble, the son-in-law and fellow copyist of André-Danican Philidor. Some *récits* 'ajustés pour être chantés à l'orgue' found their way into convent repertories. There is one example of an entire motet, *O filii et filiae*, in a reduction for soprano solo and continuo, for performance at the Concert Spirituel (Bibliothèque Nationale, Paris, MS Rés.2560).

Far from representing what Bukofzer called 'the most conservative spirit of the period' (*Music in the Baroque Era*, 1947), the motets bring together totally dissimilar elements with an unprecedented depth of feeling. *Galant* 'operatic' *airs* and the pompous 'official' style of the Versailles motet stand side by side. Cantus firmus treatment of Gregorian melodies in finely wrought polyphony is found together with weighty homophonic 'battle' choruses akin to those in Lully's *Bellérophon*. Lalande was deeply imbued with the spirit of the Latin psalms he chose. The warmth of his musical language humanized the *grand motet*. A perceptive and deeply felt homage to Lalande was included in the *avertissement* of the posthumous engraved edition; it was written by a protégé of the composer, Collin de Blamont

127

(1690–1760), who shared in the preparation of the edition. Collin de Blamont described his former teacher as a 'Latin Lully' and continued:

His great merit ... consisted in wonderful choice of melody, judicious use of harmony and nobility of expression. He understood the value of the words he chose to treat and rendered (in music) the true meaning of the majestic and holy enthusiasm of the Prophets ... Profound and learned on the one hand, simple and natural on the other, he applied all his study to touch the soul by richness of expression and vivid pictorialism. The mind is refreshed by the pleasing variety not only from one piece to the next, but within the same piece, ... by the ingenious disparities with which he ornaments his works, by the graceful melodies which serve as contrasting episodes to the most complex choral sections.

Clearly, Collin de Blamont is describing here the late motets or the final versions of earlier motets that make up the posthumous edition.

Four large collections contain most of Lalande's *grands motets*: the manuscript copy of 27 motets, made in 1689 and 1690 by the Philidor atelier; the 1729 engraved edition of 40 motets; a manuscript copy of 41 motets made for (or by) a certain Gaspard Alexis Cauvin; and copies of 11 motets (both full scores and parts) which Philidor made for the Count of Toulouse beginning in 1704 or 1705. The Cauvin manuscript is a mid-18th-century copy partly based on the 1729 edition and partly on earlier copies, with a changed sequence of motets and with the addition of the instrumental inner parts (missing from the engraved edition).

Lalande constantly revised his *grands motets*; at least 25 exist in more than one version and some in more than two. According to the *Discours*,

From the time of the former king [Louis XIV], he had begun to make changes in several of his earlier motets. Noting this, His Majesty prevented him from continuing, possibly to render more obvious the progress made under his aegis by the composer, possibly to preserve the graces and naivety of the first works, or finally, because of fear that this occupation which took so much time would prevent him from composing new music.

In his *Apologie de la Musique Françoise contre M. Rousseau* (Paris, 1754), Abbé Laugier wrote that Lalande 'produced nothing that was not extremely well worked (*travaillé*). One senses that he returned many times to his motets and that he touched and retouched them'.

If the dates in the Avignon manuscript are to be trusted 30 of Lalande's motets (less than one third of the total) date from the period 1681–91, covering the first eight years of his tenure at the royal chapel. Of these, 27 are found in the Philidor copy at Versailles. This collection, then, may be said to represent Lalande's early style. These works are referred to in the *Discours* as follows: 'The first compositions of M$^r$ De La Lande are not as well worked as the last pieces; they are more simple than profound and are less the fruits of Art than of Nature'.

Most of the 'Philidor motets' exploit the vertical sonorities and syllabic treatment of text that characterize the earlier Versailles motets of Du Mont, Lully and Robert. Although some influence from French stage music may be observed in such a binary *air* as 'Asperges me' or a rondeau *air* such as 'Amplius lava me' (both from the *Miserere*), many *récits*, often accompanied by five-part strings, are open-ended and elide or alternate with choral sections. The large four-

and five-part choruses are generally homophonic. On the other hand, a shift towards a more polyphonic style may be seen in such a chorus as 'Ascendit Deus in jubilo' from *Omnes gentes*. In his polyphonic choral settings in the 'Philidor motets', Lalande often represents two independent and clearly defined motifs in a solo *récit* (or an opening *symphonie*) and then combines them in a chorus. In the hymn *Veni Creator Spiritus*, the music assigned in the opening tenor *récit* to each part of the paired text of the fifth verset, 'Hostem repellas longius, Pacemque dones protinus', is quite different, these two are then combined in a ten-voice double chorus. A similar practice is used in the *Miserere* where the two motifs occurring in succession in the introductory *symphonie*, are worked together in the chorus which follows, the second motif being used as a counter-subject to the first. In Lalande's later music such textual counterpoint is used with much subtlety. In the eighth verset of the *De profundis*, 'Et ipse redimet Israel, Ex omnibus iniquitatibus ejus', two motifs are used to represent the two parts of the text (ex.1); motif *a* ascends and *b* descends. They were clearly chosen for use either consecutively or simultaneously. Most tutti passages combine the motifs and their respective texts, as here; to assure the comprehensibility of the text Lalande restricted the opening and the end of the movement to the first and second lines respectively.

In the 'Philidor motets' the orchestra generally doubles the voices of the *grand choeur* and supplies five-part *symphonies* or three-part *ritournelles* to mark structural divisions. Like Du Mont, Lalande allowed

**Ex.1** Extract from *De profundis*

**(a)** Motifs used in passage 'Et ipse redimet Israel'

Et ip – se re – di-met, re – di-met Is – ra – ël:

Ex om – ni-bus in – i – qui – ta – ti-bus e – jus

**(b)** Motifs combined in chorus

[Petit Choeur]

Ex om – ni-bus in – i – qui – ta – ti-bus e – jus. Et

Et ip – se re – di-met Is – ra – ël: Ex

Et

Ex

ip – se re – di-met, re – di-met Is – ra – ël:

om – ni-bus in – i – qui – ta – ti-bus e – jus.

Et ip – se re – di-met Is – ra – ël:

ip – se re – di-met, re – di-met Is – ra – ël:

om – ni-bus in – i – qui – ta – ti-bus e – jus.

131

# MOTETS

## DE FEU M.[R]

# DE LA LANDE

Chevalier de L'Ordre de S.t Michel, Sur-
Intendant de la Musique du ROY
Maitre de Musique et Compositeur
Ordinaire de la Chapelle et de la
Chambre de Sa MAIESTÉ

Avec un discours sur la Vie et les
Œuvres de L'Autheur

Prix de ce Livre Contenant deux Motets. 6.tt en Blanc

Gravé Par L. Hüe

## A PARIS.

Se Vend Chez Le S.r Boivin Marchand, Rüe
S.t Honoré a la Regle d'Or.

## AVEC PRIVILEGE DU ROY. 1729

*13. Title-page of Lalande's 'Motets', i (1729)*

the second violin to elaborate the vocal line in free counterpoint. Occasionally, especially in slow-moving choruses, the orchestra is independent of the voice parts ('Exultat cantico' from *Christe Redemptor omnium*, for example).

Clearly, Lalande suffered a crisis of conflicting styles soon after the turn of the century. Changes were taking place in French stage music by such post-Lully composers as Campra, Destouches, Mouret and Montéclair; French composers had to come to terms with the Italian cantatas and sonatas 'that have flooded all Paris' (*Mercure galant*, 1714). In spite of his absorption in the style of the Versailles motet, Lalande was no stranger to Italian music. The Italophile Nicolas Mathieu, *curé* of St André-des-Arts, had established weekly concerts in his home before the turn of the century where 'only Latin music composed in Italy' was performed. Lalande (and Charpentier) were both part of the coterie surrounding Abbé Mathieu, and it was Lalande who inherited his collection of cantatas and motets.

A stylistic and chronological gap separates the Philidor copies of 1689–90 from the 1729 engraving. The Philidor–Toulouse copies of 1704 and certain isolated Philidor motet manuscripts at Versailles may be considered representative of a transition period. In the 17 years that separate the Count of Toulouse copy of *Super flumina Babylonis* from the original version in the Philidor Versailles collection, Lalande substituted an extended concert 'aria' with flute obbligato ('Ad hereat lingua') for the earlier *récit* for soprano accompanied by five-part strings. This is already an 'ingenious disparity' (*Discours*) as is the elegant duo 'Laudate, laudate Dominum' for two sopranos and obbligato violin found in the *Laudate Dominum*, which comes from the Philidor atelier and dates from 1700 (Bibliothèque Municipale, Versailles, M.M.24).

The 1729 engraved edition and the Cauvin manuscript together offer the most complete picture of the *grands motets* of the mature Lalande. The changes documented by the 40 motets of these sources take the following forms: (1) the change from a loosely organized structure with elided sectional divisions to autonomous movements (solos and ensembles interspersed between choruses), resembling the so-called 'reform cantatas' of Bach or the Restoration anthems of Humfrey or Purcell; (2) the creation out of simple *récits* with five-part homophonic accompaniment of elaborate concert 'arias' or duos, often accompanied by obbligato instruments; (3) the changing of predominantly homophonic choruses into more polyphonic ones; (4) the change from an orchestra primarily doubling choral lines to one independent of the voices; and (5) greater economy in the use of some material while other material is expanded. The 'Requiem aeternam' from the *De profundis* is a fine example of the fifth category. The Philidor version includes a *symphonie* of 14 bars, a solo *récit* of 8 bars, a second *symphonie* of 6 bars and a basically homophonic chorus of 31 bars up to the 'Et lux perpetua' (ex.2*a*). In the 1729 edition there is only one *symphonie*, of 9 bars, which merges with a 53-bar chorus up to 'Et lux perpetua'. The writing is dense, five-part polyphony of Bach-like intensity in

Ex.2 (a) First version (after Philidor copy, *F-V*)

(b) Second version (after 1729 edn.)

which both instruments and voices participate (ex.2*b*).

The harmony in Lalande's late works may owe something to his exposure to Charpentier's music. The dissonant chord of the mediant 9th with major 7th and augmented 5th, found in the music of Charpentier, is also heard in the motets of his younger contemporary (ex.3, bars 2 and 7). Like Rameau, Lalande found the diminished 7th chord compellingly dramatic. In the *Pange lingua* (ex.3), his coupling of this chord with an indicated 'silence' shows the care with which he chose the most effective musical setting for the text.

Ex.3 Extract from *Pange lingua* (after 1729 edn.)

The motets in the engraved edition vary greatly in the number of sections they have. *Regina caeli laetare* is the shortest, with only six sections (*symphonie*, duo, chorus, recitative, trio, chorus); the *Miserere*, on the other hand, has a total of 20, including 8 *récits*. A symmetrical ordering of sections like that found in many Bach cantatas, is rare; only *Deus noster re-*

*fugium* approaches an alternation of *récit* and chorus.

In 11 *grands motets* Lalande used the traditional opening formula of the Versailles motets – that is, the sharing of the same thematic material by *symphonie*, *récit* and chorus. In seven instances, Lalande introduced his motet with an autonomous *récit*: *Quare fremuerunt gentes* begins with two. More than half the *récits* found in the engraved edition are in some sort of binary form, including examples of the type *A–B–B′*, the most common binary configuration in the stage music of the Lully and post-Lully generation; in this type of air, the text is usually a quatrain. In the *B′* section the textual repetition never gives rise to an exact musical repetition although note-values and melodic shape may be similar. The example below shows the relationship between text and music in the *récit* 'Quare utilitas in sanguine meo' from the tenth verset of *Exaltabo te, Domine*:

| | |
|---|---|
| Quae utilitas in sanguine meo, | |
| Dum descendo in corruptionem? | *A*: I – V |
| Numquid confitebitur tibi pulvis, | |
| Aut annuntiabit veritatem tuam? | *B*: V – ii |
| Numquid confitebitur tibi pulvis, | |
| Aut annuntiabit veritatem tuam? | *B′*: I – I |

Operatic influence is also seen in the more than ten *récits* scored for high voice (soprano or *haute-contre*) 'accompanied' by two flutes, by two violins or by a combination of the two without continuo. There are more than 20 *récits* with a striking resemblance to the extended arias found in French cantatas or *opéras-ballets*; these, with their elaborate melismas, chains of sequences and vocal displays ('Qui posuit' from

*Lauda Jerusalem* even has a cadenza for soprano and oboe), mark the most radical break with the past. Surprisingly, there are only two genuine da capo arias in the 40 motets of the engraved edition: most *récits* of this type are in rondeau form (*A–B–A'*), with modifications in the return of *A*.

To appreciate the extent to which Lalande had absorbed the new Italianate style in his religious music, one need only compare a *récit* of an early motet with the same *récit* as revised in the engraved edition. Ex.4a shows 'Hodie si vocem ejus' from *Venite, exultemus Domino* as it appears in an early 18th-century copy from Philidor's atelier (Bibliothèque Municipale, Versailles, M.M.25); the heavy five-part accompaniment is generally homophonic, following note-against-note the baritone's vocal line. In ex.4b the conception is totally different; we have a highly developed aria for soprano with violin obbligato.

In certain of his late motets, Lalande exposed the texts of several versets in a succession of short *récits*, much as Lully or Campra constructed an operatic scene from short dialogue airs interspersed with recitatives. This procedure may be seen in *Exultate justi in Domino*, where there is a succession of five airs, three for *haute-contre* (interrupted by a brief recitative) and two for soprano, each on two lines of text.

It is not certain that the 1729 engraved edition represents an accurate final version of Lalande's motets as performed at the royal chapel or at the Concert Spirituel. Possibly Collin de Blamont was

**Ex.4** Extract from *Venite exultemus Domino: récit* 'Hodie si vocem ejus'
**(a)** First version (after *F-V* M.M.25)

Ho - di - e     si   vo - cem   e - jus   au -

- di - e - ri - tis

**(b)** Second version (after 1729 edn.)

14. *Scene from Lalande's 'Ballet de la jeunesse', Versailles, first performed 1686: engraving*

involved in the final revisions of earlier works; according to the *Discours*, he was chosen to write an introduction to the engraved edition of his former teacher's motets because 'he had the strongest ties with M. De La Lande whose disciple he was honoured to have been'. A month after his death, on 25 July 1726, Lalande's widow requested a royal patent to engrave her husband's motets. The work was done 'chez Jacques Collombat' in 1728, although the edition carries the date of 1729. This would have allowed Collin de Blamont time to amend the music; but there is no need to credit him with a part in the composition of these eloquent statements of the mature Lalande. A study of his own extant religious music reveals none of the intensity of expression or skilful polyphonic manipulation found in several of the choruses in the engraved edition. Collin de Blamont's introduction has the ring of sincerity:

I have been too much his servant and friend, and have received too many marks of his esteem and kindness through the pains he took with my education from my tenderest youth, not to sacrifice something of my own self-interest in daring to put this in writing. I can instruct you in all the perfection I have recognized in this Latin Lully.

## II  Secular music

Most of Lalande's secular music was written between 1682 and 1700. He wrote ballets, divertissements and pastorales to entertain the royalty at Versailles, Marly, Fontainebleau and Sceaux. His *Ballet de la jeunesse*, performed at Versailles on 28 January 1686, a synthesis between opera and ballet, is an important precursor of the *opéra-ballet*; its long poem is divided into three episodes, devoted respectively to Mercury, Pallas and Tircis, and the music includes eight *symphonies*, 14 *airs*, 15 choruses and 18 dances, these last including a central 'Chaconne de la jeunesse' with 61 variations on the eight-bar bass, showing how Lalande, like Lully, was able to organize an entire scene around the chaconne pattern (the theme and 28 variations are instrumental, and the remaining music is for vocal solo, ensemble and chorus).

For the first court ballet danced by Louis XV at the Tuileries, Lalande created a pastiche in five entrées, *L'inconnu*. He chose music by Campra, Bertin de la Doué, Rebel and Destouches, and himself supplied 35 *airs de danse*. On 31 December 1721, *Les éléments*, 'Troisième Ballet dansé par le Roy dans son Palais des Tuileries', was first performed. Lalande and André-Cardinal Destouches collaborated on this court ballet which with several revisions was heard at the Paris Opéra in May 1725 as an *opéra-ballet*. The distribution of labour between Lalande and Destouches remained a carefully guarded secret, although there is little doubt most of the music is by Destouches. In a letter to Prince Antoine I of Monaco, Destouches wrote:

My *amour propre* has been flattered by the praise you give to the *Ballet des Elémens*. I share the glory of pleasing you with M. de La Lande. We were ordered to work on it together. He contributed some very beautiful things the details concerning which I must pray you not [to ask me] to divulge because he has insisted that we were both covered by the same cloak.

The only clue as to Lalande's contribution is found in the 'Table des Ballets' in the manuscript collection of *Sinfonies pour les soupers du Roi* (in the Conservatoire, Paris, Rés.581), where, under the title *Ballet des Elémens*, the overture, five items from the prologue and four items from Act 1 are listed as Lalande.

Lalande extracted, and subtly varied, parts of his ballets and divertissements for use in his popular *Symphonies* 'performed every 15 days during the supper of Louis XIV and Louis XV'. The copy of the *Symphonies* made in 1745 is a true manuscript *de luxe*. This collection, though based on earlier copies (1703, 1727), carefully 'orders' the suites by key (interior movements, however, are often in related keys) and numbers the supper for which each suite was performed. Suites nos.6 to 8 are entitled 'Caprices' or 'Caprices ou Fantaisies', and are free orchestral pieces unrelated to the dance. Suite no.7 'which the king often asked for', is in five movements designated only by tempo indications which move from slow to fast. It is imaginatively scored as an orchestral 'quartet' for violins, violas, bassoons and a continuo ('figured by M. Rebel'). The final Caprice (Suite no.8) includes a fine set of free variations in concerto scoring. Contrary to normal procedures, its *tous* sections rather than its solo sections increase in complexity. Following the suites in volume one of this collection are the *Symphonies des Nöels*, settings of traditional French carol melodies, 'which were played in the king's chapel on Christmas night'.

Numbers in right-hand margins denote references in the text.

GRAND MOTETS
*(principal sources)*

P – Motets de M. De Lalande ..., MS collected by A.-D. Philidor, 1689–90, 27 motets in 10 vols., *F-V* | 126-41

T¹ – Motets de Monsieur de La Lande ..., MS copied by Philidor, 1704, 5 motets in 7 partbooks, *Pn* [formerly *GB-T*], made for the Count of Toulouse | 128, 129, 133

T² – Mottets de Monsieur de La Lande ..., MS copied by Philidor, 1706, 6 motets in 8 partbooks, *F-Pn* [formerly *GB-T*], Count of Toulouse Collection | 128, 133

T³ – 3 motets in 2 vols., collected by Philidor, ?1704, *F-Pn* [formerly *GB-T*], Count of Toulouse Collection | 128, 133

T⁴ – 8 motets in 2 vols., collected by Philidor, ?1706, *F-Pn* [formerly *GB-T*], Count of Toulouse Collection | 128, 133

H – Motets de feu Mr De La Lande ... avec un discours sur la vie et les oeuvres de l'autheur ... gravé par L. Hue (Paris, 1729–33), 40 motets and shorter works in 21 vols.; lacks instrumental inner parts (see *RISM*, Ser. A, 1/5, 203–5, 380–82) | 119, 128, 133, 134

C – Motets à grand choeur de M. de la Lande ..., MS collected by/for Gaspard Alexis Cauvin, 1742 (watermark date), 41 motets and shorter works in 21 vols.; i–xx, *F-V*; xxi, *Pn* | 128, 134

L – 9 motets in MS, *LYm*

B – 34 motets in MS, 4 vols. [a–d]; *US-BE* (closely modelled on H)

S – 5 MS motets and shorter works in Motets Delalande, Toulouse,9, Strasbourg, M. R. Lutz, private collection

A – MS, *F-A*, list dating most of printed and MS motets

For additional sources see: *Catalogue thématique des sources du grand motet français, 1663–1792* (Paris, 1984), 126–64. Volume or manuscript numbers/letters of the sources P, H, C, and B are in parentheses. Dating follows Source A unless otherwise indicated in square brackets; asterisks designate motets found in more than one version.

Ad te Domine clamabo, Ps xxviii, 1703, H(12), C(8), L, B(d)
Ad te levavi oculos meos, Ps cxxiii, c1689[P], P(9)
Afferte Domino, Ps xxix, 1683, P(6)
*Audite coeli, 1689, P(5)

Beati omnes qui timet, Ps cxxviii, 1698, H(6), C(18), B(b); ed. H. Letocart (Paris 1928)
Beati quorum, Ps xxxii, 1683, P(2); extract: Loetamini in Domino, ed. G. Roussel (Sèvres, 1951)
Beatus vir qui timet, Ps cxii, 1692, H(19), C(2), B(d); ed. J. Pagot (Paris, 1950)
Benedictus Dominus Deus Israel, Luke i.58–79, 1702, H(18), C(19), B(d); ed. Roussel (Paris, 1955)
*Benedictus Dominus Deus meus, Ps cxliv, 1695, H(1), C(7), B(a); extracts ed. F. Raugel (Paris, 1951)
Cantate Domino, Ps xcvi, 1698, S
*Cantate Domino ... quia mirabilia, Ps xcviii, 1707, H(2), C(1), L, B(a); ed. Roussel (Paris, 1956)
Cantemus Domino, 1687, P(3); ed. K. Husa (New York, 1971) | 183
Christe Redemptor, 1690, P(8); ed. Roussel (Paris, 1953)
*Confitebimur tibi Deus, Ps lxxv, 1701, H(9), C(3), T¹, T³(1), B(b); ed. A. Cellier (Paris, 1952)
*Confitebor tibi ... in consilio, Ps cxi, 1699, H(1), C(4), T¹, T³(2), L, B(a); ed. P. Oboussier (London, 1982)
Confitebor tibi ... quoniam, Ps cxxxviii, 1697, H(19), C(7)
*Confitemini Domino, Ps cv, 1705, H(7), C(6), T², T⁴(2), L, B(a)
Conserva me Domine, Ps xvi, vocal extracts only, *F-Pn* (Vm¹ 3123)
Credidi propter quod, Ps cxvi.10–16, 1697, H(13), C(13), B(c)
Cum invocarem, Ps iv, 1714, verset, 'Signatum est', *Pn* (Vm¹ 3123)
Deitatis majestatem, 1682, P(7); extract ed. Roussel (Paris, 1950)
*De profundis, Ps cxxx, 1689, P(6), H(9), C(2), B(b), S; ed. Cellier (Paris, 1944), ed. L. Boulay (Paris, c1961), ed. J. Anthony (Chapel Hill, 1980) | 130
Deus, Deus meus, Ps lxiii, 1685, P(9)
Deus in adjutorum, Ps lxx, 1691, H(4), C(15), L, B(b); ed. Cellier (Paris, 1958)
Deus in nomine, Ps liv, 1690, versets 1, 2, 4, 6, *Pn* (Vm¹ 3123)
Deus misereatur nostri, Ps lxvii, 1687, P(3) | 136-7
Deus noster refugium, Ps xlvi, 1699, H(10), C(13), B(d)
Dies Irae, 1711, 1690 [S], S
Dixit Dominus, Ps cx, 1689, P(4)

Dixit Dominus, Ps cx, 1708, H(5), C(5), B(b); ed. H. Sarlit (Paris, 1950)

Domine, Dominus noster, Ps viii, 1686, verset, 'Quoniam videbo', Pn (Vm¹ 3123)

*Domine in virtute tua, Ps xx, 1689, P(10), H(15), C(17); ed Roussel (Paris, 1952)

Domine non est exaltatum, Ps cxxxi, 1691, 1689 [P], P(2)

Domine, quid multiplicati?, Ps iii, 1691, verset, 'Tu autem Domine', Pn (Vm¹ 3123)

Domine, salvum fac Regem, 1706, T², T⁴(4, 5)

Dominus regit me, Ps xxiii, 1695, H(11), C(20), B(d)

*Dominus regnavit, Ps xcvii, 1704, H(8), C(5), T², T⁴(4), L, B(a); ed. D. Chirat (Paris, 1953)

Ecce nunc benedicte, Ps cxxxiv, 1686, P(6)

Eructavit cor meum, Ps xlv, 1697, S

*Exaltabo te, Deus, Ps cxlv, 1712, H(10), C(19), B(d), ed. Boulay (Paris, 1956)

*Exaltabo te, Domine, Ps xxix, 1704, H(17), C(12), T², T⁴(5), B(c); extract: Psallite Domino, ed. Roussel (Paris, 1952) — 137

Exaudi Deus deprecationem, Ps lxi, 1687, P(3), C(3)

Exaudiat te Dominus, Ps xx, 1688, music lost

Exultate justi in Domino, Ps xxxiii, 1710, H(15), C(15), B(b)

*Exurgat Deus, Ps lxviii, 1706, H(14), C(10), L, B(c) — 138

*In convertendo Dominus, Ps cxxvi, 1684, P(10), H(13), C(17), B(c)

Jubilate Deo, Ps c, 1689, P(8); ed. L. Sawkins (Stuttgart, 1985)

Judica me Deus, Ps xliii, 1693, H(8), C(9)

Laetatus sum, Ps cxxii, 1693, Pn (H400b)

*Lauda Jerusalem, Ps cxlvii.12–20, 1725, c1689 [P], P(10), H(4), C(21), B(a) — 138

Laudate Dominum in sanctis, Ps cl, 1697, V (M.M.18)

Laudate Dominum, omnes gentes, Ps cxvii, 1686, P(7)

*Laudate Dominum quoniam, Ps cxlvii, 1700, H(20), C(9), T¹ — 134

*Laudate pueri Dominum, Ps cxiii, 1686, P(4)

Magnificat, Luke i.46–55, 1681, music lost

Magnus Dominus, Ps xlviii, 1701, 1702 [H], H(20), C(12)

Miserere mei, Deus, Ps lvii, 1685, P(7)

*Miserere mei, Deus, Ps li, 1687, P(1), H(3), C(4), B(a); ed. Letocart (Paris, 1927) — 129, 130, 134 136

Nisi Dominus aedificaverit, Ps cxxvii, 1694, 1704 [H], H(16), C(20), B(c); ed. Boulay (Paris, 1956)

*Nisi quia Dominus, Ps cxxiv, 1703, H(18), C(1), T², T⁴(3), B(d) — 127

Notus in Judaea Deus, Ps lxxvi, 1702, H(11), C(6), L — 130

O filii et filiae, 1698, H(2), C(14); ed. Roussel (Paris, 1952)

Omnes gentes, plaudite, Ps xlvii, 1689, P(8)

Omnes gentes, plaudite, Ps xlvii, 1721, versets 1, 5, 6, 7, Pn (Vm¹ 3123)

Pange lingua, 1704, 1689 [H], H (14), C(16), B(c); ed. Sarlit (Paris, 1951) — 136

*Quam dilecta tabernacula, Ps lxxxiv, 1686, P(2), T¹, T³; ed. Roussel (Paris, 1951)

Quare fremuerunt gentes, Ps ii, 1706, H(17), C(18), B(c); L; ed. Cellier (Paris, 1949) — 137

Quemadmodum desiderat, Ps xlii, 1696, H(7), C(14), B(13); extract: Quando veniam, in Répertoire classique de musique religieuse (Paris, 1913)

Regina caeli laetare, 1698, H(3), C(11); ed. S. Spycket (Paris, 1951), ed. Roussel (Paris, 1959), ed. Boulay (Paris, 1970) — 136

*Sacris solemnis, 1709, H(16), C(16), B(c); extracts ed. Roussel (Paris, 1951)

*Super flumina Babylonis, Ps cxxxvii, 1687, P(5), T², T⁴(6) — 133

*Te Deum, 1684, P(1), H(6), C(11), T², T⁴(1), B(b); ed. H. Sarlit Paris, 1951), ed. Boulay (Paris, c1970)

Usque quo, Domine?, Ps xii, 1692, H(5), C(10), B(b); ed. F. Gervais (Paris, 1970)

*Veni Creator, 1722, 1684 [S], P(4), S; ed. Roussel (Paris, 1953) — 130

*Venite, exultemus Domino, Ps xcv, 1700, H(12), C(3), T¹; ed. Roussel (Paris, 1953) — 138

### MISCELLANEOUS SACRED

Messe des deffuns, 1v; O salutaris, Domine salvum, in Messes de plainchant musical, F-Pn

Cantemus Domino, Pc Rés.1899; ed. G. Morche, Motets à une voix et basse continue (Paris, 1975) [attrib. Lalande by Morche, formerly attrib. J. Gilles]

Cantique de Racine, 2vv, no.4 in Cantiques chantez devant le Roy (Paris, 1695), Pn

Domine, salvum fac regem, 3vv, V

5 settings of Domine salvum fac regem, Bar, Pn

Laudate pueri, 3vv, Pn

Miserere, 1v, Pn

Les III leçons de Ténèbres et le Miserere à voix seule de feu M de La Lande, H(21)

O filii et filiae, 1v, Pc

Récits from grands motets, in Les motets à voix seule à l'usage des dames religieuses and in Récits en duo, Pn

Recueil de tous les récits de Basse-Taille des Motets de Mr De La Lande ... MS copied by Le Nôtre, récits from 18 grand motets, AIXm

## STAGE

141–3

*(ballets unless otherwise stated)*

La sérénade (Abbé Genest), Fontainebleau, 1682, F-Pn

L'amour berger (pastorale), Marquis de Lomagne, Paris, Hôtel de Duras, 1683, 2 airs in *Mercure galant* (1683)

Les fontaines de Versailles (Morel), Versailles, 5 April 1683, Pn

Le concert d'Esculupe (anon.) [bound with Les fontaines de Versailles]

Epithalame (Abbé Genest), Versailles, 25 June 1685, for marriage of the Duke of Bourbon and Mlle de Nantes, music lost

Le ballet de la jeunesse (Dancourt), Versailles, 28 Jan 1686, *V*

*140, 141–2*

Le Palais de Flore (Ballet de Trianon), Trianon, 5 Jan 1689, *Pn, Pc*

Ballet de M. de La Lande, *Pn*

Ballet (or Sérénade) de M. de La Lande, Versailles, 25 Aug 1691, *Pn*

Prologue sur la Prise de Mons (or Les géants foudroyez; anon.) [incl. the overture from the 3e suite pour les soupers], *V*

Adonis (divertissement), 1696, *Pn*

L'amour, fléchy par la constance (pastorale), Fontainebleau, 1697, *LYm*

142

Intermèdes of music and dance for comedies: Mirtil et Mélicerte (Banzy), Fontainebleau, Oct 1698, Comédie des fées, Fontainebleau, Sept 1699, *Pc*

La noce de village (Rousseau), Sceaux, 21 Feb 1700, *Pn, Pc*

L'hymen champestre, Marly, home of Mme de Maintenon, 1700, *Pc*

Ode à la louange du Roy (Abbé Genest), Sceaux, home of Mme de Maintenon, 24 Oct 1704, music lost

Ballet (Divertissement) de la Paix (Longepierre), Marly, home of Mme de Maintenon, July 1713, *Pc, Pn*

L'inconnu (T. Corneille), first ballet 'dansé par Sa Majesté dans son Palais des Tuileries' (other music by Campra, Bertin de la Doué, Destouches, Rebel), Paris, Feb 1720; L'inconnu: airs à chanter (Paris, 1720)

Les folies de Cardenio (Coypel), second ballet 'dansé par le Roy', Paris, 30 Dec 1720, *Pc*

142–3

Les éléments (opera ballet, Roy), third ballet 'dansé par le Roy', most music by Destouches, Lalande composed ov. and numbers for Prologue and Act 1, Paris, Tuileries, 31 Dec 1721; Paris Opéra, 29 May 1725, *Pn*, selections (Paris, 1725)

## AIRS

Airs in the following collections:

Airs italiens (Paris, 1695)

Recueil d'airs serieux et à boire (Paris, 1699)

Le théâtre italien de Gheradi ... tome I (Paris, 1700)

Les parodies nouvelles et les vaudevilles inconnus (Paris, 1730, 1737)

Nouvelles poésies spirituelles et morales sur les plus beaux airs de la musique françoise et italiene (Paris, 1730, 1733)

Second recueil des nouvelles poésies spirituelles et morales (Paris, 1731)

Nouvelles poésies morales sur les plus beaux airs de la musique françoise et italiene, 8 vols. (Paris, 1737)

Recueil de pieces, petits airs brunettes (Paris, c1755)

## INSTRUMENTAL

143

Suite de trio de differents auteurs ..., collected by Philidor, 3 vols., (Paris, 1699) (3 trios by Lalande)

Les symphonies de M. de La Lande ... copied par ... Philidor l'aîné ... et par son fils aîné, l'an 1703 (10 suites and a Concert de trompettes), *Pn*

Airs de violons de l'inconnu (Paris, 1720)

Recueil d'airs détachés et d'airs de violons de M. De la lande ... 1727 (21 Symphonies des Noëls and 19 suites, no.19 not by Lalande), *Pn*

143

Symphonies de M. De La Lande ... mises dans un nouvel ordre, et ses augmentations, recueillés en 1736 tome I, 1745, (vol. i includes 8 suites and 20 Symphonies des Noëls, vol. ii includes 18 suites, not all by Lalande), *Pn*

143

Symphonies des Noëls; nos.1–4, ed. Cellier (Paris, 1937); nos.1, 4, ed. Roussel (Paris, 1957); no.2, ed. Schroeder (Berlin, 1968); no.3, ed. Chirat (Paris, 1957)

143

Sinfonies pour les soupers du Roi; Suite 1, ed. R. Desormière (Paris, 1947); Caprices 1, 2, ed. Paillard (Paris, 1965); Suite 4, ed. Clerisse (Paris, 1954); extracts, ed. Boulay (Paris, 1965)

143

## BIBLIOGRAPHY

M. Brenet: *La musique sacrée sous Louis XIV* (Paris, 1899)

——: *Les concerts en France sous l'ancien régime* (Paris, 1900/*R*1970)

H. Quittard: 'Notes sur Michel-Richard de Lalande', *RHCM*, ii (1902), 315

H. Leichtentritt: *Geschichte der Motette* (Leipzig, 1908/*R*1967)

A. Tessier: 'La carrière versaillaise de La Lande', *RdM*, ix (1928), 134

A. Cellier: 'Les motets de Michel-Richard de Lalande', *ReM*, no.198 (1946), 20

J. E. Richards: *The 'Grand Motet' of the Late Baroque in France as exemplified by Michel-Richard de Lalande* (diss., U. of Southern California, 1950)

N. Dufourcq: 'La musique religieuse française de 1660 à 1789', *ReM*, no.222–3, (1953–4), 89

——: 'La place occupée par Michel-Richard Delalande dans la musique occidentale aux XVIIe et XVIIIe siècles', *3e congrès international de musique sacrée: Paris 1957*, 171

——, ed.: *Notes et références pour servir à une histoire de Michel Richard Delalande* (Paris, 1957)

——: 'Quelques réflexions sur les ballets et divertisssements de Michel Delalande', *Divertissements de cour au XVIIe siècle* (Paris, 1957), 44

M. Barthélemy: 'La musique dramatique à Versailles de 1660 à 1715', *XVIIᵉ siècle*, no.34 (1957), 7

H. Bert: 'Un ballet de Michel-Richard Delalande', ibid, 58

L. Boulay: 'Les cantiques spirituelles de Racine mis en musique au XVIIe siècle', ibid, 79

F. Raugel: 'La musique à la chapelle du château de Versailles sous Louis XIV', ibid, 19

S. Spycket: 'De La Lande ou la noblesse intérieure', *L'art sacré* (1957), July–Aug, 22

H. A. Durand: 'Note sur la diffusion de M. R. Delalande dans les chapitres provençaux au XVIIIe siècle', *RdM*, xxxix (1957), 72

J. E. Richards: 'Structural Principles in the Grands Motets of Michel Richard de Lalande', *JAMS*, xi (1958), 119

N. Dufourcq: 'Michel-Richard de la Lande', *Revue de l'histoire de Versailles et de Seine et Oise*, liii (1959–60), 71

L. Boulay: 'Notes sur quatre motets inédits de Michel-Richard Delalande', *RMFC*, i (1960), 77

N. Dufourcq: 'Retour à Michel-Richard Delalande', *RMFC*, i (1960), 69

C. Masson: 'Journal du Marquis de Dangeau 1684–1720', *RMFC*, ii (1961–2), 193

G. Thibault: 'Le "Te Deum" de Lalande', *FAM*, xii (1965), 162

147

*Lalande*

J. E. Morby: *Musicians at the Royal Chapel of Versailles, 1683–1792* (diss., U. of California, Berkeley, 1971)

J. R. Anthony: *French Baroque Music from Beaujoyeulx to Rameau* (London, 1973, rev.2/1978, rev. Fr. trans., 1981, as *La musique en France à l'époque baroque*)

B. Stein: *The French Te Deum from 1677–1744: its esthetic, style and development* (diss., U. of Illinois, 1974)

J. R. Anthony and N. Dufourcq: 'Church music in France, 1661–1750', *NOHM*, v (1975), 437–492

L. Sawkins: 'Lalande and the Concert Spirituel', *MT*, cxvi (1975), 333

P. Oboussier: 'Lalande's Grands Motets', *MT*, cxvii (1976), 483

L. Sawkins: 'An encore to the Lexicographer's dilemma, or de Lalande et du Bons Sens', *FAM*, xxviii/4, (1981), 319 [see response by J. Anthony, *FAM*, xxix/3 (1982), 141]

J. R. Anthony: 'La structure musicale des récits de Michel-Richard de Lalande', *Le grand motet français (1663–1792): CNRS Paris 1984*, 119

L. Sawkins: 'L'interprétation des grands motets de Michel-Richard de Lalande d'après le minutage de l'époque', *Le grand motet français (1663–1792): CNRS Paris 1984*, 105

C. J. Moomaw: *Augmented Mediant Chords in French Baroque Music* (diss., U. of Cincinnati, 1985)

B. Coeyman: *The Secular Music of Michel-Richard Delalande in the musical–cultural context of the French Court, 1680–1720* (diss., City U. of New York, in preparation)

L. Sawkins: *The Sacred Music of Michel-Richard De Lalande (1657–1726)* (diss., U. of London, in preparation)

# FRANÇOIS COUPERIN

## Edward Higginbottom

CHAPTER ONE

# Life

François Couperin – *le grand* – is the most important member of the Couperin dynasty. He wrote some of the finest music of the French classical school, and, with Charpentier, may be reckoned the most important musical figure in France between Lully and Rameau.

Couperin was born on 10 November 1668 into an organist's milieu: most immediately that of St Gervais, where his uncle, Louis Couperin, had been organist, and where since 1661 his father, Charles Couperin, had held the post. It seems reasonable to suppose that he received his first musical instruction from his father. Charles died in 1679, when François was ten; according to Titon du Tillet, Jacques Thomelin, the famous organist of St Jacques-de-la-Boucherie and *organiste du roi*, took the young but promising François under his wing and became 'a second father to him'. The church council of St Gervais agreed that François should inherit his father's post on his 18th birthday, provided he attained the requisite proficiency, securing Lalande's services for the interim. During this period François probably often deputized at St Gervais for Lalande (who held two other church appointments in Paris); by 1683, the year of Lalande's appointment as *sous-maître* of the royal chapel,

François must have been organist of St Gervais in all
but name. On 1 November 1685 the church council
decreed that he should receive 300 livres a year until
a formal contract was made with him.

Since François was to inherit his father's post, the
churchwardens of St Gervais permitted him and
Marie (his mother) to continue to live in the organist's house attached to St Gervais after Charles'
death. Marie died in 1690. However, Couperin's
domestic circumstances had already changed in the
previous year upon his marriage to Marie-Anne An-
sault (in the contract, dated 26 April, he is styled
'Sieur de Crouilly'; he also used the title on his *Pieces
d'orgue* of 1690). Marie-Anne had influential family
connections in the business world by which Couperin
was subsequently able to profit: the dedicatees of the
first two of his harpsichord books, C. A. Pajot de
Villers and F. Pratt, both held important and lucrative administrative positions in government de-
partments. There were at least four children of the
marriage: Marie-Madeleine, also known as Marie-
Cécile (baptized Paris, 11 March 1690; *d* Maubuisson,
16 April 1742), a nun, possibly organist at Maubuisson; Marguerite-Antoinette (*b* Paris, 19 Sept 1705;
*d* Paris, *c*1778), who on 16 February 1730 was granted
the reversion of the post of *ordinaire de la chambre
pour le clavecin* from her father, who for health
reasons was unable to continue, a position she held
until 1741 when she sold it, again for reasons of
failing health; François-Laurent (*b* before 1708, *d*
after 1735), who according to an inventory taken after
Couperin's death deserted his parents; and Nicolas-

Louis (baptized Paris, 26 July 1707; *d* probably in infancy).

In the year after his marriage Couperin obtained his first royal privilege to print and sell his music. This licence was valid for six years, and he used it to publish a collection of *Pieces d'orgue*, consisting of two organ masses. Only one copy of the original publication (held in the Bibliothèque Inguimbertine et Musée de Carpentras) is known to exist: it takes the form of a manuscript bound with an engraved title-page, *approbation* and *privilège*, a not uncommon procedure for limited editions (the expense of having the music pages hand-copied, even several times, was considerably less than having them engraved). Another manuscript copy of the masses (in the Bibliothèque Municipale, Versailles) may predate the 1690 issue, possibly representing an earlier version (Gilbert and Moroney, 1982). If the form of the 1690 publication speaks of Couperin's fairly straitened financial circumstances at the time, a less parsimonious note is sounded in Lalande's *approbation*, which describes Couperin's pieces as being 'fort belles et dignes d'être données au public'. Clearly Couperin had not been slow in turning his acquaintance with the now celebrated Lalande to good use, nor for that matter in turning his early musical training to good account.

The organ music in this collection is both the first and the last that Couperin is known to have written. But, following a centuries-old essentially improvisatory tradition of organ music for the liturgy, Couperin was active as an organist for many years to come, almost until his death. It was as an organist, with duties for the first quarter of each year, that he first gained a foothold at court, being Louis XIV's choice in 1693 as successor to his former teacher, Thomelin: an appointment that surely must have satisfied the sentimental as well as pleasing the musically discerning. His fellow royal organists were Buterne, Nivers and Lebègue.

About this time Couperin seems to have been at work on a set of trio sonatas, three of which, under different names, were later incorporated in the publication *Les nations* of 1726. These three – their original titles are *La pucelle*, *La visionnaire* and *L'astrée* – appear with a fourth sonata, *La Steinquerque*, in a manuscript in the Brossard Collection at the Bibliothèque Nationale, Paris; two others, *La sultane* (actually a sonata *en quatuor*) and *La superbe*, are to be found in manuscript partbooks in the Bibliothèque Municipale, Lyons.

The four sonatas in the Brossard MS are thought to date from about the same year, 1692, partly on account of topical allusion (*Steinquerque* probably commemorates the French military victory of that year), and partly on account of the group's stylistic unity. Opinions differ on the dating of *La sultane* and *La superbe*: Tessier favoured *c*1695, while Citron suggested a date as late as 1710 for *La sultane*. Neither manuscript is in Couperin's hand.

To appreciate the motive behind the composition of the earliest sonatas, and their significance, it is necessary to look ahead a number of years and examine the preface to *Les nations*:

It is now several years since some of these trios were composed. There have been several manuscript copies of them in circulation, though untrustworthy through the negligence of copyists. From time to time I have added to their number; and I believe they will please the discriminating. The first sonata in this collection is also the first that I composed, and [moreover] the first composed in France. Its history is curious:

Charmed by the sonatas of Signor Corelli, whose works I shall love as long as I live, just as I do the French works of Monsieur de Lully, I attempted to compose one myself which I [then] had performed in the concert series where I had heard those of Corelli. Knowing the keen appetite of the French for foreign novelties above all else, and being unsure of myself, I did myself a very good turn through a little 'technical' deceit. I pretended that a relation of mine [his cousin Marc Roger Normand], in very truth in the service of the King of Sardinia, had sent me a sonata by a new Italian composer. I rearranged the letters of my name to form an Italian one, which I used instead. The sonata was devoured with eagerness, and I need not trouble to defend myself. However, I was encouraged. I composed others, and my italian-ized name brought me, in disguise, considerable applause. My sonatas, fortunately, won enough favour for me not to be in the least embarrassed by the subterfuge.

These early sonatas are thus the first fruits of Couperin's admiration for the Italian Baroque masters, and for Corelli in particular, an admiration he was eventually to express in overt terms in his *Apothéose de Corelli* of 1724, but which he demonstrated more profoundly in his lifelong effort to unite in his music the best of the French with the best of the Italian.

Couperin's appointment as an *organiste du roi* (26 December 1693), with a salary of 600 livres for the quarter, was perhaps the most important event of his career, for it opened up opportunities and emoluments available nowhere else. Shortly after his arrival at court he was engaged to teach the harpsichord to the Duke of Burgundy and several other princes and princesses, including the Count of Toulouse, the dowager Princess of Conti and Mlles de Bourbon and de Charolais, daughters of the Duke of Bourbon. Couperin acquired his own coat-of-arms after only three years at court, taking advantage of Louis XIV's edict of 1696 offering ennoblement to people in respectable employment who could afford to pay for the privilege. A further honour followed about 1702, when he was made Chevalier de l'Ordre de Latran. His rising fortune is also evident in his move in 1697 from the organist's house at St Gervais into a larger apartment in the rue St-François.

After his initial period at court Couperin's activities became more diversified. From about 1700 there are several references to his participation in concerts at Versailles, Fontainebleau and Sceaux, and probably he stood in for the younger D'Anglebert, officially *ordinaire de la musique de la chambre du roi pour le clavecin*, with increasing regularity as D'Anglebert's eyesight failed. By now Couperin was also active as a court composer, not only of chamber music, some of which appeared in print much later in the *Concerts royaux* (1722) and *Les goûts-réünis* (1724), but also of sacred music for use in the royal chapel. In 1703, 1704 and 1705 Ballard published three sets of psalm versets composed by order of the king; numerous other motets, probably written for the most part in the late 1690s, are extant only in manuscript. During the first decade of the 18th century Couperin was also engaged in writing for the harpsichord. Several of the pieces in his first harpsichord book (1713) were clearly in circulation in manuscript long before that date; a few were even printed anonymously in Ballard's *Pièces choisies pour le clavecin* (1707).

During this period, covering the last 15 or so years of Louis XIV's reign, Couperin established himself as one of the leading French composers of his day, earning the admiration of his contemporaries, and finding himself the dedicatee of several of their works. Yet he received none of the eight most important musical offices that fell vacant at court between 1693 and 1715. Perhaps Lalande, who took six, and who was once so disinterested a mentor to Couperin, was now too much his rival. Perhaps Couperin refused to play the courtier; or perhaps he was simply unwilling to take on new responsibilities. However, in 1717 it was finally recognized that D'Anglebert had long been unable to fulfil his duties as king's harpsichordist, and Couperin was offered the right to inherit the post on D'Anglebert's death. In effect it meant that from 1717 Couperin replaced D'Anglebert as *ordinaire de la musique de la chambre du roi pour le clavecin.*

At the height of his career, Couperin was considered second to none as a harpsichord and organ teacher, with the possible exception of Louis Marchand; even before the turn of the century, Du Pradel's *Le livre commode contenant les adresses de la ville de Paris* (1692) had placed him third among Parisian harpsichord and organ teachers (the first two were Lebègue and Thomelin). But these activities were a considerable drain on his time and energies. He blamed the tardy appearance of his first harpsichord book partly on his teaching commitments at court and in Paris. As for his duties as organist, although his royal appointment was only for the first quarter of the year, for the rest of the time he was of course expected back at St Gervais.

It was alongside these commitments that Couperin had to find time to compose his music and to prepare it for the engravers. In 1713 he took out a printing licence for 20 years which, as it turned out, was to cover the publication of his music up to the end of his life. The dissemination of his harpsichord pieces was his first concern, beginning in 1713 with his *Pieces de clavecin ... premier livre*, and then proceeding to a treatise on playing the harpsichord, *L'art de toucher le clavecin*, first published in 1716, and followed by a second, substantially revised edition in 1717. His *Second livre de piéces de clavecin* also probably dates from that year. In addition, some important sacred vocal music, *Leçons de tenébres*, came out during this phase of printing. Only the first three lessons are set of a projected nine; the last six were never published, nor have they survived in manuscript.

How far circumstances changed for Couperin after the death of Louis XIV in 1715 is uncertain. It is reasonable to suppose that he preferred the seriousness of the old regime to the relative flippancy of the new and although he still had duties to perform at court (among his royal pupils in the early 1720s was the Polish princess Maria Leszczyńska, betrothed to Louis XV), it is probable that he was less involved in the musical activities of the regency than he had been in those of the court of Louis XIV. More or less coincident with the regency, within the space of 11 years, Couperin moved house three times before settling in a spacious apartment in the rue Neuve des Bons-Enfants in 1724 (it still exists, on the corner of the rue Radziwill and the rue des Petits Champs). The year before, his health becoming increasingly fragile, he sought help with his duties at St Gervais by arranging for his cousin Nicolas Couperin to be his assistant, and eventually his successor.

Meanwhile the publication of his music continued, a steady stream of prints being issued between the appearance of the third (1722) and fourth (1730) harpsichord books. The *Concerts royaux* (comprising four works) were sold as the second part of the *Troisiéme livre de piéces de clavecin*; *Les goûts réünis, ou Nouveaux concerts* came out in 1724 as a sequel to the *Concerts royaux*, taking the numbering already begun in the earlier publication as far as 14, and finishing with 'une grande Sonade en Trio intitulée Le Parnasse ou l'Apothéose de Corelli'. In the following year, 1725, appeared the natural successor to the Corelli sonata: *Concert instrumental sous le titre d'Apothéose composé à la mémoire immortelle de l'incomparable Monsieur de Lully*.

The publication *Les nations* (1726), described on the title-page as 'Sonades et suites de simphonies en trio', has already been mentioned in connection with the early trio sonatas: three of them, *La pucelle*, *La visionnaire* and *L'astrée*, are incorporated in this publication under the titles *La françoise*, *L'espagnole* and *La piemontoise* respectively. But each forms only the first half, the Italian half as it were, of a diptych, the second half of which is in each case a newly composed suite (or *ordre*) in the French style. A fourth diptych, *L'impériale*, boasts a trio sonata not in the early extant manuscripts, and which is probably a later work, perhaps contemporary with the rest of the new music in *Les nations*.

Last to appear before the *Quatriéme livre de piéces de clavecin* of 1730 were Couperin's *Pieces de violes* (1728).

In the preface to his fourth harpsichord book, Couperin wrote of his health failing him 'day by day'. In the same year he gave up both his court appointments, arranging for his talented daughter Marguerite-Antoinette Couperin to take over as harpsichordist and Guillaume Marchand to replace him in the royal chapel. Three years later in Paris, on 11 Sept 1733, Couperin died.

Shortly before his death, he took out a new privilege for ten years (that of 1713 being on the point of expiring) to cover the printing of his remaining unpublished work. Unfortunately no-one in Couperin's family, to whom the task fell, showed sufficient interest to carry through the project. Since none of Couperin's manuscripts has survived, this inaction has caused the loss, if not of a significant number of his works for harpsichord (his last harpsichord book has the appearance of assembling what remained), then of a substantial amount of his chamber music, both instrumental and vocal, and of his sacred music (perhaps even the other six *leçons de ténèbres*).

Biographers of Couperin, and those who wish to penetrate the composer's personality, have to work

*15. François Couperin: engraving (1735) by Jean-Jacques Flipart after André Boüys*

161

from surprisingly little material. None of his correspondence has survived: letters he is supposed to have
exchanged with Bach were allegedly used as jampot
covers some years later. Contemporary and near-
contemporary accounts of him are rare, and he clearly
did not cut the kind of dashing figure in public life as
did his colleagues – among them Louis Marchand
and Antoine Forqueray. From Couperin's prefaces,
and his work, one may gain an impression of a man
untainted by national prejudices, careful in his work,
capable of forthrightness, and not lacking in self-
esteem. His lack of formal education may account
for the diffidence with which he approached the task
of writing his prefaces. Whatever the gaucheries of
his prose, his music does not lack fluency and poise,
but rather demonstrates elements of satire and wit
that show Couperin refusing to take at face value the
times in which he worked. The engraving by Flipart
after a portrait by André Boüys (fig.15) gives him an
air of quiet confidence; his features are solid and
composed; in his large eyes one may perhaps catch a
trace of that wistfulness which is also found in the
restrained expressiveness of his music. Nothing in this
portrait betrays the illness that Couperin mentioned
several times in his prefaces, and which appears to
have tried him sorely in his old age.

Of his high standing among his contemporaries
there is no doubt. Siret, Dornel and Montéclair dedicated works to him; Dagincour paid him tribute in
the preface to his *Livre de pièces de clavecin* (1733);
Titon du Tillet (1755) told how Calvière expressed his
indebtedness to Couperin's art; and numerous con-

temporary poetasters reflected the popularity of his harpsichord music in their parody settings. If the currency of the epithet 'le grand' during Couperin's lifetime is uncertain, La Borde's reference (1780) to 'François Couperin, surnommé le grand' has the ring of established usage.

According to Titon du Tillet, Couperin's harpsichord music was well known abroad, in Italy, England and Germany. Gerber claimed that in his playing Bach used many of Couperin's mannerisms; Bach certainly knew Couperin's music, as may be judged from his copy of *Les bergeries* (*ordre* no.6) in Anna Magdalena's music-book, and his arrangement for organ of the F major rondeau from *L'impériale* (BWV587). As to his posthumous reputation, both Debussy and Ravel felt a close affinity with his music, which seemed to them to epitomize the spirit of French art: the first contemplated dedicating his *Etudes* to Couperin, and the second paid a more open tribute to his clarity, poise and refinement in his *Le tombeau de Couperin*. More surprising is the interest shown on the one hand by Brahms, who with Chrysander prepared the first complete edition of Couperin's harpsichord music (1871–88, following partial ones by Laurens in 1841 and Farrenc in 1862–9), and on the other by Richard Strauss, who freely arranged some of the harpsichord pieces in his Dance Suite for small orchestra (1923) and returned to the same source for material for his Divertimento (1941). The publication of Couperin's collected works in 1933 (by Editions de l'Oiseau Lyre) came late by comparison with the first modern editions of Bach and

Handel; but its sumptuous presentation was an appropriate act of homage to one of France's greatest composers.

CHAPTER TWO

# Works

## I  Style

Couperin's art derives from several sources. His early
training as an organist equipped him above all with
solid contrapuntal skills, and although he was never
to equal Bach or Handel as a contrapuntist – such an
idea would in any case have been abhorrent to French
taste – his competence contributed significantly to the
firm linear qualities in much of his writing. He was
also heir to the qualities of *douceur* and naturalness
that the French considered the hallmarks of their
style. Nor could any French composer at that time
avoid being influenced by that cynosure of French
music, Lully: by the intensely pathetic but discreet
vocal writing of his *tragédies lyriques*, the imposing
orchestral style of his overtures, or the beautifully
turned dance music of his ballets.

Couperin's enthusiasm for Italian music, and in
particular the trio sonata, throws these French qualities into relief. Late in his career he made clear his
intention to effect a union between French and Italian
music. His collection *Les goûts-réünis* and his celebration of the reception of Corelli and Lully on
Parnassus in the two *Apothéose* sonatas appear as a
bold affirmation of that purpose. But the fertilization
of his style by Italian elements dates from the earliest

165

stages of his career, bearing most immediate fruit in his first trio sonatas.

Conservative French opinion was unconvinced that such a union of French and Italian styles could be achieved. Le Cerf de la Viéville took the view that they were 'so different that it is difficult to link and intermingle them without spoiling the two'. But he was unwilling to be sympathetic to Couperin's cause, whom he considered a 'serviteur passionné de l'Italie' who had renounced his national heritage. Despite these censures Couperin can be said to have achieved in part a synthesis. But while he adopted the outward forms of the Italian sonata, increasingly used driving sequences to expand and reinforce his musical argument, and introduced a more idiomatic instrumental style, he never deserted the basic canons of French art: a natural and flowing melody, a richly expressive but not excessively chromatic harmony (Neapolitan 6ths, for example, are rare in his music) and a basic simplicity in musical design that generally avoided virtuosity, whether in performance or in composition.

The 'paradox of sensuous purity' (Mellers, 1950) in Couperin's music springs from the conjunction of a restrained and simple melodic style with a rich and diversified harmonic vocabulary; the poignancy in Couperin's music derives more often from expressive dissonances, particularly 7ths and 9ths, than 'affective' melodic intervals. Mellers has also emphasized the close connection between Couperin's music and the poetry and painting of his contemporaries. Even before the writings of Dubos and Batteux there was never any doubt that music was attempting exactly the same thing as the other arts: a true imitation of nature. It fell under the same restraints as poetry and painting, and partook of the same aspirations. The close links between Racine, Watteau and Couperin represent a triumph of the civilization to which they belonged.

## II  Organ music

Couperin's early maturity as a composer is astonishing. He was only 21 when his *Pieces d'orgue* (1690) were offered to the public; and yet they show every mark of a thoroughly assured compositional technique, and stand with Grigny's *Premier livre d'orgue* (1699) at the apex of the French classical organ tradition.

The *Pieces d'orgue* consist of two masses. The first, 'à l'usage ordinaire des paroisses', is the more majestically conceived, intended for use on principal feasts in churches when the plainchant setting *Cunctipotens genitor Deus* was sung for the Ordinary. Couperin, following in part the stipulations of the *Caeremoniale parisiense* (1662), set this plainchant as a cantus firmus in the opening versets to each item, the Kyrie, Gloria, Sanctus and Agnus Dei (the last Kyrie verset is also a cantus firmus setting). The Mass 'propre pour les convents', which has no cantus firmus settings, is much more intimate in character: its key structure suggests that it was used with one of the many *messes en plainchant musical* composed in France towards the end of the 17th century and popular in religious communities. Nivers was very

16. St Gervais–
St Protais,
Paris:
engraving,
'Prospect of St
Gervais', from
'Topographia
Galliae', i
(Paris, 1655)

168

actively involved in the editing of such new liturgical chant books; his setting of the Ordinary for use at feasts of the first class (published in his *Graduale romano-monasticum*, 1658) is an obvious example of the sort of chant which may have been used with Couperin's organ versets, being compatible both in key and in musical effect.

The skills in composition that Couperin acquired during his organist's training covered a wider range of formal possibilities than simply fugue. In the works of Nivers and Lebègue, particularly, concertante forms such as the 'Récit en taille' and the 'Basse de trompette' had become an established part of the repertory; in Couperin's work they tend to take pride of place by virtue of his gift for characterful melodic lines, sometimes poignantly expressive as in the beautiful 'Récit de Tierce en taille' from the Gloria of the Mass 'des paroisses', sometimes irresistibly ebullient as in the 'Dialogue sur les trompettes' from the preceding Kyrie. At the same time Couperin could sport his contrapuntal skill in the canonic statement of the cantus firmus in the first verset of the 'paroisses' Sanctus. The offertories of both masses are written on a grandiose scale, Couperin taking full advantage of the lengthy liturgical ceremonies at this point. The C major 'Offertoire sur les grands jeux' of the 'paroisses' Mass is an impressive tripartite piece, passing from the pomp of the French overture to the *gravitas* of fugue, and then the high spirits of a rollicking gigue.

These pieces show Couperin's musical range: the *récits* bear eloquent testimony to his melodic gift, and the cantus firmus settings and fugues bring to the fore his contrapuntal skills, which he always wore lightly and which are firmly controlled by his melodic instinct. If his harmonic vocabulary was not yet fully developed, it is at times quite as audaciously expressive as in his more mature writing.

## III  Instrumental chamber music

The instrumental chamber music falls into two categories: the trios and the solo (*à* 2) pieces. The first category includes all the early trio sonatas (including for convenience the four-part *La sultane*), the *Apothéose* sonatas and *Les nations*; the second category comprises the *Concerts royaux*, continued in *Les goûts-réünis* as 'nouveaux concerts', and the *Pieces de violes*. Couperin was not generally specific about the instrumentation of his chamber music. He wrote that the *Concerts royaux* might be played on the harpsichord, or on the violin, oboe, flute, viol and bassoon. The trios, according to the preface to the *Apothéose de Lully*, might be played either on two harpsichords or on 'tous autres instruments'; violins would have been the norm, but flutes and oboes were not excluded.

Brossard, writing of the mid-1690s, observed that 'every composer in Paris, and above all the organists, was madly writing sonatas in the Italian manner' (*Catalogue des livres de musique*, MS, 1724). Couperin was no exception; in the preface to *Les nations* he claimed priority in the field. In the same preface he cited Corelli as his principal source of inspiration. By the early 1690s, the date of Couperin's first essays in sonata writing, three of Corelli's sets of sonatas had appeared in print. Of these, opp.1 and 3 were collections of *sonate da chiesa*, and it was that type that Couperin followed in his trios, renouncing binary dance forms for a sequence of contrasted movements composed for the most part in unitary structures.

However, the composition of three-part instrumental music was not without its difficulties for Couperin; and his first efforts reveal a certain strain in handling the idiom. Part of the problem was textural: the common tessitura of the upper two parts was difficult if one had been brought up on simple treble-and-bass-orientated structures. Often, in the early trios, the second *dessus* plays a subservient role, rarely rising above the first, and seldom assuming equal importance in the texture. Raguenet complained that in French trios 'the first upper part is generally beautiful enough, but then the second descends too low to deserve our attention'; he might have been thinking of certain movements in *La pucelle* or *La visionnaire*.

The nature of Corelli's trios is also defined by the balanced interplay of musical ideas between the three voices, this interplay deriving much of its force from a fairly tight motivic consistency; this too was not easily grasped by Couperin. Nor was the central role of tonality in shaping the unitary structures of *sonata da chiesa* movements. Indeed, of all Couperin's trio sonatas, perhaps only *L'impériale* (clearly a work of his maturity) shows a complete understanding of the mechanics of the Italian trio sonata style: its last movement in particular, with its athletic seven-bar theme, its lively interplay of ideas and firm tonal logic, stands with the trios of Bach and Handel as one of the 18th-century works closest to the Corellian ideal.

It would, however, be foolish to judge Couperin's achievements solely by comparison with Corelli. Often in treating the trio texture more as in two parts than three, with the second *dessus* added somewhat in the manner of a *contre-partie*, providing harmonic depth as well as the occasional rhythmic and melodic variety, he established a no less viable idiom in which melody is paramount. The exquisitely yearning *air* which stands as the third movement of *La visionnaire* provides a model of such an added part, inserted by Couperin for the publication of this sonata (as *L'espagnole*) in *Les nations*. More to the point, perhaps, is the type of writing encountered in the second movement (Vivement) of *L'astrée*: it purports to be three-part, but for substantial stretches the second *dessus* consistently shadows the first in 3rds or 6ths, enriching the texture and harmony but not the musical argument. This technique appears even more strikingly in the *ordres* of *Les nations*; almost every piece of the *ordre* in *L'impériale* demonstrates its use.

There are also other ways in which the early trio sonatas (*La pucelle*, *La visionnaire*, *L'astrée*, *La Steinquerque*, *La superbe* and *La sultane*) do not slavishly strive to imitate Corelli. For instance, besides tempering the Italian instrumental style, Couperin included in each sonata at least one typically French *air*. He also avoided being too clearcut in design (as opposed to expression): the final movement of *La visionnaire*, with its rattling harpsichord 'badinage' added for *Les nations*, offers an excellent example of an attempt to suggest clear formal structures while in fact avoiding them: the piece constantly alludes to the chaconne but remains free of a ground-bass structure.

The sonatas *La pucelle*, *La visionnaire* and *L'astrée* (respectively *La françoise*, *L'espagnole* and *La piemontoise* in *Les nations*) were seen by Couperin, along with the sonata *L'impériale*, to serve merely as preludes or 'espèces d'introductions' to the ensuing *ordres* specially composed for *Les nations*. If this seems to minimize the importance of the *sonate da chiesa*, particularly that of *L'impériale*, it accurately reflects the greater length of the *ordres*. The latter, distinctly French and conservative in style, balance out the ultramontane influences at work in the sonatas. The dances themselves are Couperin's most beautifully turned in the old style: discreet and flowing, but with a wealth of expressive detail, and at times a force that belies their surface charm. The chaconnes of the first two *ordres* (*La françoise* and *L'espagnole*) are superb examples of Couperin's treatment of the form, grandiose in design though still tender in expression, rich in detail though forceful in their drive.

In the two *Apothéose* sonatas Couperin was perhaps at his most authentic in the trio medium. While in *Les nations*, published just after the *Apothéose* sonatas, he sought to counter-balance the Italianisms of his earlier *sonate da chiesa* by accompanying each with a French *ordre*, in the *Apothéose* sonatas the balance is, as it were, achieved internally. The programmatic element, particularly in *L'apoth-*

*éose de Lully*, is a powerful factor in this synthesis, since in the final stages of Lully's reception on Parnassus he and Corelli play respectively first and second *dessus* in a French overture, and in the four-movement 'Sonade en trio' that follows. This partnership is at the instigation of Apollo, who persuades the two musicians that 'la réunion des Goûts François et Italien doit faire la perfection de la Musique'. The reunion, however, does not exclude a telling juxtaposition of their styles: first in the welcome accorded to Lully by Corelli and the former's gracious acknowledgment, and even more neatly in two duos where, with all the appropriate modifications in the style, first Lully takes the *premier dessus* with Corelli accompanying, and then the roles are reversed. The programmatic nature of this sonata led Couperin to draw heavily on French opera conventions. *L'apoth-éose de Corelli* relies less heavily on such conventions, being cast, appropriately enough, in the mould of a seven-movement *sonata da chiesa*.

The distinction made between three- and two-part textures should not be seen to imply the use of a radically different compositional technique in Couperin's *Concerts* and *Pieces de violes*. Even in the trio textures the essentials may often be reduced to a treble and bass; but in renouncing them Couperin found himself speaking with a more pronounced French accent.

The 14 *concerts* of the *Concerts royaux* and *Les goûts-réünis* are among Couperin's most naturally conceived instrumental compositions, attempting little that is profound, striving simply to accommodate civilized tastes at a high artistic level. Some at least were written to entertain an aging and highly conservative Louis XIV (in the preface to the *Concerts royaux* Couperin mentioned performances during 1714 and 1715). Although they are for the most part written out on two staves, and although Couperin mentioned the possibility of performing them on the harpsichord (the *Concerts royaux* did after all appear in the same publication as the third harpsichord book), there is no doubt from the texture, the right-hand compass, and some specific indications concerning instrumentation (including a reference to the original performers), that they were intended primarily for performance on treble (violin, oboe or flute) and bass (viol or bassoon) instruments with continuo. The *Concerts royaux* are *ordres* of five to seven pieces for such instrumental combinations. The 'nouveaux concerts' of *Les goûts-réünis* continue on the same lines, with substantially more ambitious schemes only for the eighth and ninth *concerts*.

The preface to *Les goûts-réünis* carries what might be considered Couperin's clearest statement on his approach to national styles:

The Italian and the French styles have for a long time shared the Republic of Music in France. For myself, I have always highly regarded the things which merited esteem, without considering either composer or nation; and the first Italian sonatas which appeared in Paris more than 30 years ago, and which encouraged me to start composing some myself, to my mind wronged neither the works of M de Lully, nor those of my ancestors, who will always be more admirable than imitable. And so, by a right which my neutrality gives me, I remain under the happy influence which has guided me until now.

French and Italian interests are clearly represented in *Les goûts-réünis* but, partly because of the two-part texture, a preference is often shown for busy contrapuntal writing in which bounding quaver figures and regular semiquaver patterns predominate. The allemandes are almost without exception treated in this way. Only in the 11th *concert* is there a typically French version of this dance, measured and aristocratic; in the others the tempo is fast, the mood airy and gay, and the musical gestures, often including developed imitative writing, distinctly Italian.

The eighth *concert*, 'dans le goût théatral', is the most impressive – an undisguised tribute to Lully, beginning with a French overture and 'Grand ritournéle', and continuing with a rich diversity of veritable *airs à danser*. Of this *concert*, Holman (1986) has argued persuasively that the published version represents a reduced scoring of a lost fully orchestrated setting (*à* 5), similar in design to the orchestral dance suites of Georg Muffat and Lalande. The immediate juxtaposition of the ninth 'Ritratto dell'Amore', might lead one to expect a sequence of pieces as Italian as those of the previous *concert* are French. But Couperin did not attempt a consistently Italian style. This *concert*, with its descriptive titles (the only one to have them), recalls the more stylistically balanced world of his late harpsichord *ordres*, and some pieces, *La douceur* and *L'et coetera* in particular, employ a distinctly harpsichord-like texture.

The 1728 *Pieces de violes*, for solo viol and continuo, are among Couperin's last works. That he should turn to the bass viol so late is interesting in itself, and seems to indicate a wish to pay homage to a glorious but waning tradition; 1728 had witnessed

the death of Marin Marais, alongside Antoine Forqueray the greatest viol player among Couperin's
colleagues at court. The *Pieces de violes* are arranged
in two suites, the first a traditional French *ordre*, the
second (consisting of only four pieces against the
seven of the first suite) a remodelled *sonata da chiesa*.
This is among the most assured music that Couperin
wrote; it is as though the mellow sonority of the viol
itself called forth a musical utterance no less mature.
The first suite is retrospective in character, beautifully
expressive in the accentuated dissonances of the
Gavotte, and richly varied in the glorious concluding
*Passacaille*. The second suite is more Italianate: the
*Pompe funèbre* (compare the 'Pompe funèbre' in
Lully's *Alceste*) is unusually lucid in its sense of tonal
direction, almost Handelian, but still French in its
quiet intensity; and the enigmatic *La chemise-blanche*,
puzzling in name only, is a *moto perpetuo* piece carried
to audacious lengths and demanding, for once, virtuoso playing of a high order. Couperin's viol music
may not be the most idiomatic for this instrument,
but with that by Marais it is certainly the most
accomplished in the French tradition.

## IV Vocal music

Couperin's sacred vocal music is an unjustly neglected
part of his output, filling in, as it were, the history of
his compositional career between his appointment as
*organiste du roi* in 1693 and the death of Louis XIV.
This repertory shows that Couperin's duties at the
royal chapel were by no means confined to playing
the organ.

Much of Couperin's sacred music is found only in

manuscript (besides the early trio sonatas and organ masses the only significant body of his music to be extant other than in printed form). The two principal sources are a collection of 13 motets in score (Bibliothèque Municipale, Versailles, 59) and a set of partbooks containing 25 items now at the Bibliothèque Nationale, Paris, formerly at St Michael's College, Tenbury. According to Oboussier these two sources, whose contents largely overlap, are in the same hand. The Tenbury partbooks are believed to have been copied between 1702 and 1706. *Laudate pueri Dominum*, one of the motets in this collection, also appears in another source, copied in 1697 (Bibliothèque Municipale, Versailles, 18). It is likely that most of these pieces were composed in the late 1690s, and probably none after 1703, the date of Couperin's first published sacred music.

The predominant influence in these works is Italian, Couperin's extant motets being closer to the small-scale vocal forms used by Carissimi and his French pupil M.-A. Charpentier than to the massive style cultivated by Du Mont and Lully in their *grands motets*. The scoring is generally for one to three solo voices and continuo, sometimes with concertante instruments (mainly violins) and a chorus. The dozen motets 'à grand choeur' which according to Titon du Tillet were left in manuscript at Couperin's death may have been in the French tradition, but none has survived.

Couperin's understanding of Italian idioms can be seen to have matured since the early trio sonatas. He is now fully assured in his treatment of driving sequences, in moving from one tonal centre to another, in the handling of instrumental ritornellos and in enriching his harmonic vocabulary with such chords as diminished 7ths as well as other extremes of chromatic harmony (see for instance the section 'O mors coeca' from *O Jesu amantissime*). Also frequent are sequential 7ths (bass falling by 5ths and rising by 4ths), affective intervals (diminished 5ths and 7ths) and vocal melismas. Indeed, in the light of Couperin's florid and regular ground bass for a section of *Quid retribuam*, his vocal virtuosity at the opening of *Victoria: Christo resurgenti*, or his entirely instrumental treatment of the voice in *Regina coeli laetare*, Le Cerf's description of him as 'un serviteur passionné de l'Italie' does not seem all that wide of the mark. The motet *Regina coeli laetare* might almost have been written as an exercise in eliminating everything French from his style; certainly its central recitative is without parallel in Couperin's music, completely instrumental in conception, its concluding phrase somersaulting from *g″* to *d′* in less than a bar. That, however, is an extreme case. Much of Couperin's vocal writing is properly vocal and syllabic, the phrases generally short, and much of the instrumental writing is nicely balanced between vocal and instrumental idioms. The opening 'simphonie' of *Laudate pueri Dominum* is a good example of instrumental writing controlled by the vocal line of the solo soprano entry.

The published church music consists of three sets of versets that appeared in successive years, 1703, 1704 and 1705, and the *Leçons de tenébres*. If it is assumed that the manuscript motets were written for use at court, the courtly function of the versets is indisputable: they were written 'by order of the king', so the title-page proclaims, and were doubtless performed in his presence. The printed score also gives the names of the soloists who took part in the first performances in the royal chapel. The *Quatre versets* (1703) are scored exclusively for two soprano soloists – one of them specifically Couperin's cousin Marguerite-Louise Couperin – with flutes, violins and two-part soprano chorus. They begin unusually enough with a duet for the soloists 'sans Basse Continüe ny aucun instrument'. The verset *Adolescentulus sum* is no less remarkable in sonority, being for soprano solo and flutes, with *dessus de violons* playing the continuo line. The consistently high tessitura and the limpid interweaving phrases of the flutes and voice create an unforgettably ethereal effect.

In contrast, the solos in the *Sept versets* of the next year are almost exclusively for men's voices (including *haute-contre*) with tenor and baritone chorus, transverse flutes, oboes and violins; only the last two versets include a soprano solo. The verset *Ostende nobis* must be mentioned for its audacious chains of parallel 6ths, including a long sequence of 6 – 4 chords, a harmonic gesture that Couperin often made to invoke gentle pathos but nowhere else on this scale. The French idioms are stronger in several of the versets in this collection, tempering the Italianisms. The *Sept versets* of 1705 strike a balance in the disposition of forces. At the same time they are much more wrought: the 'symphonies' include a fiery

French-overture movement, and in the bass verset *Dux itineris* a 'symphonie à deux choeurs' provides sharp contrasts in instrumental colour. Contrasts are also sought in the solo soprano verset *Operuit montes*, with the accompaniment divided between rapid violin scales and gently caressing phrases for two flutes.

The three *Leçons de tenébres* are arguably Couperin's finest vocal works, indeed among his finest in any medium. They appeared in print between the publication of the first and second harpsichord books (1713–17). The first two *leçons* are for soprano solo (and continuo), the third for two soprano soloists. The text, from the *Lamentations of Jeremiah*, was traditionally sung at Matins on Maundy Thursday. Other sections of the *Lamentations* were sung at Matins on Good Friday and Holy Saturday, making a total of nine 'lessons'. The heading 'pour le Mercredy' at the beginning of the published *leçons* refers to the practice, widespread at the time, of advancing the office of Matins on each of these days to the previous afternoon. It is puzzling that Couperin did not publish all nine *leçons*, since in the preface to his extant set he made a clear reference to the imminent appearance of the others; indeed, he disclosed that three *leçons* for Good Friday had been composed some years previously. The preface to his second harpsichord book, which mentions the recent publication of the Wednesday set, also refers unequivocally to the composition of nine *leçons*. The lost Good Friday set was composed for the nuns of the abbey of Lonchampt, just outside Paris, which enjoyed a fashionable reputation for its Holy Week

Offices, not least because the leading singers of the day were invited to perform at the services. Le Cerf disapproved of this practice on the grounds that celebrities from the Opéra could not be relied on to maintain the decorum appropriate to such occasions; Couperin, in scoring his extant *leçons* for soprano soloists and continuo, clearly did not share Le Cerf's misgivings.

The emphasis on solo declamation in Couperin's settings, however, transcends whatever superficial attraction this may have held for the fashionable, and carries the music to the heart of Jeremiah's anguish. The exterior brilliance and sensuous charm of the versets are left far behind. In this intensely personal world Couperin had recourse to the declamatory recitative and arioso of the *tragédie lyrique*. But he conformed to convention in adopting the traditional plainchant formula as the basis for the opening phrase 'Incipit Lamentatio Jeremiae'. This, and the no less traditional melismas on the initial Hebrew letters that punctuate the text (only the first melisma of each *leçon* is based on plainchant), are set to easily flowing but highly decorative lines which, juxtaposed with the settings of the main text, sound almost nonchalant. The contrast is intended: the two-soprano vocalise of the letter 'Jod' at the beginning of the third *leçon*, with its interweaving lines, crushed 2nds, and regular crotchet tread in the bass, evokes the relatively impersonal idiom of Corelli's sonatas precisely in order to act as a foil to the overt expressiveness of the ensuing recitative.

The main sections of the *leçons* are set either in a

measured but freely declamatory style, which Couperin indicates as 'récitatif', or in more tightly organized *airs*. The latter form the emotional core of each *leçon*. The most rigorously organized is 'Recordata est' of the second *leçon*, a ground bass in B minor – Couperin's most passionate key – in which rising diatonic movement to the dominant is balanced against a descending chromatic tetrachord. The technique of approaching the dominant alternately from one direction and the other is common in Couperin's chaconnes; but nowhere else did he treat the form in so disciplined a manner, and it is that discipline that makes the movement, with its intense sequences of 7ths and 9ths, cunning examples of cadence evasion, and beautifully articulated melodic line, so emotionally charged. Within its slender resources this piece achieves a truly Purcellian power. Of the other *airs*, 'Plorans ploravit' (first *leçon*) is in an *ABACC* form, while 'O vos omnes' (third *leçon*) has no distinct returns. In the latter the impassioned cry 'attendite et videte' for the two sopranos seems to owe something to Monteverdi in its emphasis on simple vocal declamation and sonority, and in the heightening of drama through transposed repetition. The 'Jerusalem convertere' sections that conclude each *leçon* are also set to superbly expressive music. The final two-part setting has an inexorable drive of a force perhaps unique in Couperin's music.

The harmonic language of this music is not only rich in dissonances but also in such chromatic chords as diminished 7ths and even Neapolitan 6ths. In spite of the highly charged atmosphere this creates, the

*Leçons de tenébres* remain an exquisitely civilized expression of the grief and bitter anguish of the prophet.

The extant secular vocal music is found mainly in the popular *Recueils d'airs sérieux et à boire* published by Ballard between 1697 and 1712. It includes eight *airs sérieux*, among them *La pastorelle* and *Les pellerines*, which appeared in 1713 as harpsichord pieces, and a two-part *air à boire*. While these *petits riens* occupy a humble place in Couperin's canon, they reveal much about the sources of his melodic style. Overtly more popular, less recherché than the 17th-century *air de cour*, they are nevertheless closely related to that tradition in their discreetly flowing vocal lines and simple phrase structure. Moreover, *La pastorelle* and *Les pellerines* emphasize just how far the melodic style of Couperin's instrumental music was derived from the vocal. The intimacy of this relationship is also revealed in the number of parody settings of his popular harpsichord pieces, a practice to which Couperin alluded – not without some satisfaction – in the preface to his third harpsichord book.

In addition to the printed music, three three-voice catches, two of them in canon, are extant in manuscript. Tessier located a reference to an otherwise unknown cantata *Ariane abandonée* in an Amsterdam catalogue of 1716. Titon du Tillet referred to cantatas among the works of Couperin not engraved and printed.

## VI  Harpsichord music

The four books of harpsichord music (some 220 pieces, excluding the separate movements to some of the titles and the eight preludes in *L'art de toucher le clavecin*) represent his crowning achievement. Part of their stature must be attributed to a particularly happy union between the composer's personality and the harpsichord as a musical medium. It was a medium he understood and loved deeply; and it was natural for him to grace his worldly progress with music for the instrument which had, so to speak, made his fortune. When Couperin published his first book of harpsichord pieces in 1713, most of the important harpsichord collections of the French classical school had already appeared. The first decade of the 18th century in particular, when Couperin was assembling material for his own publication, witnessed a striking proliferation of harpsichord books, those of Louis Marchand, Clérambault, J. F. Dandrieu, Gaspard le Roux, Rameau and Elisabeth-Claude Jacquet de la Guerre appearing within five years.

These collections consolidated the external characteristics of the French keyboard suite: a sequence of seldom more than ten dances arranged in a fairly predictable order in the same key. It is thus surprising that Couperin's first collection, the *Pieces de clavecin* of 1713, reverted to the motley nature of D'Anglebert's 1689 publication: so much so that Couperin seems to have felt constrained to adopt a new term, *ordre*, to designate the groupings of pieces within the book. The first *ordre* contains no fewer than 18 items, the second a record 23, the third 13, the fourth 4, and the fifth 14. In his second book (*ordres* 6 to 12) the average number of pieces in an *ordre* falls from 15 to 8. It seems clear that in his first book Couperin

17. Title-page of Couperin's 'Pieces de clavecin ... premier livre' (Paris, 1713)

was ridding himself of a backlog of harpsichord music. This impression is reinforced by the increased sensitivity he showed in his second book and thereafter towards maintaining a certain homogeneity of mood throughout each *ordre*. In the remaining two books the average number of pieces in an *ordre* drops to six.

The second book shows a decisive move away from the traditional sequence of dance movements. Even in the first collection the sequence is distorted by the inclusion of so many 'optional' dances. In the second book only the eighth *ordre* retains the Allemande–Courante–Sarabande grouping in any recognizable form. This rupture with tradition is reflected in the increasing emphasis on character-pieces. It is not that a significant number of the 1713 *Pieces de clavecin* lack descriptive titles, but rather that, from the second book onwards, Couperin abandoned many of the stereotyped gestures of dance pieces in an attempt to diversify and enrich the character of his music.

Couperin wrote clearly about the use of descriptive titles in the preface to his 1713 collection:

In composing these pieces, I have always had an object in view, furnished by various occasions. Thus the titles reflect ideas which I have had; I may be forgiven for not explaining them all. However, since among these titles there are some which seem to flatter me, it would be as well to point out that the pieces which bear them are a kind of portrait which, under my fingers, have on occasion been found fair enough likenesses, and that the majority of these flattering titles are given to the amiable originals which I wished to represent rather than to the copies which I took from them.

This was a natural enough habit of mind in a tradition which saw the role of music as that of arousing specific feelings and thoughts in the hearts and minds of listeners. Nor, of course, was Couperin an innovator in this respect. Where he did contribute in a new way was in the force and intensity of his musical characterizations, and in the manner in which his pieces were freed from dance prototypes.

When Charles Batteux (*Les beaux-arts réduits à un même principe*, 1746) discussed the theory of imitation as it related to music, he distinguished between imitations of sounds which were 'animés' and those which were 'non-passionnés'; the distinction is between qualities attributable to people and those attributable to natural phenomena, or events. An examination of Couperin's use of descriptive titles and their relation to his harpsichord music may usefully employ this distinction. Foremost in the category of 'sons animés' come the musical portraits of Couperin's friends, pupils and royal masters. There are a number of readily identifiable sitters: Gabriel Garnier, Couperin's colleague at the royal chapel (*La Garnier, ordre* no.2); Antoine Forqueray, the great viol player (*La superbe ou La Forqueray*, no.17); Mlle de Charolais, one of the daughters of the Duke of Bourbon and pupil of Couperin (*La Charoloise*, no.2); the Polish princess Maria Leszczyńska, another pupil of Couperin and fiancée of Louis XV (*La Princesse Marie*, no.20). There is even what may be a self-portrait, *La Couperin* (no.21). These, and many other portraits, make their point by reflecting the personal qualities of their subjects in appropriate musical gestures. *La Garnier*, in its apposition of dark-hued textures and expressive *ports de voix*, combining solemnity with tenderness, conjures up a personality at once noble and sensitive. Forqueray, self-assured and brilliant, is epitomized in a proud Allemande movement, a firmly treading bass against an alert, driving treble. And turning to *La Couperin*, one may read into its spacious sequences, its firm linear quality and strong tonal architecture a high seriousness of purpose.

Other portraits not immediately connected with the musical world seem more obscure in origin. However Clark (1980) has uncovered a number of plausible identities which demonstrate how closely Couperin attached his work to the artistic and social milieu of his day. For example, *La fine Madelon* and *La douce Janneton* (*ordre* no.20) may refer to the celebrated actress Jeanne de Beauval, who was generally known as Jeanneton, and who would be known also for her playing of Madelon in Molière's *Les Précieuses Ridicules*. Both pieces mirror feminine lightness and grace in their high tessitura and triple metre, the first is delicate, the second – portraying de Beauval herself and marked 'plus voluptueusement' – distinctly more sensuous in its melodic line and texture. Contrasting personalities provide an obvious opportunity for neat musical antitheses: *Les vieux seigneurs* and *Les jeunes seigneurs* (no.24) counterpose halting gravity and nimble high spirits, the first a 'Sarabande grave', the second a leaping and agile movement in two-part writing. But there may be a sharper edge to Couperin's wit to be found in these pieces. *Les nonètes: Les blondes – Les brunes* (no.1) may be intended in its burlesque sense: nuns were not all disdainful of a young man's advances. Satire is more obvious in *Les fastes de la grande et anciénne Mxnxstrxndxsx* [*Ménestrandise*] from *ordre* no.11 where the company of Ménétriers is mercilessly portrayed as a disreputable rabble of street entertainers finally routed by their own bears and monkeys. (This guild of musicians had previously attempted – unsuccessfully – to place the king's organists, including Couperin, under their jurisdiction.) *Les folies françoises* (no.13) reveals a more refined satirical art, but still barbed. The work comes at the end of an *ordre* which Clark interprets as Couperin's commentary on the moral state of the Regency; these are *les folies françoises* rather than *les folies d'Espagne*. Each piece in this set of variations is a character study, brilliant in its precision and conciseness, delineating Virginity, Modesty, Ardour, Hope, Fidelity, Perseverance, Languor, Coquetry, and so on. The characters in this masked ball 'work their way to their inevitable doom' (Clark), the *ordre* ending with *L'âme-en peine*, the soul in torment, a piece which with its enriched B minor harmony and drooping phrases evokes intense melancholy.

The second category of descriptive pieces, those which imitate 'les sons non-passionnés' (natural phenomena, events and ideas rather than humanity), ranges from the bluntly naive description of *Les petits moulins à vent* (no.17), with its whirling semiquaver scales, to *L'amphibie* (no.24), whose title seems to play on the notion of the transformations inherent in its loose ground bass structure. But things are not always what they seem. *Les papillons* (no.2) may refer to a fashionable ladies' hairstyle rather than butterflies, and *Le rossignol-en-amour* (no.14) along with the other birds in this *ordre* may have more to do with anthropology than ornithology. On the other hand, pieces such as *Le réveil-matin* (no.4) and *Le moucheron* (no.6) are no doubt what they appear to be: a musical portrayal of a couple of life's irritations. If with *Les baricades mistérieuses* (no.6) we seem to enter the world of metaphor, Couperin had on another occasion the directness of mind to call a favourite piece – indeed the one he included in his portrait by André Boüys – quite simply *Les idées heureuses* (no.2).

A greater understanding of the topicality of these titles, and the burlesque or satirical tone that lies behind some of them, sharpens the music's effect on our senses. These pieces are not all benign and charming portraits, agreeably presenting the sitters. From them Couperin emerges as a keener critic of his age than at first sight he would appear. The tone of irony and satire creates an altogether more complex picture of his musical language.

Structurally, Couperin's harpsichord pieces divide into three main types: the binary movement, the rondeau and the chaconne. (It is interesting to note that he never felt confident enough of the abilities of his public to leave any unmeasured preludes, a semi-improvisatory genre which went back to the beginning of the French harpsichord tradition.) His use of binary form in his harpsichord music is interesting in several respects, some of them typifying the distinctions between French compositional techniques of his time and those of German and Italian early 18th-century composers. First sections are often markedly shorter than second (*La florentine* and *Les papillons, ordre* no.2); and initial (or final) bars of sections are not often directly related motivically. Indeed, rather than underline structure through motivic references, Couperin often favoured a flexible development of musical ideas (articulated at the double bar) in which motifs acquire definition only as the piece progresses. Occasionally this will lead to a second section that introduces new material, sometimes making no further motivic reference to the first half of the piece (e.g. *La ténébreuse*, no.3).

The rondeau form, along with the chaconne, permitted the composition of pieces of greater length and diversity than was possible with simple binary structures. The rondeau was evidently a form that Couperin found congenial; many of his most striking and popular pieces such as *Les baricades mistérieuses* and *Les bergeries* (no.6) conform to it. The rondeau section itself is normally a regular four- or eight-bar theme, the episodes (*couplets*) being distinctly freer, sometimes contrasted in other senses too, but also sometimes texturally and motivically undifferentiated. The episodes in *Soeur Monique* (no.18) strike a nice balance between unity and contrast, the later episodes gaining increasing independence. This process is also at work in *La tendre Fanchon* and *Les ondes* (no.5).

Two of the three pieces that carry the title 'chaconne' or 'passacaille' are in fact in rondeau form, a treatment often met in earlier French harpsichord chaconnes (for example in those of Chambonnières and Louis Couperin). They are the superbly intense B minor *Passacaille* of *ordre* no.8 and the chaconne *La favorite* (no.3). While the episodes of the *Passacaille* are strongly and individually characterized, those of *La favorite* hark back in allusive fashion to the descending tetrachord bass of the opening bars. The art of allusion achieves its greatest expression in *L'amphibie* 'mouvement de Passacaille' (no.24). Various sorts of bass are heard with strong ground bass associations, the sections being of various lengths and highly differentiated: the object appears to be to convey the sense of a chaconne rather than its outward and visible form, the spirit rather than the letter. Behind this suggestive art and chameleon structure lies a piece of immense poise and strength. Only in one piece, *Les folies françoises* (no.13) does Couperin adopt the format of a series of pieces 'en variation' (the allusion to modish sets of variations on *La folia* is clear); these variations take the harmonic scheme of the opening piece rather than its melodic contour.

The textures Couperin used in his harpsichord pieces are no less important than the formal structures. Pride of place goes to the *style luthé*. Some of his best pieces are built exclusively on this 'broken style': *Les idées heureuses* (no.2), *Les charmes* (no.9), *La Mézangére* (no.10) and of course *Les baricades mistérieuses*. It is also the predominant stylistic feature of many of his allemande-type movements. The technique is finally sublimated in such pieces as *La convalescente* (no.26). This texture played an important role in the formation of Bach's mature keyboard style; Couperin came closest to Bach in his keyboard writing when he supported the *luthé* style with firm contrapuntal lines. By contrast, simple two-part textures constituted no less critical a part of Couperin's technical vocabulary. He recognized that they were less idiomatic but believed them adaptable to the harpsichord provided 'le dessus, et la basse travaillent toujours' (*L'art de toucher*). The high motivic consistency in most of these two-part pieces springs from Italian roots. Several good examples of this style of writing are to be found in the second book, in particular *La Bersan* and *La commére* (no.6), and *La coribante* and *L'atalante* (no.12); it was generally associated with brilliant and fast pieces. But the significance of Couperin's two-part technique extends beyond the examples cited, since a firm grasp of the contrapuntal relationship between treble and bass parts underpins his whole style. The solo line against accompaniment, as used in such pieces as *Les bergeries*, represents a third important type of texture. In some examples, like *Le moucheron* (no.6), the lower part gains independent status through its strong linear character in spite of a musically predominant right hand. Couperin's use of texture shows his keen awareness of the particular sonorities of the harpischords produced by French workshops of this period: his second book is remarkable for the number of pieces (see *ordre* no.7) using only the lower half of the keyboard, which was specially full and sonorous on French instruments.

Couperin's use of keyboard ornaments shows another important aspect of his handling of the harpsi-

18. *Part of the table of ornaments from Couperin's 'Pieces de clavecin . . . premier livre'* (1713)

chord (see fig.18). He took infinite pains over the notation of his ornaments (expecting the performer to respect his signs to the letter); and in 1733 he was credited by Dagincour (in the preface to his harpsichord book of that year) with the standardization of

195

a system that had by that time gained universal currency in France.

In its wealth of ideas, range of expression, and relationship to the culture from which it sprang, Couperin's harpsichord music stands unequalled in 18th-century France. At the same time it is an intensely personal testimony, revealing the most intimate aspects of his art. If elsewhere he may at times have matched the wit, the urbanity, the sombre passion, the easy charm, the melancholy or the high spirits of his harpsichord music, in no other medium did he combine those qualities to so remarkable a degree.

## VI  Theoretical works
Couperin spent much of his time teaching the harpsichord (perhaps too much, if one is to judge from the delays in the publication of his music). But it is precisely that immersion in the daily routine of teaching that makes his *L'art de toucher le clavecin* (1716, rev. 2/1717) so valuable a document. Unlike Saint-Lambert in his *Principes du clavecin* (1702), the only previous French keyboard tutor of any pretension, Couperin did not set out to cover the subject methodically from beginning to end. Rather, his treatise is a series of reflections on certain aspects of teaching, and on certain aspects of performing the pieces from his first two harpsichord books. The layout of his remarks is somewhat haphazard but, broadly speaking, they begin with comments on the initial stages in a pupil's training; a central section touches on fingering, ornamentation and other

questions related to performance; and finally, suggested fingerings are given for difficult passages in
the first and second harpsichord books. Eight
preludes are included as teaching material. Couperin
seems to have been diffident about his literary skills.
But his admirable directness makes his observations
on harpsichord touch and demeanour at the keyboard
essential reading for anyone who plays the instrument. His comments on fingering reveal him
faithful to the old system of crossing the third finger
over the second or fourth in scale passages, but enthusiastic about certain innovations that had come into
use in his day – principally the change of finger on
the repeated note of a prepared *port de voix*, and the
use of legato fingering for double 3rds. The most
widely quoted passages of *L'art de toucher* have been
those on the use of ornaments, *notes inégales*, and
general stylistic conventions in performance. These
are valuable remarks, but general laws should not too
readily be adduced. Too much is left unsaid. No less
valuable as insights into Couperin's world are his
comments on the harpsichord as a medium, its capa-
bilities, and the music which best suits it. He even took
the trouble to compose a two-voice Allemande to illustrate the manner in which that idiom could best be
adapted to the harpsichord. The eight preludes are
designed not only as teaching material but also as
introductory preludes to the *ordres* of the first and
second harpsichord books; Couperin did not conceal
his lack of faith in the ability of harpsichordists to
improvise such pieces. In order that the improvisatory
flavour of his notated preludes be retained, he in-

197

structed the performer to be rhythmically flexible, at least where the piece was not marked 'mesuré'. The general impression gained from this tutor is of Couperin's love for the harpsichord, his enthusiasm for its precision, neatness, brilliance and range, his wish to make it as expressive as other instruments (for example through introducing the *aspiration* and *suspension*), and his earnestness in attempting to convey to others a sensitivity about its use. The care he took over the printing of his harpsichord music reflects the same dedicated spirit.

A short manuscript *Regle pour l'accompagnement* is Couperin's only other extant theoretical work: it is a concise exposition of the rules of figured bass and of the treatment of chromatic dissonances. Its principal interest lies in the richness of the harmonic vocabulary demonstrated, a richness Couperin did not fail to exploit in his music.

Numbers in right-hand margins denote references in the text.

Editions: F. Couperin: *Oeuvres complètes*, ed. M. Cauchie and others, i–xii (Paris, 1932) [C]; rev. K. Gilbert and D. Moroney, ser. I–V and suppl. (Monaco, 1980– ) [GM; vols. n square brackets are in preparation]

F. Couperin: *Leçons de ténèbres à 1 et à 2 voix*, ed. P.-D. Vidal, Le pupitre, viii (Paris, 1968) [V]

F. Couperin: *Pièces de clavecin*, ed. K. Gilbert, Le pupitre, xxi–xxiv (Paris, 1969–72) [G xxi–xxiv]

F. Couperin: *Neuf motets*, ed. P. Oboussier, Le pupitre, xlv (Paris, 1972) [O]

F. Couperin: *Pièces de violes (1728)*, ed. L. Robinson, Le pupitre, li (Paris, 1974) [R]

## SACRED VOCAL     177–84

MS sources: Elevat[ions] de Couperin (score), *F-V* 59    178
Motets a voix seule, 2 et 3 parties et Symphonies de Mr Couperin, *F-Pn* Rés. F1679 (score), *Pn* Rés. F1680 [a–e] (5 partbooks) [formerly *GB-T* 1432–7]    178
Scores copied by S. de Brossard, *F-Pn* Vm¹ 1630
Motets de Messieurs Lalande, Mathau, Marchand Laisné, Couprin et Dubuisson, copied by Philidor, 1697, *V* 18    178

4 versets (from Ps cxviii) d'un motet composé de l'ordre du roy ... On y joint le verset 'Qui dat nivem' du psaume 'Lauda Jerusalem' (Paris, 1703): Tabescere me, S, S; Ignitum eloquium tuum, S, S, 2 vn, bc; Adolescentulus sum, S, 2 fl, vn; Justitia tua, S, S, SS, bc; Qui dat nivem, S, 2 fl, vn; C xi, GM [V/i]    179, 180

7 versets (from Ps lxxxiv) du motet composé de l'ordre du roy (Paris, 1704): Converte nos, B, fl, bc; Numquid in aeternum, T, Bar, bc; Ostende nobis, haute-contre, fl/vn, bc; Audiam quid loquatur, B, 2 vn, bc; Misericordia et veritas, T, T, bc; Veritas de terra, vn, bc; Et enim Dominus, S, 2 ob, 2 fl; C xi, GM [V/i]    180

7 versets (from Ps lxxxix) du motet composé de l'ordre du roy (Paris, 1705): Qui regis Israël, haute-contre, T, B, 2 vn, bc; Excita potentiam tuam, haute-contre, B, bc; Vineam de Aegypto, B, vn, bc; Dux itineris fuisti, B, 2 vn, 2 fl, 2 ob, bc; Operuit montes, S, vn, 2 fl, bc; Extendit palmites suos, S, vn, 2 fl, bc; Deus virtutum convertere, haute-contre, fl, ob, b viol, bc; C xi, GM [V/i]    181

Leçons de ténèbres a 1 et a 2 voix ... premier jour (Paris, between 1713 and 1717): première leçon, S, bc; seconde leçon, S, bc; troisième leçon, S, S, bc; C xii, GM V/ii, V    158, 179, 181–4
6 leçons de ténèbres, lost    160, 181

Accedo ad te, Dialogus inter Deum et hominem, haute-contre, B, bc, *F-Pn* Rés. F1679–80, *V* 59; C xii, GM V/ii

Ad te levavi oculus meos, B, 2 vn, bc, *Pn* Rés. F1679–80; GM [suppl.], O

Audite omnes et expanescite, haute-contre, 2 vn, bc, *V* 59; C xii, GM V/ii

Domine salvum fac regem, S, B, bc, *Pn* Rés. F1679–80; GM [suppl.], O

Exultent superi, motet for Ste Suzanne, inc., S, A, B, ? 2 vn, bc, *Pn* Rés. F1679–80; GM [suppl.]

Festiva laetis, motet for Ste Anne, S, T, B, bc, *Pn* Rés. F1679–80, *V* 59; C xii, GM V/ii

Jucunda vox ecclesiac, motet for St Augustin, S, S, B, bc, *Pn* Rés. F1679–80, *V* 59; C xii, GM V/ii

Laetentur coeli, motet for St Barthélemy, S, S, bc, *V* 59; C xii, GM V/ii

Lauda Sion salvatorem, elevation, S, S, bc, *Pn* Rés. F1679–80; GM [suppl.], O

Laudate pueri Dominum, S, S, B, 2 vn, bc, *Pn* Rés. F1679–80, *V* 18; C xii, GM [V/i]    178, 179

Magnificat, S, S, bc, *Pn* Rés. F1679–80, *V* 59; C xii, GM V/ii

O amor, O gaudium, elevation, haute-contre/T, B, bc, *Pn* Rés. F1679–80, *V* 59; C xii, GM V/ii

O Domine quia refugiam, B, B, B, bc, *Pn* Rés. F1679–80, *V* 59; C xii, GM V/ii

O Jesu amantissime, haute-contre, T, bc, *Pn* Rés. F1679–80, *V* 59; C xii, GM V/ii    179

O misterium ineffabile, elevation, S, B, bc, *Pn* Rés. F1679–80, *V* 59; C xii, GM V/ii

Ornate aras, inc., haute-contre, ? 2 vn, bc, *Pn* Rés. F1679–80; GM [suppl.]

Quid retribuam tibi Domine, haute-contre, bc, *Pn* Rés. F1679–80, *V* 59; C xii, GM [V/i]    179

Regina coeli laetare, S, S, bc. *Pn* Rés. F1679–80; GM[suppl.], O

Resonent organa, motet for Ste Cécile, inc., S, S, B, ? 2 vn, bc, *Pn* Rés. F1679–80; GM [suppl.]

Respice in me, haute-contre, bc, *Pn* Rés. F1679–80; GM [suppl.], O

Salve regina, haute-contre, bc, *Pn* Rés. F1679–80; GM [suppl.], O

Salvum me fac Deus, B, 2 vn, 2 fl, b viol, bc, *Pn* Rés. F1679–80; GM [suppl.], O

Tantum ergo sacramentum, S, S, B, bc, *Pn* Rés. F1679–80; GM [suppl.], O

Usquequo, Domine, haute-contre, bc, *Pn* Rés. F1679–80; GM [suppl.], O

Veni sponsa Christi, motet for Ste Suzanne, S, haute-contre, B, 2 vn, bc, *Pn* Vm¹ 1630, Rés. F1679–80; C xi, GM [V/i]

Venite exultemus Domine, S, S, bc, *Pn* Rés. F1679–80, *V* 59; C xii, GM V/ii

Victoria: Christo resurgenti, motet for Easter Day, S, S, bc, *Pn* Rés. F1679–80, *V* 59; C xii, GM V/ii

Other motets, incl. 12 à grand choeur, cited by Titon du Tillet, lost

## SECULAR VOCAL

In Recueil d'airs sérieux et à boire (Paris, 1697–1712) unless otherwise stated, dates in parentheses; all in C xi, GM [V/i]

Qu'on ne me dise, air serieux, T, bc (1697)

Doux liens de mon coeur, air sérieux, S, bc (1701)

Jean s'en alla, epitaphe d'un paresseux, air à boire, S, B, bc (1706)

Il faut aimer, La pastorelle, air sérieux, S, B, bc (1711)

Dans l'Isle de Cythère, Les solitaires, air sérieux, S, B, bc (1711)

À l'ombre d'un ormeau, musette, air sérieux, S, S, bc (1711)

Zephire, modere en ces lieux, brunete, air sérieux, S, bc (1711)

Faisons du temps, vaudeville, air sérieux, S, S, B, bc (1712)

Au tempe de l'amour, Les pellerines, air sérieux, S, B, bc (1712)

Trois vestales champetres et trois Poliçons, trio, S, S, S, in Recueil de trio de differens auteurs, *F-Pc*

La femme entre deux draps, canon à 3, S, S, S, in 1er recueil d'airs a boire en duó et trió, *Pc*

A moy! Tout est perdu!, canon à 3, S, S, S, in 1er recueil d'airs a boire en duó et trió, *Pc*

Ariane abandonée, cantata, cited in Amsterdam catalogue, 1716, see Tessier

Cantatas, cited by Titon du Tillet, lost

## CHAMBER MUSIC

170–77

MS sources: Scores copied by S. de Brossard, *F-Pn* Vm¹ 1156

Set of 4 partbooks, *LYm* 129.949

Concerts royaux, hpd/(vn, fl, ob, viol, bn), in Troisième livre de pièces de clavecin (Paris, 1722): 1e concert (G); 2e concert (D); 3e concert (A); 4e concert (e); C vii, GM IV/i — 156, 159, 170, 174-5

Nouveaux concerts, unspecified insts, in Les goûts-réunis ou nouveaux concerts (Paris, 1724): 5e concert (F); 6e concert (Bb); 7e concert (g); 8e concert dans le goût théatral (G); 9e concert intitulé Ritratto dell'Amore (E); 10e concert (a); 11e concert (c); 12e concert à 2 violes ou autres instrumens à l'unisson (A); 13e concert, a 2 instrumens à l'unisson (G); 14e concert (d); C viii, GM [IV/ii] — 156, 159, 165, 170, 174, 175-6

Le Parnasse, ou L'apothéose de Corelli, grande sonade en trio, 2 vn, bc, in Les goûts-réünis (Paris, 1724); C x, GM [IV/iv] — 155, 165, 170, 173-4

Concert instrumental sous le titre d'Apothéose composé à la mémoire immortelle de l'incomparable Monsieur de Lully, 2 vn, 2 fl, other insts (unspecified), bc (Paris, 1725); C x, GM [IV/iv] — 159, 165, 170, 173-4

Les nations: sonades et suites de simphonies en trio, 2 vn, bc (Paris, 1726): La françoise [La pucelle]; L'espagnole [La visionnaire]; L'impériale; La piemontoise [L'astrée]; C ix, GM IV/iii — 154, 159–60, 170, 171-3

Pieces de violes avec la basse chifrée, b viol, bc (Paris, 1728): 1ere suite (e); 2eme suite (a); C x, GM [IV/iv], R — 160, 170, 174, 176-7

La pucelle (e), 2 vn, bc, *F-Pn* Vm⁷ 1156, *LYm* 129.949; C ix, GM IV/iii — 171, 172, 173

La visionnaire (c), 2 vn, bc, *Pn* Vm⁷ 1156, *LYm* 129.949; C ix, GM IV/iii — 171, 172, 173

L'astrée (g), 2 vn, bc, *Pn* Vm⁷ 1156, *LYm* 129.949; C ix, GM IV/iii — 172, 173

La Steinquerque (Bb), 2 vn, bc, *Pn* Vm⁷ 1156, *LYm* 129.949; C x, GM [IV/iv] — 154, 172

La superbe (A), 2 vn, bc, *LYm* 129.949; C x, GM [IV/iv] — 154, 172

La sultane (d), 2 vn, b viol, bc, *LYm* 129.949; C x, GM [IV/iv] — 154, 170, 172

## HARPSICHORD

Pieces de clavecin . . . premier livre (Paris, 1713); C ii, GM II/i, G xxi — 184-96, 247

1e ordre, g/G: Allemande l'auguste; Premiere courante; Seconde courante; Sarabande la majestueuse; Gavotte; La milordine, gigue; Menuet (with double); Les silvains; Les abeilles; La Nanète; Les sentimens, sarabande; La pastorelle; Les nonètes: i Les blondes, ii Les brunes; La bourbonnoise, gavotte; La Manon; L'enchanteresse; La fleurie ou La tendre Nanette; Les plaisirs de St Germain en Laye — 156, 158, 185-7, 189

201

22e ordre, D/d: Le trophée; Le point du jour, allemande; L'anguille; Le croc-en-jambe; Menuets croisés; Les tours de passe-passe

23e ordre, F: L'audacieuse; Les tricoteuses; L'arlequine; Les gondoles de Délos; Les satires, chevre-pieds

24e ordre, a/A: Les vieux seigneurs, sarabande grave; Les jeunes seigneurs; Les dars-homicides; Les guirlandes; Les brinborions; La divine-Babiche ou Les amours badins; La belle Javotte, autre fois l'infante; L'amphibie, mouvement de passacaille — 189, 190; 193

25e ordre, Eb/C/c: La visionaire; La misterieuse; La Monflambert; La muse victorieuse; Les ombres errantes

26e ordre, f#: La convalescente; Gavote; La Sophie; L'epineuse; La pantomime — 193

27e ordre, b: L'exquise, allemande; Les pavots; Les chinois; Saillie

Sicilienne, G, F-Prthibault, A. Tessier's private collection, ?Paris; C ii, GM II/i

ORGAN

Pieces d'orgue consistantes en deux messes: 'à l'usage ordinaire des paroisses'; 'propre pour les convents de religieux et religieuses' (Paris, 1690); C vi, GM III — 120–21, 153; 167–70

WRITINGS

L'art de toucher le clavecin (Paris, 1716, rev. 2/1717); C i, GM [I] — 196–8
Regle pour l'accompagnement (MS, F-Pn); C i, GM [I] — 198

### BIBLIOGRAPHY

*FétisB* [but see *Ongaku gaku*, xix (1973), 113]; *GerberL*; *GerberNL*

J. Raguenet: *Parallèle des italiens et des français* (Paris, 1702)

J. L. Le Cerf de la Viéville: *Comparaison de la musique italienne et de la musique françoise* (Paris, 1704–6/*R*1972)

E. Titon du Tillet: *Le Parnasse françois* (Paris, 1732/*R*1971; suppl. ii, 1755)

J.-B. de La Borde: *Essai sur la musique ancienne et moderne* (Paris, 1780/*R*1972)

H. J. Taskin: *Notice sur la famille Couperin* (Paris, 1850)

A. Jal: *Dictionnaire critique de biographie et d'histoire* (Paris, 1867, 2/1872)

A. Guilmant, ed.: *Archives des maîtres de l'orgue* (Paris, 1904)

C. Bouvet: *Une dynastie de musiciens français: les Couperin, organistes de l'église Saint-Gervais* (Paris, 1919)

A. Pirro: *Les clavecinistes: étude critique* (Paris, 1924)

A. Tessier: 'François Couperin à l'orgue de Saint-Gervais', *RdM*, v (1924), p.56

——: *Couperin . . . biographie critique* (Paris, 1926)

J. Tiersot: *Les Couperin* (Paris, 1926/*R*1976)

A. Tessier: 'Un exemplaire original des pièces d'orgue de Couperin', *RdM*, x (1929), no.30, p.109

C. Bouvet: *Nouveaux documents sur les Couperin* (Paris, 1933)

M. H. Reimann: *Untersuchungen zur Formgeschichte der französischen Klaviersuite mit besonderer Berücksichtigung von Couperins Ordres* (Regensburg, 1940)

P. Brunold: *François Couperin* (Monaco, 1949)

M. Cauchie: *Thematic Index of the Works of François Couperin* (Monaco, 1949)

W. Mellers: *François Couperin and the French Classical Tradition* (London, 1950/*R*1968, rev. 2/1986)

M. Antoine: 'Autour de François Couperin', *RdM*, xxxi (1952), no.103, p.109

P. Citron: *Couperin et La Fontaine* (Manosque, 1953)

M. Antoine: 'Un acte inédit de François Couperin', *RdM*, xxxvii (1955), no.112, p.76

P. Citron: 'Autour des "Folies françaises" de François Couperin', *ReM*, no.226 (1955), 89

P. Hardouin: 'Quelques documents relatifs aux Couperin', *RdM*, xxxvii (1955), no.112, p.111

P. Citron: *Couperin* (Paris, 1956)

S. Hofman: *L'oeuvre de clavecin de François Couperin* (Paris, 1961) [with thematic catalogue]

M. Thomas: 'A travers l'inédit: archives paroissiales de Chaumes-en-Brie – les Couperin', *RMFC*, iii (1963), 221

——: 'Chaumes-en-Brie, pépinière d'organistes avant et après les Couperin', *RMFC*, vii (1967), 75

M. Antoine, M. Benoit, N. Dufourcq and others: *Mélanges François Couperin* (Paris, 1968) [on whole family; incl. exhaustive bibliography to 1966]

M. Pincherle: 'François Couperin et la conciliation des "goûts" français et italien', *Chigiana*, xxv (1968), 69

*Colloque international Couperin: Paris 1969*

T. Dart: 'On Couperin's Harpsichord Music', *MT*, cx (1969), 590

M. Benoit: *Musiques de cour: chapelle, chambre, écurie, recueil de documents, 1661–1733* (Paris, 1971)

P. Oboussier: 'Couperin Motets at Tenbury', *PRMA*, xcviii (1971–2), 17

K. Gilbert: 'Les livres de clavecin de François Couperin: note bibliographique', *RdM*, lviii (1972), 256

J. R. Anthony: *French Baroque Music from Beaujoyeulx to Rameau* (London, 1973, rev. 2/1978, rev. Fr. trans., 1981 as *La musique en France à l'époque baroque*)

M. Thomas: *Les premiers Couperin dans la Brie* (Paris, 1978)

B. Gustafson: *French Harpsichord Music of the 17th century: a Thematic Catalogue of the Sources with Commentary* (Ann Arbor, 1979)

P. Beaussant: *François Couperin* (Paris, 1980)

J. Clark: 'Les folies françoises', *Early Music*, viii (1980), 163

K. Gilbert and D. Moroney: preface to *François Couperin: Oeuvres complètes*, iii, *Pièces d'orgue* (Monaco, 1982)

D. Tunley: *Couperin* (London, 1982)

P. Holman: 'An orchestral suite by François Couperin?' *Early Music*, xiv (1986), 71

D. Fuller: *French Harpsichord Music* (Cambridge, in preparation)

# JEAN-PHILIPPE RAMEAU

Graham Sadler

Albert Cohen

# CHAPTER ONE

# Life

## I  Early life

Jean-Philippe Rameau was baptized in Dijon on 25 September 1683. His father Jean, a local organist, was apparently the first professional musician in a family that was to include a number of notable keyboard players: Jean-Philippe himself, his younger brother Claude and sister Catherine, Claude's son Jean-François (the infamous 'neveu de Rameau' of Diderot's novel) and Jean-François's half-brother Lazare.

Jean Rameau, the founder of this dynasty, held various organ appointments in Dijon, several of them concurrently; these included the collegiate church of St Etienne (1662–89), the abbey of St Bénigne (1662–82), Notre Dame (1690–1709) and St Michel (1704–14). Jean-Philippe's mother, Claudine Demartinécourt, was a notary's daughter from the nearby village of Gémeaux. Although she was a member of the lesser nobility, her family, like that of her husband, included many in humble occupations. Jean-Philippe, the seventh of their 11 children and the fourth to survive infancy, was the eldest surviving son. His birthplace in the cour Saint-Vincent on the rue Saint-Michel still remains (now 5–7 rue Vaillant). Despite only modest means, the family maintained influential connections; the composer's godparents, for example, were both from noble families connected with the Burgundian *parlement*.

The first 40 or more years of Rameau's life can be reconstructed only sketchily. Most of this period was spent in the comparative obscurity of the French provinces; it was not until his 40th year that he began to make his mark as a theorist and later still as a composer. He himself was secretive about the whole of the first half of his life: according to Chabanon, 'he never imparted any detail of it to his friends or even to Madame Rameau his wife'.

Rameau *père* apparently took responsibility for the early musical education of his children: 'he taught them music even before they had learnt to read' (Maret). It is possible that in 1692 or later Jean-Philippe also had lessons from Claude Derey, organist of the Sainte-Chapelle, Dijon. Eventually, perhaps as late as the age of 12, he was sent to the Jesuit Collège des Godrans. There he would have encountered the didactic music-theatre that was an important element in the contemporary Jesuit curriculum; indeed, it was quite probably the experience of taking part in such productions that sparked off his enthusiasm for opera which, he later admitted, had begun when he was 12. No precise details of the Dijon school productions have come to light, however. In view of his later achievements as a scholar, it is surprising that the young Rameau did not distinguish himself at the college; according to a classmate, he would sing or write music during lessons, and he left without completing the course. Certain anecdotes suggest that his written French was seriously defective at this time and indeed his prose style in the theoretical works and elsewhere is notable for its lack of clarity.

After leaving school, Rameau went to Italy. The date of his departure from Dijon is not known; Maret presumed that it was before his 19th year, but Decroix, in a biographical article (1824) based on material collected as much as 50 years earlier, states that the composer was 18. The visit was short – perhaps only a few weeks or months – and he never went beyond Milan. In later life he confided to Chabanon his regrets at not having stayed longer in Italy, where he believed he might have 'refined his taste'. Decroix claims that Rameau returned to France as a violinist with a touring theatrical troupe that performed in various towns in Provence and Languedoc. If this is true, the troupe concerned was almost certainly that of the Lyons Opéra (Zaslaw, *Dijon 1983*), in which case Rameau must have joined it in southern France (not in Milan, as Decroix maintains; the troupe never visited Italy).

On 14 January 1702 Rameau was temporarily appointed *maître de musique* at the Cathedral of Notre Dame des Doms, Avignon. By 1 May, however, he had taken up a longer-term post as organist at Clermont Cathedral. The contract, signed on 30 June, was for six years, though in fact Rameau served no more than four. By 1706 he had moved to Paris, where he is said to have lodged opposite the monastery of the Grands Cordeliers (Franciscans) to be near the church where Louis Marchand was organist. By the time his *Premier livre de pieces de clavecin* was published in 1706, he had succeeded Marchand

as organist at the Jesuit College in the rue Saint–
Jacques (the famous Collège Louis-le-Grand, the
pupils of which at that time included his future collaborator Voltaire); he was also organist to the Pères
de la Merci (Mercedarians). On 12 September 1706
he won a competition for the post of organist at Ste
Madeleine-en-la-Cité, but when the judges learnt that
he was unwilling to give up his other two posts they
appointed Louis-Antoine Dornel. Rameau still held
the same posts in July 1708.

In 1709 he returned to Dijon to succeed his father
as organist at Notre Dame, at that time the town's
principal church. On 27 March he signed a six-year
contract with the church authorities, sharing the post
with Lorin *fils*. Rameau was required to play only on
solemn feast days, at performances of the *Te Deum*
and at public ceremonies. It is clear, though, that
when Lorin succeeded to the post (2 July 1713),
Rameau had relinquished it some time before.
Probably he had already moved to Lyons: by 13 July
he had been there long enough to be described as
'maistre organiste et musicien de cette ville' when the
Lyons authorities paid him for organizing a concert
to celebrate the Peace of Utrecht (the concert never
took place). Rameau's compositions at this time
probably include motets: the library catalogue of the
Lyons Concert, a concert-giving society founded in
August 1714, lists his *Deus noster refugium* among its
earliest acquisitions; the piece may even have been
written specially for the Concert. (Although the
catalogue includes three more of his motets, among
them the lost *Exultet coelum laudibus*, their position

in the catalogue suggests that they were acquired after Rameau had left Lyons.) By 1 July 1714 he was organist at the Dominican convent known as the Jacobins, the organ of which had only recently been rebuilt; it is possible that he had already been there for a year or more. On 13 December, the day of his father's death, he drew his salary and journeyed to Dijon, remaining there for the wedding of his brother Claude in January 1715. When he returned to Lyons, he organized and composed music for a concert at the Hôtel de Ville (17 March 1715) in honour of the new archbishop. By this date he had been succeeded at the Jacobins by Antoine Fioco (presumably Antonio Fiocco) and Etienne Le Tourneur.

The following month, Rameau signed a second contract as organist at Clermont Cathedral, this time to run for 29 years from 1 April 1715. A contemporary description of the organ reveals that it had 15 stops on the *grand orgue*, ten on the *positif* and four each on the pedals and echo organ. As in 1702, his duties included the instruction of one chorister (according to Suaudeau (1958), there existed autograph teaching materials from 1717, but none is now known). Rameau briefly revisited Dijon for the baptism on 31 January 1716 of his brother Claude's eldest son Jean-François. Maret claims that three of Rameau's cantatas – *Médée*, *L'absence* (both lost) and *L'impatience* – were composed at Clermont. Four others – *Thétis*, *Aquilon et Orithie*, *Orphée* and *Les amants trahis* – survive in copies made during his time there. It was at Clermont, too, that the greater part of his *Traité de l'harmonie* must have been written.

*19. Jean-Philippe Rameau: portrait by Jacques Aved (1702–66)*

212

From 22 August 1721 until his departure about a year later, Rameau seems to have shared his cathedral post with an organist named Marchand, a member of a local family of musicians.

Rameau was still at Clermont on 11–13 May 1722, when he was paid for taking part in three Rogation Day processions. He finally left for Paris shortly afterwards, once again well before his contract expired (on this occasion it still had 21 years to run). It is alleged that at first the cathedral authorities refused him permission to go, and consequently that during the Octave of Corpus Christi he selected the most disagreeable stop-combinations and the most unpleasant discords until the authorities relented. It is possible, however, that this incident took place (if at all) before Rameau first left Clermont in 1705 or 1706 (Zaslaw, *Dijon 1983*). There is, in any case, a well-documented account of a similar occurrence at Dijon in 1736, when the organist was his brother Claude.

## II 1722–32

Rameau probably arrived in Paris in late May or in June 1722. He was to live there for the rest of his life. The immediate cause of his move seems to have been a desire to eliminate numerous errors from his *Traité de l'harmonie* which, he states, had been typeset in Paris while he was still at Clermont. Before the work was issued, he included a lengthy supplement of corrections, a revised or possibly new preface and other changes. The *Traité* must eventually have been issued soon after his arrival in the capital, since the first review appeared in the October-

November issue of the *Journal de Trévoux* (familiar title of *Memoires pour l'histoire des sciences et des beaux-arts*).

Rameau was virtually unknown in Paris. The appearance of this monumental 450-page treatise immediately earned him a formidable reputation, soon to be consolidated by the publication of the *Nouveau système de musique théorique* (1726). It has recently been discovered that shortly after publication Rameau sent a copy of the *Nouveau système* to the Royal Society in London, where a review by the mathematician Brook Taylor was read on 18 January 1727/8 (Miller, 1985); Rameau's attempts to gain international recognition for his work thus began more than ten years earlier than was previously thought.

The controversial nature of some of Rameau's theories, in particular that of the *basse fondamentale*, led to a public debate with 'a second musician' in Paris on 8 May 1729, continuing into the following year as a series of polemical exchanges in the *Mercure de France*. Rameau's opponent has sometimes been tentatively identified as Jacques de Bournonville, but is far more likely to have been the composer and theorist Michel Pignolet de Montéclair. Meanwhile, the firm of Ballard, which had published the *Traité* and the *Nouveau système*, was in the process of printing the *Dissertation sur les différentes méthodes d'accompagnement pour le clavecin, ou pour l'orgue* when Rameau broke off relations with them. The *Dissertation*, first mentioned in the preface to his *Pieces de clavessin* (1724), was eventually published by Boivin and Le Clerc in 1732. Thereafter, Rameau changed publisher with almost every new theoretical work.

Incongruous as it may seem in view of his new-found eminence as a theorist, Rameau's first compositions in Paris consisted of incidental music to a farcical and somewhat vulgar *opéra comique*, *L'Endriague*, at one of the Fair theatres (3 February 1723). The suggestion that he should provide music to supplement the well-known tunes traditionally used in such plays came from the author, Alexis Piron, a fellow-Dijonnais and one of the few people in Paris that he would already have known. Rameau's music, of which there was a considerable quantity, is now lost. In his three subsequent collaborations with Piron at the Fair theatres, he contributed much less. In spite of the lack of prestige attached to the Fairs, he was to make useful contacts there, among them Louis Fuzelier, future librettist of *Les Indes galantes*.

On 10 September 1725 Rameau attended a performance by two Louisiana Indians at the Théâtre Italien; he was soon to characterize their dancing in the harpsichord piece *Les sauvages*, later published in his *Nouvelles suites de pieces de clavecin*. *Les sauvages* was one of the works that Rameau referred to in his oft-quoted letter (25 October 1727) to the dramatist Antoine Houdar de La Motte, the text of which shows that he was already actively planning his operatic début, that La Motte had already refused him a libretto and had cast doubts on his chances of success. Evidently stung by this, Rameau set out with unusual clarity his credentials as a potential opera composer, but to no avail.

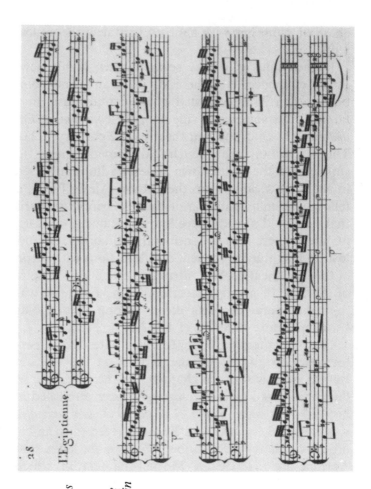

20. Part of 'L'égiptienne' from Rameau's 'Nouvelles suites de pieces de clavecin', published by the composer, Boivin and Le Clerc, c1729–30

216

During the middle and late 1720s, more of his music appeared in print. A second keyboard collection, the *Pieces de clavessin*, was issued in 1724, followed by the *Nouvelles suites de pieces de clavecin* and the *Cantates françoises à voix seule*. Recent research has resulted in the redating by Bruce Gustafson of the *Nouvelles suites* and by Neal Zaslaw (*Dijon 1983*) of the *Cantates françoises* both to 1729 or 1730, a year or two later than has long been assumed. One of the cantatas, *Le berger fidèle*, had been performed at Philidor's Concert Français on 22 November 1728 by Mlle Le Maure.

On 25 February 1726, now aged 42, Rameau married the 19-year-old Marie-Louise Mangot, an accomplished singer and harpsichordist and possibly already one of his pupils. She bore him four children. Her father, Jacques, was one of the *symphonistes du roy*, while her brother, Jacques-Simon, was later to make Rameau's music known at the court of Parma and to act as intermediary in correspondence between Rameau and Padre Martini.

In spite of his growing reputation as a theorist, composer and teacher, especially of harmony and continuo playing, Rameau was unable to secure an organist's appointment of any importance for many years after reaching Paris. The title pages of his music printed in the 1720s, unlike those of his previous publications, give no current post; that of the *Nouveau système* describes him as 'formerly organist of Clermont Cathedral'. He is not mentioned by Nemeitz (1727) or Valhebert (1727) in their listings of prominent Parisian organists. He competed for the post of organist at the parish church of St Paul (28 April 1727), but lost to Louis-Claude Daquin. By 1732, however, Rameau had become organist at Ste Croix-de-la-Bretonnerie and, by 1736, at the Jesuit Novitiate ('les Jésuites de Collège'). In 1738 he still held the former appointment but not the latter. (According to Decroix (1824), after his defeat in the St Paul competition in 1727 the disillusioned Rameau left Paris to become organist at St Etienne, Lille. This is unlikely: Rameau was in Paris for the baptism of his son Claude-François on 3 August 1727, and his subsequent publications give Paris addresses. In any case, Decroix's placing of the St Paul competition – before Rameau's arrival at Clermont – is far too early. Yet the claim cannot be ignored: Decroix, a native of Lille, was in frequent contact with Claude-François Rameau after the composer's death and had access to sources unavailable to other early biographers. Unfortunately, the relevant church archives were destroyed in 1792.)

## III  1733–44

Although Rameau did not make his operatic début until he was 50, it is clear from passages in the *Traité*, from his letter to La Motte in 1727 and from certain later remarks that it had long been his ambition to write for the Paris Opéra. The final impetus, it was widely claimed, was provided by Montéclair's *Jephté* (February 1732), the power of which had greatly moved Rameau. Although he had earlier quarrelled publicly with its composer, he refers admiringly to this work in his later writings.

The impact of Rameau's first opera, *Hippolyte et Aricie* (1733), was immense. Initial reactions ranged from excitement and admiration to bewilderment and disgust. The work gave rise to a long-running dispute between the conservative *lullistes*, as the anti-Rameau faction was to be christened, and the composer's supporters, known as *ramistes* (or, more provocatively, *ramoneurs*: chimney sweeps). The *lullistes*, who formed a powerful and vociferous cabal, were variously motivated by a distaste for the quantity, the complexity and the allegedly Italianate character of Rameau's music and by fear that the new style would annihilate the traditional repertory, above all the works of the revered Lully. There was a strong element of professional jealousy on the part of certain composers and librettists, and Rameau also had to contend with the ill will of some of the Opéra performers. The dispute raged around Rameau's second opera two years later ('The music is a perpetual witchery ... I am racked, flayed, dislocated by this devilish sonata of *Les Indes galantes*', complained an anonymous contributor to the *Observations sur les écrits modernes* in 1735) and reached its height with the production of his fifth, *Dardanus*, in 1739. Although the dispute abated during the following decade as the public gradually came to terms with the composer's powerful and sophisticated idiom, and accepted that a great theorist could also be a great artist, echoes could still be heard in the 1750s and beyond. Despite the controversy, Rameau's first five operas were by no means failures. *Castor et Pollux* and *Dardanus*, the two least successful at their first appearance, had runs of 21 and 26 performances respectively. The two earliest *opéras-ballets* proved even more popular: *Les Indes galantes* was performed 64 times between 1735 and 1737, *Les fêtes d'Hébé* 71 times in 1739 and 1740.

In December 1733, Rameau made his first visits to the court. Between then and 1740, all the operas he had so far written were given concert performances attended by the queen, Maria Leszczyńska, and occasionally by Louis XV. The singers sometimes included Rameau's wife; the *Mercure de France* (February 1734) reports that 'the Queen highly praised her voice and her tasteful ornamentation'.

Almost immediately after the première of *Hippolyte et Aricie*, Rameau began the first of three collaborations with Voltaire. The libretto of the ill-fated *Samson* had been sketched between October and December 1733, and the composer had written enough of the music by the following October for a rehearsal to take place at the home of the *intendant des finances*, Louis Fagon. By then, however, the Sorbonne had begun to take an unwelcome interest in an opera based on scripture by a writer known for his outspoken criticism of the religious and political establishment; further, Voltaire had enemies at court. Thus, despite the successful precedent of Montéclair's biblical opera *Jephté*, fears of censorship beset the project. At the beginning of 1736 Voltaire was still keen to see it through, but Rameau appears to have lost interest and the opera was subsequently abandoned. Voltaire later stated that music from *Samson* had eventually found its way into 'Les Incas' (the second *entrée* of *Les Indes galantes*), *Castor et Pollux* and *Zoroastre*. Fragments may also be identified in *La princesse de Navarre* and in the 1753 version of *Les fêtes de Polymnie*.

At the time of his first collaboration with Voltaire, Rameau was beginning his last with Piron – not this time at the Fair theatres but on the exalted stage of the Comédie Française. *Les courses de Tempé*, one of the few pastoral plays staged there, was given a single performance, on 30 August 1734. The Marquis D'Argenson described Rameau's divertissement (now largely lost) as 'pretty and well performed'.

During the 1730s, Rameau came under the protection of the tax-farmer A.-J.-J. Le Riche de La Pouplinière and acted as his director of music. La Pouplinière was one of the richest men in France and an influential patron of the arts. The accepted date for this development, 1731, was based on a collection of Voltaire's letters, the first of which is now believed to have been written in October 1733. Rameau had not by then joined La Pouplinière's entourage. Evidence for earlier contacts between the two (a rehearsal of *Hippolyte* said to have been held in La Pouplinière's home in the spring or summer of 1733 and his 'loan' of Rameau during September to the financier Samuel Bernard) is not trustworthy. Moreover, in a letter to Rameau of around December of that year, Voltaire refers to the composer as being under the protection of the Prince of Carignan, and it seems he continued so for some time since for well over a year Voltaire sent messages to Rameau, not through his own agent, Formont (who lived at La Pouplinière's house), but

21. Marie Sallé:
engraving (1733) by
Nicolas IV de
Larmessin after N.
Lancret; two of
Sallé's greatest
triumphs were as the
Rose in 'Les Indes
galantes' (1735) and
as Terpsichore in
'Les fêtes d'Hébé'
(1739)

by way of Berger, the prince's secretary. It is in any case more probable that the fashion-conscious La Pouplinière would have interested himself not so much in Rameau the eminent theorist and teacher as in Rameau the newly famous (or infamous) opera composer. Significantly, it was in 1734 or shortly after that the financier took as mistress Thérèse des Hayes, a devoted pupil of Rameau and one of his most enthusiastic champions; it may even have been Thérèse, whom La Pouplinière later married, who introduced Rameau to the household. At all events, Rameau cannot with any certainty be said to have joined the financier's circle until after 1734.

Rameau's association with La Pouplinière, which lasted until 1753, was of the utmost importance to his career. The financier's home was 'a meeting-place for all classes. Courtiers, men of the world, literary folk, artists, foreigners, actors, actresses, *filles de joie*, all were assembled there. The house was known as the menagerie and the host as the sultan' (Grimm; see Tourneux). It was there that Rameau met most of his future librettists, while the house became 'la citadelle du Ramisme' (Cucuel, 1913). Yet remarkably little is known about the terms of Rameau's appointment or, before 1751, the size and constitution of his patron's musical establishment. In 1741, La Pouplinière took over some of the Prince of Carignan's players, including the violinist Joseph Canavas, possibly the flautist Michel Blavet and (more doubtfully, despite his signing himself in 1751 'chef des violons de M. de la Pouplinière') the violinist Jean-Pierre Guignon. Singers and dancers from the Paris Opéra were frequent dinner guests and took part in concerts and theatrical entertainments. In the later 1740s, La Pouplinière was to import from Germany and Bohemia virtuoso players of the clarinet and orchestral horn. These instruments were then new to France, and Rameau was the first to use them at the Paris Opéra.

A second polemic on the subject of music theory erupted in the mid-1730s, this time between Rameau and his former friend, the Jesuit Louis-Bertrand Castel, mathematician, physicist and scientific journalist. The history of their association dates back to 1722 with the publication of the *Traité de l'harmonie*. Castel had been captivated by the treatise and had sought Rameau out through a mutual friend 'M. B.' (perhaps the Borin whose book *La musique théorique et pratique*, published anonymously in 1722 shortly after the *Traité*, is full of praise for Rameau's book). Castel took harmony lessons with Rameau, and may also have introduced him to the work of the mathematician and acoustician J. Sauveur. Castel's enthusiastic review of the *Traité* (*Journal de Trévoux*, October–November 1722) brought Rameau's work to the attention of a wide – indeed, a European – readership. Reviewing the *Nouveau système* six years later, Castel had become markedly less enthusiastic. By the early 1730s, his views had diverged sharply from Rameau's. It was for this reason, he was later to claim, that he had refused the offer of all Rameau's research work, around 1733, when the composer had considered abandoning music theory to concentrate on his newly launched operatic career. That was apparently their last meeting. Two years later, Castel's article 'Nouvelles expériences d'optique & d'acoustique' (*Journal de Trévoux*, August–December 1735) contained an implication that Rameau had not sufficiently acknowledged his debt to certain earlier scholars. Rameau and Castel exchanged open letters, the stiffly courteous tone of which suggests that their friendship had not completely broken down. But when Castel finally wrote a grudging and equivocal review of *Génération harmonique* (1737), Rameau unleashed a riposte of such withering sarcasm that, it seems, the Jesuit *Journal de Trévoux*, which had hitherto published the entire polemic, refused to print it; it appeared instead in the Abbé Prévost's independent *Le pour et contre* (1738). Voltaire's characteristically witty 'Lettre à Mr. Rameau' congratulating Orpheus Rameau on vanquishing Euclid Castel appeared later the same year.

*Génération harmonique* is Rameau's only major theoretical work of the period 1733–49. It was dedicated to the members of the Académie Royale des Sciences, who responded by commissioning a report on the work from three of their foremost academicians, R.-A. Ferchault de Réaumur and J.-J. Dortous de Mairan, both physicists, and the scholar E. S. de Gamaches. The two latter had already discussed music theory with Rameau, Mairan as much as 12 years earlier. The report was complimentary and Rameau proudly included in his treatise the 'Extrait des registres de l'Académie Royale des sciences' which echoed the sentiments of the report and was signed by the academy's eminent secretary, Bernard Le

Bovier de Fontenelle. Shortly after publication, Rameau sent a copy of the treatise to the distinguished English scientist Sir Hans Sloane, President of the Royal Society, together with a letter inviting his opinion of the work. It is not known whether Sir Hans replied.

Between 1737 and 1741 Rameau's views on temperament were criticized by Louis Bollioud-Mermet in lectures at the Lyons Académie des Beaux Arts. In a letter to Jean-Pierre Christin, secretary of the academy (3 November 1741), Rameau defended himself sharply; he may even have been responsible for the open letter 'from a person interested in Rameau's works' threatening to publish Bollioud's paper 'in the public interest' unless the writer did so himself. Other academicians, notably Charles Cheinet and Jacques Mathon de la Cour the elder, were staunch supporters of Rameau's theories.

In December 1737, the *Mercure de France* carried Rameau's announcement that he was establishing a school of composition. Up to 12 pupils would meet each week for three two-hour classes. In this way, Rameau claims, a thorough grasp of the theory and practice of harmony could be gained in six months at the most, even by those who could not already read music. Around this time, four reviews of *Génération harmonique* appeared in the leading Parisian periodicals. That in *Le pour et contre* was written by 'a young muse', almost certainly Thérèse des Hayes, who was by now Mme de La Pouplinière and renowned for her sharp intellect. (Maret, however, claimed that the author was 'Mme de Saint-Maur, née Aléon', another of Rameau's pupils.) Thérèse and her husband were among the godparents of the composer's third child, born in 1740. The following year, Rameau honoured her husband by giving one of the *Pieces de clavecin en concerts* the title 'La Lapopliniere' [*sic*].

The period 1740–44 was uncharacteristically slack by the standards of Rameau's mature years. He produced no theoretical writings – indeed, nothing of this kind between 1738 and 1749 – while his musical output was limited to the publication of the *Pieces de clavecin en concerts* (1741) and the revision for their first revivals of *Hippolyte et Aricie* in 1742, *Les Indes galantes* in 1743 and *Dardanus* (this revision admittedly involving much new music) in 1744. Circumstantial evidence hints at a quarrel with the Opéra management. Such a quarrel might also explain his marked lack of enthusiasm for a libretto, *Pandore*, that Voltaire offered him in 1740, though Rameau might equally have refused it because he sensed the controversial nature of the work and its librettist or wished to avoid another, possibly fruitless collaboration. At all events, Rameau's productivity revived sharply soon after Thuret was replaced by Berger as Opéra director in May 1744.

## IV  1745–51

The immediate stimulus to Rameau's creative activity was a series of commissions, three of them from the court, resulting in the production of no fewer than four dramatic works in 1745. For the festivities surrounding the Dauphin's wedding he composed *La princesse de Navarre* (his second collaboration with Voltaire) and *Platée*; for the court celebration of the victory of Fontenoy he wrote *Le temple de la Gloire* (again with Voltaire); for the Paris Opéra commemoration of Fontenoy he provided *Les fêtes de Polymnie*, adding a celebratory prologue to a work that, like *Platée*, was probably already in progress. *Les fêtes de Polymnie* was the first of at least seven collaborations with Louis de Cahusac. Apart from Voltaire and J. F. Marmontel, no other librettist worked with Rameau on more than two operas.

On 4 May, shortly after the Dauphin's wedding, Rameau received a royal pension of 2000 livres and the title *compositeur de la musique de la chambre du roy* (in some sources *compositeur du cabinet du roy*): an exceptional honour, for the title was normally conferred only on a member of the king's musical establishment.

Thus began a closer association with the court: from 1745 onwards, more than half of Rameau's stage works were intended for court premières. One, *Les surprises de l'Amour* (1748), was even written as a vehicle for Mme de Pompadour's theatrical talents in her Théâtre des petits appartements. There is evidence that, at the time of his first royal pension, Rameau had not been financially well off. After *Le temple de la Gloire*, Voltaire generously donated his own fee to Rameau, since 'his fortune is so inferior to his talents' (on the other hand, Rameau was already said to have worked with librettists only if they surrendered their fees to him). In 1750, the king accorded him a further pension of 1500 livres payable by the Opéra out of its

*22. Performance of Rameau's comédie-ballet 'La princesse de Navarre' at the Théâtre des Grandes Ecuries at Versailles on 23 February 1745 to celebrate the marriage of the Dauphin Louis to Maria Teresa of Spain: engraving by Charles-Nicholas Cochin (the younger)*

revenue. There is, however, some doubt as to whether this was honoured, at least before 1757.

The five years 1745–9 were Rameau's most productive. No fewer than nine new works were performed, including the *tragédie Zoroastre*, the *comédie Platée*, two pastorales and three *opéras-ballets*. By 1749 his works dominated the stage to such an extent that the Marquis D'Argenson, who had supervisory responsibility for the Opéra and who disliked Rameau and his music, felt compelled to forbid the management to stage more than two of his works in any one year.

Around 1750 Rameau had the support of a wider cross-section of the French public than ever before. His position at court was secure, he enjoyed the esteem of most of the intellectuals (including many who were later to side against him), and his works were widely performed in the provinces. The extent to which he had won over the audiences and performers at the Opéra can be judged by a report in the *Mercure de France* for May 1751:

At Wednesday's performance [*Pigmalion*] M. Rameau, who had only just recovered from a long and dangerous illness, appeared at the Opéra in one of the rear boxes. His presence aroused a murmur that began in the stalls and spread rapidly throughout the whole audience. Then suddenly there broke out a general applause and – something that had never been seen before – the assembled orchestra added their rapturous cheers to those of the *parterre* . . . [Rameau] shared with the public the pleasure of an excellent performance. That night it seemed that all the actors were striving to excel themselves.

Such spontaneous demonstrations of respect and affection were to become more common during the

1750s and after. Even so, audiences were still slow to respond to new works; it was frequently observed that Rameau's operas were really successful only when they were revived.

One operatic casualty of the period was the *tragédie Linus*. Decroix, who acquired and had a copy made of the first violin part (now virtually the sole contemporary source of the music known to survive), was told by the composer's son Claude-François that the opera was being rehearsed at the home of the Marquise de Villeroi when the Marquise was suddenly taken seriously ill. In the confusion, the score and all the other parts were lost or stolen. The rehearsal must have taken place by 1752; the Abbé de Laporte alludes to it in a book published that year. In 1760 he was to state that the opera was never performed because of flaws in the music of the fifth act. Collé had claimed in 1754 that Rameau had never quite completed the music after La Bruère had made changes to his libretto. The libretto survives in manuscript.

Rameau's operatic activities in the mid- and later 1740s had left little time for theoretical work, but in 1749 he broke an 11-year silence in this field with some minor writings. (The long silence supports Castel's claim that in the mid-1730s Rameau had felt he could develop his theoretical work no further.) The following year he published the far more important *Démonstration du principe de l'harmonie*. Here he had the 35-year-old Denis Diderot as collaborator: hence the clarity and elegance of what is generally regarded as one of his best and most mature theoretical works.

The *Démonstration*, approved by members of the
Académie Royale des Sciences, including D'Alembert,
was dedicated to the Count D'Argenson, himself a
member of the academy. Though the book was
widely reviewed, no copy – surely deliberately – was
sent to the *Journal de Trévoux*.

In 1745, two events took place that were to sow
the seeds of Jean-Jacques Rousseau's undying hatred
of Rameau. Rousseau had completed an opera *Les
muses galantes*, modelled on *Les Indes galantes*, and
tried to elicit Rameau's opinion of it. Although
Rameau at first refused, a performance of excerpts
was arranged at La Pouplinière's. Rameau listened
with growing impatience and, according to Rousseau,
finally declared that 'part of what he had heard was
by someone who was a master of the art and the rest
by an ignoramus who did not understand the first
thing about music' (the stylistic discrepancy he noted
is explained by the fact that the young F. A. Danican
Philidor had composed some of the accompaniments
and inner parts). 'Admittedly', Rousseau continued,
'my work was unequal and inconsistent . . . Rameau
claimed that he could see in me nothing but a little
plagiarist without talent or taste'. Later in the year,
while Voltaire and Rameau were busy on *Le temple
de la Gloire*, the Duke of Richelieu commissioned
Rousseau to complete *Les fêtes de Ramire*, the libretto
of which had been written by Voltaire to re-use
Rameau's divertissements from *La princesse de
Navarre*. The task evidently involved writing verse as
well as music, and Rousseau maintained that it cost
him much effort. But the result was so harshly criti-

cized by Richelieu's mistress (the scarcely impartial Mme de La Pouplinière) that the work was sent back to Rameau. Rousseau claimed to have composed the overture and recitatives, but surviving sources suggest that his musical contribution to the work as finally performed consisted of little more than the undistinguished monologue 'O mort, viens terminer les douleurs de ma vie'. At all events, Rousseau gained no credit from the episode. From then on, he seldom missed an opportunity to speak in scathing or hostile terms of the compositions, and to a lesser extent the theories, of his former idol.

When Rameau's troublesome nephew Jean-François was sent to the prison of For l'Evêque in 1748 for insulting the Opéra directors, the composer was asked by the authorities 'how long he deemed it fitting that [the nephew] should stay there'. Rameau evidently suggested that Jean-François be deported to the colonies. In his reply, the Secretary of State, Phelypeaux, sympathized that Jean-François had not profited more from the good education procured for him by his uncle, but makes it clear that deportation was out of the question; the nephew was released three weeks later.

## V 1752–64

During his final 13 years, Rameau's operatic activity declined sharply. Apart from two major works, *Les Paladins* and *Les Boréades*, his composition was limited to small-scale pastorales and *actes de ballet* and to the revision of earlier works for revivals, notably *Castor et Pollux* and *Zoroastre*. Of the new works, only *Les Paladins* was given at the Opéra; the rest were performed solely at court. *Les Boréades* is now known to have been prepared for performance not at the Opéra but at Choisy in June 1763; it was rehearsed two months earlier in Paris and Versailles by a mixture of court and Opéra personnel, but subsequently abandoned and never performed in the 18th century (Bouissou, 1983). Up to his last years, Rameau continued to take an active part in new productions and in revivals, giving his views on the distribution of roles and attending rehearsals.

No doubt advancing age and the ill health that Rameau and others increasingly allude to were in part responsible for the slackening of the rate, if not necessarily the quality, of his compositions. But this slackening coincides with a remarkable resurgence of activity in his theoretical work. From 1752 he produced some 23 writings. Many are short pamphlets; but more weighty works include the *Observations sur notre instinct pour la musique* (in part a reply to J.-J. Rousseau's notorious *Lettre sur la musique françoise*), the *Code de musique pratique* and the recently discovered *Vérités également ignorées et interressantes tirées du sein de la nature*, Rameau's last work (formerly known only in the fragmentary form, *Vérités interessantes*; see Schneider, 1985).

The dissemination of his theories was given powerful impetus in 1752 when D'Alembert, acting on Diderot's suggestion that 'someone should extract [Rameau's] admirable system from the obscurities that enshroud it and put it within everyone's reach', produced his *Eléments de musique théorique et pratique suivant les principes de M. Rameau.* Here the master's theories are expounded with lucidity and elegance. The book was translated into German by Rameau's lifelong admirer F. W. Marpurg (Leipzig, 1757). A letter of about 1750 from the 33-year-old D'Alembert to the 67-year-old Rameau reveals that the two were on extremely cordial terms. The *Mercure de France* of May 1752 contains an open letter in which Rameau touchingly acknowledges his deep gratitude to D'Alembert.

By contrast, he could be brusque to the point of rudeness with a little-known provincial like 'M. Ducharger of Dijon', whose niggling criticism of his ideas Rameau had apparently promised to answer in a forthcoming book. When Ducharger inquired when this would appear, he received the following reply (13 June 1754) which he later published:

Sir, The book in question is now in print. It is entitled *Observations sur notre instinct pour la musique.* I have neither time nor health to think or to reflect. Forgive me, sir; I am old, you are young, and I am your very humble and very obedient servant, RAMEAU.

The *Observations* contain a dismissal of Ducharger's ideas but without even mentioning him by name.

Evidence of Rameau's contacts with foreign scholars increases markedly in this period as he sought wider recognition. Beginning in 1750 he entered successively into correspondence with Gabriel Cramer (Geneva), Johann II Bernoulli (Basle), Christian Wolff (Halle), Leonhard Euler (Berlin), Giovanni Poleni (Padua), J. B. Beccari and Padre Martini (both at Bologna). Although he had also communicated with many French scientists and scholars over the years, the list now widened to include the aesthetician Charles Batteux, the architect Charles-Etienne Briseux and the scholar François Arnaud, all of whom were to prove influential.

With the obvious exception of Rousseau, Rameau still had the support of most of the intellectuals at the start of the decade. During the Querelle des Bouffons (1752–4), however, Melchior Grimm and others found it expedient, partly at least for extra-musical reasons, to side against the principal living exponent of French music; and Rameau was soon to break with Diderot and D'Alembert in a polemic concerning the articles on music in the *Encyclopédie*. When Diderot had asked him to write some of these, Rameau had regretfully declined but had offered to comment on the manuscripts before they were printed. Eventually it was Rousseau who wrote these articles. He later complained that Diderot had allowed him only three weeks and that this had impaired their quality. Rameau, however, was never shown them before publication (possibly Rousseau had seen to that). His pride doubtless hurt, he kept silence for some time, but eventually felt compelled to point out their failings in a series of pamphlets. By the time Diderot and D'Alembert had been fully drawn into the conflict, when they defended Rousseau in the preface to volume six of the *Encyclopédie* (1756), Rameau had alienated all the principal *philosophes*. Even without this quarrel, however, these men could not have allied themselves with some of the latest developments in

23. Autograph MS from Rameau's pastorale-héroïque
'Daphnis et Eglé', first performed in 1753

Rameau's thinking, in particular when it took on a metaphysical or a theological tone.

The break with the *philosophes* must have been desperately disappointing to Rameau, since it had long been his principal ambition to be accepted as a thinker. 'Can it not be clearly seen', he wrote to Diderot and D'Alembert in 1757, 'that in honouring me with the titles "artiste célèbre" and "musicien" you wish to rob me of the one [i.e., "philosophe"] which I alone among musicians deserve, since I was the first to have made music a science by the discovery of its natural principle?' He must have been equally disappointed never to have been elected to the Académie Royale des Sciences despite the high regard that the academy had shown for his work. The nearest he came to such an honour was in 1752 when, with several other distinguished Burgundians, he was elected an associate member of Président Richard de Ruffey's Dijon literary society. When that society ceased to exist in 1761, he was elected to its victorious rival, the Académie des Sciences, Arts et Belles-Lettres de Dijon.

After nearly two decades, Rameau's association with La Pouplinière came to an end in 1753. Although the financier had separated from his wife five years earlier, the composer and Mme Rameau stayed on, spending each summer at his country home in Passy and even living for a time in an apartment in his Paris residence. But in 1753 La Pouplinière's new mistress established herself there and soon made life unbearable for a number of the residents, including the Rameaus. At the same time, the financier seemed anxious to replace his venerable, 70-year-old music director with a more fashionable musician. Maret claimed that the final rift came when La Pouplinière installed another composer in his house. If so, that composer cannot (as has been conjectured) have been Johann Stamitz; Stamitz was eventually to succeed Rameau at La Pouplinière's, but arrived in Paris only in 1754.

Rameau's activities in the 1750s still included teaching. In addition to those already mentioned, his pupils over the years had included Diderot and possibly D'Alembert, the future Mme Denis (Voltaire's niece and mistress), Anne-Jeanne Boucon (later to marry the composer Mondonville) and the composers Claude Balbastre, Pierre-Montan Berton, Antoine Dauvergne, Pietro Gianotti and Jean-Benjamin de La Borde.

In his last years, aware that time was running out, he made feverish attempts to finish his theoretical work, now more important to him than composition. A rare glimpse of the aged Rameau is contained in his letter of November 1763 to the businessman Casaubon. He begins with profuse apologies for having seemed brusque or even insulting in a previous letter, but 'the time that I take up to write concerning my domestic affairs is very precious to me since I steal it from Him whom I fear and who does not fail me, so that I can bring to light new discoveries'. He was forced to communicate his thoughts in abbreviated form, he says, because of 'a lack of brainpower, of eyesight, and because I cannot concentrate nowadays more than two hours during the daytime'.

Very few personal letters of this sort have survived. According to Claude-François Rameau, who in his youth had often served as a messenger boy, his father burned much (Schneider, *RMFC*, 1985).

By now Rameau was comparatively rich, having for some time had a respectable income from his royal pensions, pupils' fees, payments from the Opéra, the court and, until 1753, La Pouplinière. There was also revenue from the sale of books, scores and pamphlets. Details survive of a number of his investments. In 1757, the Opéra belatedly granted him a pension of 1500 livres, though Rameau justifiably claimed that he had never been adequately recompensed by the management, considering the revenue his works had brought them. Three years earlier, he helped his son Claude-François buy the much-prized title of *valet de chambre* in the king's service, providing 17,500 of the necessary 21,500 livres. On several other occasions he gave financial help to members of his family circle (for the most recent evidence see Bouquet-Boyer, *Dijon 1983*).

He died at his home in the rue des Bons Enfants on 12 September 1764, three weeks after contracting a violent fever. He was buried the next day in his parish church of St Eustache. Five months earlier, he had received from the king letters patent of nobility; among the papers found after his death is proof that the necessary registry fees were paid, but only during his final illness and probably on his wife's or eldest son's initiative. The inventory of his estate, valued at almost 200,000 livres, reveals a sparsely furnished apartment containing only one musical instrument ('un vieux clavecin à un clavier en mauvais état'). Yet money bags in the writing desk in his wife's room contained coins worth 40,584 livres. Mme Rameau was able to provide a grand 'society' wedding for her 20-year-old daughter Marie-Alexandrine (according to Collé, Rameau had sworn that she would never marry in his lifetime) less than four months after the composer died.

Three memorial services were held in Paris. The first, at the church of the Pères de l'Oratoire (27 September 1764), involved nearly 180 musicians from the Opéra and from the *musique du roi* and was attended by perhaps 1500 people. Other services were held at the Carmelite church ('les Carmes du Luxembourg') on 11 October and again at the Pères de l'Oratoire on 16 December. Similar commemorations took place in various provincial towns, among them Marseilles, Orleans and Avignon. Dr Hugues Maret, secretary of the Dijon Academy of which Rameau had been a member, delivered a carefully researched *éloge* (25 August 1765) that was published the following year and is one of the most valuable sources of information on the composer's life.

Descriptions of Rameau's physique agree on his height and build: 'his stature was extremely tall; he was lean and scraggy, with more the air of a ghost than of a man' (Chabanon); 'though much taller than Voltaire, he was as gaunt and emaciated' (Grimm; see Tourneux); 'like a long organ pipe with the blower away' (Piron; see Proschwitz). Collé and Grimm give extremely unflattering and doubtless jaundiced accounts of his personality. 'Rameau was by nature harsh and unsociable; any feeling of humanity was foreign to him . . . His dominant passion was avarice' (Grimm); 'he was a difficult person and very disagreeable to live with; . . . he was, furthermore, the most uncivil, the most unmannerly and the most unsociable man of his day' (Collé). Almost all accounts are by those who knew him only as an old and evidently eccentric man; the picture that they give is thus almost certainly distorted. There are, sadly, scarcely any comparable accounts from his earlier years to provide balance. He was undoubtedly a difficult man to work with, as numerous scholars, librettists and others discovered. His shyness and modesty are attested by various anecdotes. The charge of avarice cannot be dismissed, but against it must be set his acts of generosity to members of his family.

As a keyboard player he excelled in continuo realization. Although he never acquired an organist's post of any great prestige in Paris, his playing at Ste Croix-de-la-Bretonnerie attracted many music lovers there. Marmontel describes him, on the organ at La Pouplinière's house at Passy, playing 'pieces of astonishing vitality'. Maret's assessment, though second-hand, derives from those well acquainted with Rameau's playing: 'Less brilliant in execution, perhaps, than Marchand's, but more learned, his touch yielded nothing in delicacy to that of Clérambault'.

CHAPTER TWO

# Works

Rameau has long been recognized as one of the greatest figures in French musical history. A theorist of European stature, he was also France's leading 18th-century composer. Although he made important contributions to the cantata, the motet and, more especially, keyboard music, many of his finest and most ambitious compositions are in the field of dramatic music, where they stand alongside those of Lully and Gluck as the pinnacles of pre-Revolutionary French opera. While his interests in music theory and opera both date from boyhood, his first theoretical work did not appear until he was nearly 39, his first opera until he was 50; it is to the second half of his long life that all but a small proportion of his works belong.

## 1 Cantatas and motets

Rameau's first sojourn in Paris (c1706–9) coincides with the remarkable first outpouring of French cantata publications from Morin, Bernier, J. B. Stuck, Campra and others. If Rameau experimented with the new genre in those years, the results have been lost. Most of his surviving cantatas – all but *Le berger fidèle* (c1728) and the recently identified *Cantate pour le jour de la Saint Louis* (probably c1745) – seem to

243

have been written in the provinces during the following decade, or at least before his return to Paris in 1722.

For much of the present century, Rameau's cantatas have been regarded as mere prentice works, insipid and somewhat anonymous beside the powerful and individual creations of his maturity. While it may be true that only *Orphée* and *Le berger fidèle* contain hints of the emotional force of the future opera composer, that has much to do with the fact that the cantata was always a relatively lightweight genre, decorative and largely undramatic. There is accordingly little of profundity here, but much that is charming, witty and thoroughly refined.

To his immediate forerunners Rameau owes not only his conception of the cantata but to a large extent its musical style, a peculiar amalgam of French and Italian elements that tends strongly towards the latter. Among the distinctive features of Rameau's cantatas are the many energetic and technically demanding obbligato lines, in particular the concerto-like bass viol parts of *L'impatience* and *Les amants trahis* and the fiery *tirades* in *Thétis*. Not surprisingly, his work tends to be harmonically less bland than that of his contemporaries, especially in such poignant movements as the first air of *Le berger fidèle* or the central monologue, 'Emu par des nouveaux accords', in *Orphée*.

Rameau's only other secular vocal music consists of convivial drinking songs and some canons, genres that for him as for others of his epoch were not mutually exclusive. (For a newly identified canon see fig.24.)

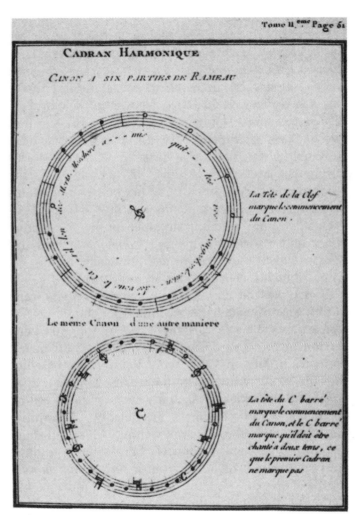

24. Canon by Rameau from 'Essai sur la musique ancienne et moderne' by J.-B. de La Borde, published in Paris in 1780

For one who was employed as a church musician for at least 26 years, even if mainly as organist rather than as *maître de musique*, Rameau appears to have written remarkably little sacred music. Apart from a lost *Exultet coelum laudibus*, there is no evidence of any *petits motets*. Only four *grands motets* survive, two of them incomplete. The collector Decroix, who searched assiduously for missing Rameau works during the later 18th century, was unable to locate anything further. Likewise, the organizers of various memorial services to the composer in 1764 and 1765 evidently found nothing suitable among his sacred music and resorted to making *contrafacta* from his operas which they performed alongside works by Gilles, Philidor, Rebel, Giroust and others.

It may well be that Rameau's *grands motets* were in any case intended not so much for church as for concert use. This is certainly true of the surviving version of *In convertendo*, performed at the Concert Spirituel in Paris in 1751, while *Deus noster refugium* was probably written for the Lyons Concert. Like *Quam dilecta tabernacula*, both have a quasi-secular character with frequent graphically descriptive passages and bold orchestral writing. All are substantial works (except 'Laboravi', an isolated quintet almost certainly detached from a lost *grand motet*). In their use of clearcut, autonomous movements, elaborate arias and ensembles, predominantly contrapuntal choruses and a vigorously independent orchestra, they resemble, and in some works perhaps even anticipate, the *grands motets* of Lalande's later years. Solos and to a lesser extent choruses tend to be more brilliant and technically demanding than those of Lalande and other older contemporaries. *Deus noster* and *In convertendo* each contain significant cross-references between movements.

## II  Keyboard music

Until recently, Rameau's output of keyboard music was believed to consist of three solo collections (1706, 1724, *c*1729–30), a volume of accompanied keyboard music (the *Pieces de clavecin en concerts*, 1741) that also contained five solo arrangements, and the independent *La Dauphine* (?1747). To these must now be added some two dozen harpsichord arrangements of orchestral music from *Les Indes galantes* (1735) and, if the attribution is reliable, the recently identified *Les petits marteaux* (Fuller, 1983). Some 18th- and 19th-century writers claimed that Rameau composed for the organ, but no such works have been discovered.

This corpus of music, containing Rameau's first known compositions as well as works of his full maturity, naturally exhibits considerable development of style and approach. The 1706 book consists of a single suite much in the tradition of Lebègue, Louis Marchand and Gaspard Le Roux. Beginning with an old-fashioned, partly unmeasured prelude (one of the last of its kind printed in Rameau's day), it consists mainly of the standard dances – two allemandes, courante, gigue, two sarabandes, gavotte and menuet – and contains only one genre-piece, 'Vénitiénne'.

In the next two keyboard collections, this type of suite coexists with a newer one: each contains a pair of suites contrasted both in tonality and character.

The first of each pair is dominated by dances (not all
of them the traditional ones) and includes only two
or three genre pieces; the second consists almost exclusively of pieces with genre titles. In their make-up,
if not in their style, these latter suites are closer to the
*ordres* of François Couperin, 19 of which (books 1–3)
were published between the appearance of Rameau's
first two collections. Given that this newer type was
to dominate French harpsichord publications,
Rameau can be seen to be a little conservative in
devoting half of each collection to the older type. The
traditional dance movements of the third book, and
particularly the monumental allemande and courante,
are in fact among the finest and most highly developed in the entire French repertory. It may be that
Rameau's interest in such dances was prolonged by
the example of Handel whose first book of suites,
published in 1720, he appears to have known.
Kenneth Gilbert (1979) points out the remarkable resemblance between the Gavotte with six *doubles* in
the third collection *c*1729–30 and the Air with five
*doubles* in Handel's Suite no.3. The structure of
Rameau's theme closely follows Handel's, as do the
textures and figuration of the first three variations.
His intention seems to be to emulate and, in the
amazing display of virtuosity in the last three variations, to surpass his model.

If the new prominence given to genre pieces represents one of Rameau's few important debts to
Couperin, an equally important influence in this
respect may have been Castel. Castel claims that he
introduced Rameau, soon after the composer had

settled in Paris in 1722, to the 'birdsongs noted in Kircher' (i.e. in *Musurgia universalis*, 1650), among which he specifically mentions the hen and the nightingale; with Kircher as his example, Castel claims to have given Rameau 'the outlines of pieces which imitate the truth of Nature'. While Rameau's birds in *Le rappel des oiseaux*, *La poule* and elsewhere do not in fact sing the same songs as Kircher's, the composer was undoubtedly stimulated in the mid-1720s to produce his series of magnificent descriptive pieces drawn not only from nature (as in the bird pieces, *Les tourbillons* and others) but also from the theatre: *Les sauvages*, the popularity of which was to be unrivalled in the 18th century, characterizes the dancing of two Louisiana Indians at the Théâtre Italien in 1725; *Les cyclopes* may well have been inspired by the portrayal of the one-eyed giant in Lully's *Persée*, revived in November 1722 and probably one of the first operas Rameau saw on returning to Paris. Many titles (e.g. *Les soupirs*, *La joyeuse*, *Les tendres plaintes*) evoke a mood. Some (*La vilageoise*, *La follette*, *L'egiptienne*) are character studies. Others (*Les trois mains*, *L'enharmonique*) allude to compositional technique.

Rameau's final collection, the *Pieces de clavecin en concerts* (1741), incorporates several features, most obviously the inclusion of additional instruments, that set it apart from the earlier ones. There is also the internal organization of the collection: whereas the suites of the first three books each comprise between seven and ten movements, the *concerts* of the fourth contain only three or five. Moreover, dance movements are almost entirely supplanted by genre pieces; of the 19 movements, all but the two menuets and tambourins have characteristic genre titles. By this time, however, Rameau's approach to titles had also changed. While five movements still bear such titles as *La timide*, *La pantomime* or *L'indiscrette*, nine are named after pupils, patrons, fellow composers and others, a fashion he had hitherto ignored. The link between title and piece may not, in any case, be strong: according to Rameau's preface, many titles were suggested, after the pieces were composed, by 'persons of taste and skill'.

Not surprisingly, all four books consist almost exclusively of binary and rondeau forms (there are no chaconnes). But whereas the first and third books are composed mainly of binary movements, more than half the pieces in the second are rondeaux. In the *Pieces . . . en concerts*, binary movements outnumber rondeaux by two to one. Rameau's handling of binary form shows a steady development. In 1706 he still occasionally used the traditional French technique of balancing elegant phrases that are rhythmically connected but otherwise largely independent. In the later collections, motivic organization becomes increasingly tighter, and the integration of the two sections by rhyming terminations, structural symmetry and other means becomes far closer. None of the solo pieces, however, comes as close to sonata form as *La pantomime* in the *Pieces . . . en concerts*, with its brief but unmistakable development section and clearcut recapitulation.

In all three of his mature collections, Rameau

provides lengthy prefaces that give invaluable insights
into the performance and composition of his harpsichord music. Among other things, the 1724 preface
draws attention to two features of his keyboard
writing: *roulements* – virtuoso scale passages of the
sort found in *Les tourbillons*, *Les trois mains* or *La
Cupis* and often involving hand-crossing; and *batteries* – rapid, disjunct figuration of which five main
varieties may be distinguished: (1) the same note or
notes are struck alternately by the two hands (ex.1);
(2) the hands play rapidly in turn, the left alternately
above and below the right (ex.2); (3) the hand rotates
around the thumb in widely-spaced figures of various
shapes (ex.3); (4) one hand is required to make two
successive wide leaps in the same direction (ex.4); and
(5) the hands share brilliant arpeggio figures spanning
up to four octaves. None of these may be found in
the 1706 book but are common from 1724 onwards.

Ex.1 Gavotte, 4me double

Ex.2 *Les cyclopes*

Ex.3 *Les cyclopes*

Ex.4(a) *Les niais de Sologne*

(b) Gavotte, 5me double

Although Rameau's claim to have invented the first two of these may not be entirely justified, his use of such virtuoso figuration is both more extensive and more imaginative than that of any French predecessor and contributes to the muscular yet spacious character of such pieces as the A minor Gavotte and *Les niais de Sologne* (with their multiple *doubles*), *Les cyclopes* and many of the *Pieces . . . en concerts*.

While Rameau's keyboard idiom shows a remarkable flexibility and variety of texture, overt examples of the classic *style luthé* beloved of Couperin and his predecessors are strikingly rare, at least from the second book onwards. Apart from the extraordinarily Couperinesque *Les soupirs*, or *La Livri* from the *Pieces . . . en concerts*, it may be found only fleetingly in the mature collections. Broken-chord figures, often slurred to indicate that notes should be held beyond their written value, continue to form an important element of his style, however. Although the compass required for his works gradually increases from just over four octaves in 1706 to a full five octaves in 1741, Rameau is unusual among the French harpsichord composers in being relatively indifferent to the exploration of unfamiliar keyboard sonorities. He more than compensates, however, in harmonic boldness, at least from the third book (c1729–30) onwards. Examples include the strange progressions of the A major Sarabande, the quirky chromaticisms in *La triomphante* and the G minor Menuet of 1741, and above all the frankly experimental *L'enharmonique*.

On at least 20 occasions Rameau borrowed harpsichord pieces for use in his operas. More numerous are his keyboard arrangements of orchestral originals, even apart from those pieces in the 1724 book (e.g. the musette, tambourin and rigaudons) that are almost certainly derived from the incidental music to *L'Endriague* (1723). In 1735 or 1736 Rameau made harpsichord transcriptions of about two dozen movements from *Les Indes galantes*; these were published in a multi-purpose volume where the opera's set pieces are regrouped into four concert suites. In his arrangements, Rameau uses harpsichord-style ornament signs rather than those normal in opera scores; the arrangements were, however, intended to be played either as solos or as ensemble pieces, and this dual purpose prevented Rameau's using keyboard figuration that could not easily be adapted by other instrumentalists. Even so, many of the pieces are no less idiomatic than, say, *La follette*, *L'indifferente* or the rigaudons of earlier collections. The best of them, the 'Air gratieux pour les Amours', the menuets, the rigaudons and, above all, the 'Air vif pour Zéphire et la Rose', make attractive additions to the repertory. The arrangements make more use of full block chords and left-hand octave passages than do Rameau's earlier keyboard works, foreshadowing the greater use of such features in the *Pieces . . . en concerts.*

In permitting other instrumentalists to double the harpsichord, the arrangements from *Les Indes galantes* might be considered Rameau's first contribution to the genre of accompanied keyboard music. Far more important in this respect, however, is his final collection, the *Pieces de clavecin en concerts*, in which the harpsichord is partnered by a violin or flute and a seven-string *basse de viole* or second violin. From his preface it is clear that the immediate stimulus was Mondonville's *Pieces de clavecin en sonates* op.3 (1734), for harpsichord and violin, though the composer must have been aware of a longer tradition of accompanied keyboard music.

Rameau's technical demands on the players, of harpsichord and viol especially, are high. Indeed, the viol part is one of the most taxing in the repertory: the instrument spends so little time doubling the bass and so much in the higher registers that the composer's alternative part for second violin involves remarkably little adaptation. The collection was published in score, Rameau states, 'because not only must the three instruments blend but . . . the violin and viol must above all adapt themselves to the harpsichord, distinguishing what is merely accompaniment from what is thematic, in order to play still more softly in the former case'. In spite of the subtle and intimate interplay between the three instruments, the harpsichord remains the dominant partner. Indeed, the composer states that the pieces could be played by harpsichord alone; his preface gives detailed instructions as to what small changes would be necessary if this were done, and the volume includes solo arrangements of five pieces that required more extensive adaptation. Although we might not agree with Rameau that such solo versions 'lose nothing', a number of movements, notably those of no.2, deserve to be heard more often in this guise.

Apart from the 1706 collection, surviving exemplars of which are so rare that it was long considered lost, Rameau's harpsichord publications circulated widely. Although there were people who preferred such music 'free of that affected harmony and those risky and brilliant passages that astonish the mind more than they touch and charm the heart' (Titon du Tillet, *Suite du Parnasse françois jusqu'en 1743*, 1743), the collections proved at least as influential as Couperin's. There can be little doubt, however, that they contributed to an emphasis, in the works of his successors, on virtuosity at the expense of emotional depth and intellectual weight. Indeed, Rameau's own last surviving harpsichord pieces, *La Dauphine* and *Les petits marteaux*, cannot escape the same criticism.

## III  Dramatic music

By French standards, Rameau's operatic output was large. Taking into account lengthy prologues and works now lost, it amounts to the equivalent of more than a hundred separate acts. This quantity is the more astonishing in view of the composer's late start at the Opéra and his continued production of theoretical writings.

The operas may be grouped into three periods: 1733–9, 1745–51 and 1753–63. To the first belong five works, the *tragédies Hippolyte et Aricie, Castor et Pollux* and *Dardanus* and the *opéras-ballets Les Indes galantes* and *Les fêtes d'Hébé*. All are now considered among his finest achievements, controversial though they may have been at their first appearance. The second period, more prolific, includes 12 varied and attractive works but few, apart from *Platée* and *Pigmalion*, that are the equal of those of the first. In his final period, Rameau's rate of production slackened as he devoted more of his by now limited energies to theoretical writing. Most of the operas of this period are one-act ballets and pastorales, but there are also two full-length works, including one of his finest, *Les Boréades*. This and the major revisions of *Castor* (1754) and *Zoroastre* (1756) demonstrate that his creative powers had by no means failed.

Rameau's *oeuvre* includes virtually all the subspecies of French opera then current, but is perhaps most remarkable for its emphasis on the *tragédie*. At a time when most composers were paying scant attention to this weightiest and most demanding of French operatic genres, Rameau devoted to it almost a quarter of his output. Only four of his seven *tragédies* were staged during his lifetime (*Samson, Linus* and *Les Boréades* were for various reasons abandoned), but *Dardanus* and *Zoroastre* were so extensively revised for their first revivals that these later versions can almost be considered new works. Rameau himself, in fact, described the revised *Dardanus* as a 'nouvelle tragédie' when he published it in 1744.

Revolutionary though they may at first have seemed, Rameau's *tragédies* now appear firmly rooted in French operatic tradition. This is true of their subject matter (only *Samson* and *Zoroastre* depart from classical myth and legend or medieval romance), of their dramatic structure and organization (all are in five acts, each involving a spectacular *fête* or *divertissement*) and of many important musical details. Rameau's achievement was to invigorate the native tradition by bringing to it a musical imagination of unrivalled fertility, a harmonic idiom of greater richness and variety than that of any French predecessor, and a forcefulness of expression that can still seem astonishing or even over-powering. He may never have been as fortunate as Lully in his choice of librettist (he is known to have shied away from the idea of re-setting Quinault), but the librettos of several of his *tragédies*, notably those by Pellegrin, Bernard and of course Voltaire, are among the finest of the 18th century.

Of the five surviving *tragédies*, the most successful in their integration of music and drama are *Hippolyte et Aricie*, *Castor et Pollux* and *Les Boréades*. There is about *Hippolyte* a tragic grandeur that few of Rameau's other works possess (significantly, the libretto's ancestry can be traced to Euripides by way of Seneca and Racine). This is in no small measure due to the scope that Pellegrin provided for characterization, his eye for impressive and dramatic

257

set-pieces and his skill in placing the obligatory divertissements so that they enhance rather than weaken the action.

In spite of the opera's title, it is not the youthful lovers Hippolytus and Aricia that dominate the drama but rather the tragic figures of Theseus and Phaedra. That of Theseus is the more extensive and powerful. It gains immensely by Pellegrin's decision to devote the whole of Act 2 to the king's selfless journey to Hades, his eloquent pleas for the life of his friend Peirithous and his trial by Pluto's court. In Act 3, Theseus is forced by the welcoming of his loyal subjects to suppress his reactions to what seems an attempt on his wife's honour by his own son; the delay, subtly engineered by Pellegrin, gives extra force to Theseus's eventual outburst, the tragic consequences of which are felt in Act 4. Finally, his attempted suicide when he discovers Hippolytus's innocence, and his dignified acceptance of the punishment exacted by Neptune provide a fitting end to one of the most moving and monumental characterizations in Baroque opera.

The smaller role of Phaedra naturally suffers from comparison with Racine's altogether more subtle study in the psychology of jealousy. But the queen's revelation of her guilty love for her stepson is certainly worthy of Racine, while her expression of remorse at his apparent death is among the outstanding passages in 18th-century opera. Nevertheless, *Hippolyte* was never considered Rameau's finest work during the composer's lifetime. This was undoubtedly the result of the savage cuts, made early in the first run and never restored, that severely weakened the characterization and blunted the opera's impact.

It was, in fact, *Castor et Pollux* that was generally regarded as Rameau's crowning achievement, at least from the time of its first revival (1754) onwards. The opera's subject matter – the brotherly love of the twins Castor and Pollux, the one mortal, the other immortal – was unusual in French opera of the period, which normally concerned itself with romantic love. The central theme of the plot is the generosity of Pollux in renouncing his immortality so that his mortal twin might be restored to life. This provides the motivation for more genuine conflicts of feeling than can be found in any other Rameau opera: the struggle between Pollux's own inclination and his duty, the complication of his love for Castor's bereaved Telaira, the jealousy of the spurned Phoebe and the conflict of the brothers' mutual affection, where neither can be persuaded to return to Earth while the other is condemned to remain in Elysium. This last is particularly marked in the revised, dramatically more taut version of 1754, arguably the best constructed libretto Rameau set.

*Dardanus* and *Zoroastre* are both marred by serious defects in their librettos. The former suffers from an inept and puerile plot. The latter, though its theme is ostensibly the conflict of Good and Evil as found in the dualist religion of ancient Persia (Cahusac's libretto also has masonic overtones), is weakened by various structural flaws and by the introduction of a conventional love element that implausibly involves the great prophet Zoroaster himself. Both works also

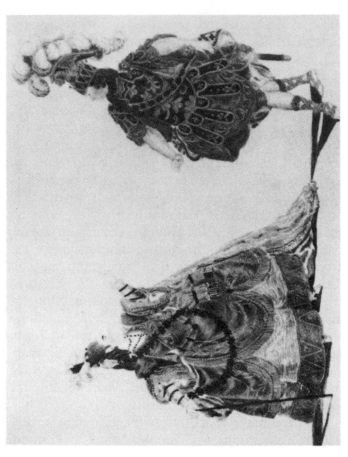

25. Rameau's
'Castor et
Pollux' (Paris,
Opéra, 1737):
costumes for
Phoebe and
Pollux (this
page) and
Telaira and
Castor (p. 261)

261

make excessive use of the supernatural. Although many of the worst failings of these operas were eliminated or lessened at their first revivals, neither opera succeeds more than fitfully in dramatic terms. Yet they are full of music that is at times awe-inspiring in its power and seldom below Rameau's best.

If *Les Boréades* is not quite on the level of *Hippolyte* and *Castor*, it avoids most of the failings of the other *tragédies*. The plot may be conventional but it is competently constructed and is swept along by music so lively and inventive that it is astonishing to realize that Rameau was in his late 70s when he wrote it. Much of the work's character derives from the frequent representations of storms, whirlwinds and the like (the plot involves Boreas, god of the North Wind, and his descendants). Though much of this tempestuous writing is directly linked to the action, it may also be found in the decorative music of the divertissements (e.g. those of Acts 1 and 2) and thus provides a unifying element. Why the opera was abandoned in 1763 is still not known. Doubtless the explanation has to do with changing musical tastes in the 1760s or with the fact that the music is phenomenally difficult to perform on mid-18th-century instruments, particularly the woodwind. It may even be connected with the disastrous fire which burned down the Opéra a few weeks before the two rehearsals that the work is known to have received.

The six *opéras-ballets* belong to the years 1735–48. Rameau was, however, sporadically concerned with the form during his final decade or so, refurbishing earlier works and composing numerous one-act ballets and pastorales that may be considered isolated *opéra-ballet* entrées, to be loosely combined as 'fragments' or 'spectacles coupés', or, like *Les sibarites*, eventually subsumed into an existing *opéra-ballet*.

Cahusac (1754) neatly characterized the differences between *opéra-ballet* and *tragédie*: if the latter was 'un tableau d'une composition vaste' like those of Raphael or Michelangelo, the former comprised 'de jolis Watteau, des miniatures piquantes' that demanded great precision of design, graceful brush-strokes and a brilliant palette of colours. Unlike the *tragédie* with its continuous action, the *opéra-ballet* is made up of three or four acts or entrées, each with its self-contained plot. The subject matter of these is linked to some general theme hinted at in the title (or more often, in Rameau's case, in the subtitle – e.g. *Les fêtes de l'Hymen . . . ou Les dieux d'Egypte*) and expounded during the prologue. In each case, a slender thread of plot leads up to the all-important divertissement, dominated by spectacle, chorus and, above all, ballet.

It would be a mistake to imagine that the limitations of such a genre preclude dramatic interest. The subject matter of *Pigmalion*, for example, is ideally suited to the medium in this respect. The legend is familiar: the sculptor Pygmalion falls hopelessly in love with his own creation, implores the aid of Venus, and is eventually rewarded when the statue comes to life. This simple plot gives rise to a surprisingly wide range of moods – the deeply-felt yearning of Pygmalion's opening monologues, his wonderment and elation as the statue comes to life, the almost uninhibited joy of the final divertissement. It also gives a central position to the obligatory ballet: soon after the statue has come to life, she naturally tries out her steps, at first haltingly but then with growing confidence, until she has encompassed almost the entire range of dance steps.

Spectacle in these works is often suggested by exotic locations. Like all the *entrées* in *Les fêtes de l'Hymen*, 'Canope' is set in ancient Egypt; the action involves preparations for a human sacrifice and culminates in the overflowing of the River Nile. Equally exotic are the locations of *Les Indes galantes*. The four entrées are set respectively in a Turkish garden, a desert in the Peruvian mountains, a Persian market and a village in the North American forests. Three of the entrées culminate in a ritual act: the adoration of the Sun in 'Les Incas du Pérou', a Persian flower festival in 'Les fleurs' and the ceremony of the Great Pipe of Peace in 'Les sauvages'. The librettist cleverly uses these ethnic elements to develop fashionable Enlightenment themes involving the interaction of and contrast between European and other cultures, not always to the former's advantage. In its choice of modern characters, *Les Indes galantes* was reverting to an earlier style of *opéra-ballet* pioneered by Campra in *L'Europe galante* (1697). Rameau's other works in this genre all derive from the more orthodox oriental and Greek myths or legends.

As a genre, the *opéra-ballet* was ideally suited to Rameau's musical talents, and he responded with an almost inexhaustible stream of first-rate and by no means merely decorative music. Not surprisingly, many of the *opéras-ballets* and isolated entrées have proved to be among his most popular and enduring works.

Among Rameau's remaining operas, two principal species may be distinguished: the *pastorale héroïque* and the *comédie lyrique*. Both differ from *opéra-ballet* in their use of a single continuous plot and from *tragédie* in their division usually into three rather than five acts and in their subject matter. This last is self-evident in the *comédies*; for their part, the pastorales lack the sustained dramatic tone of the *tragédie* and place greater emphasis on the decorative divertissement. They are 'heroic' only in that they happen to involve the actions of heroes and gods.

Although none of the pastorales contains any serious emotional conflict or much attempt at characterization, their straightforward plots usually prove adequate to sustain interest from one divertissement to the next. The plots also provide dramatic justification for the divertissements, which are cleverly varied and rich in colour. Those of *Naïs*, for example, involve the ancient Isthmian Games, a country grotto (where the blind soothsayer Tiresias predicts the future by interpreting the song of the birds) and Neptune's undersea palace. Supernatural elements, strong in *Naïs*, are even stronger in *Zaïs* and *Acante et Céphise* which are set in the enchanted world of Middle Eastern mythology, inhabited by spectacular aerial beings. Not surprisingly, all these operas contain an abundance of pastoral music, much of it in the languorous yet wistful mood so characteristic of Rameau.

The *comédie lyrique* was the least established of all the genres that Rameau cultivated. Since the mid-1670s, when Lully eliminated comic roles from his operas, instances of deliberate humour were rare at the Paris Opéra. Isolated examples may be found by Campra (1699), Destouches (1704), La Barre (1705), Mouret (1714 and 1742) and Boismortier (1743). It was perhaps the example of these last two more recent works (Mouret's *Les amours de Ragonde* and Boismortier's *Don Quichotte chez la duchesse*) that stimulated Rameau to choose a comic subject, *Platée*, for the celebration of the Dauphin's marriage in 1745. Much of the humour derives from the ugliness and incongruous behaviour of the marsh-nymph Plataea: a travesty role created by the *haute-contre* Pierre Jélyotte. To the 20th-century mind the choice of subject may seem distasteful or even mischievous (the Dauphine herself is said to have been plain). But Rameau's contemporaries were less fastidious and apparently voiced no such criticism. Though not immediately successful, *Platée* came to be regarded as a masterpiece. That is not an unjust view, for there can be no denying the work's skilful construction and dramatic pace nor the high level of musical and comic invention. Few of these qualities, however, may be found in *Les Paladins*, Rameau's only other essay in the genre. Only the musical invention, astonishing in a septuagenarian, remains as fresh as ever.

Rameau's debt to the French operatic tradition extends to most of the musical forms found in his dramatic works and also to many elements of his style. Few of these elements, however, escaped without reappraisal or intensification. In his recitative, for example, he accepted the fundamental character of the Lullian model, with its meticulously notated declamatory rhythms, its active bass-line and frequent changes of metre; he even accepted many of its turns of phrase. Yet compared with that of his predecessors, Rameau's recitative seems far more flexible and varied. It makes greater use of syncopation, cross-accents and, in later works, triplets, and contains a wider variety of note-values (ex.5). Bold leaps, especially those involving augmented or diminished intervals, are frequent (ex.6), while the severely syllabic style of word-setting is increasingly relieved by discreet use of decorative or expressive detail (ex.7). Above all, Rameau brings to the recitative one of the richest harmonic idioms of his age, full of 7ths, 9ths

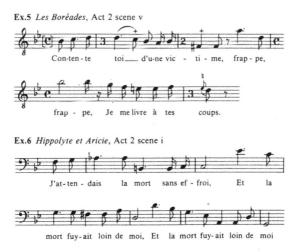

Ex.5 *Les Boréades*, Act 2 scene v

Con-ten-te toi____ d'u-ne vic - ti - me, frap-pe, frap - pe, Je me livre à tes coups.

Ex.6 *Hippolyte et Aricie*, Act 2 scene i

J'at-ten - dais la mort sans ef - froi, Et la mort fuy-ait loin de moi, Et la mort fuy-ait loin de moi

267

Ex.7 *Castor et Pollux* (1754 version), Act 3 scene iii

and other dissonant chords, numerous appoggiaturas, frequent modulations often to remote keys and even occasional enharmonic progressions.

Many of these developments arise from a desire to enhance and intensify the declamation. At the same time, Rameau could not help allowing purely musical considerations to invade his recitative: 'Lully needs actors', Voltaire reports him as saying, 'but I need singers'. It was this greater musical elaboration and complexity that caused many contemporaries to compare his recitative style unfavourable with 'le beau naturel' of Lully's.

Accompanied recitative, though by no means absent from the operas of his predecessors, is used by Rameau with increasing frequency, especially from the mid-1740s onwards. In style it is uniquely French.

The vocal line remains much as in simple recitative, while the accompaniment generally takes one of two principal forms: the first, reserved for solemn pronouncements, consists of organ-like sustained chords involving double-stopped strings and, occasionally, independent lines for woodwind; the second, found in agitated contexts, consists of tremolandos, scales and a variety of energetic figures demanding considerable orchestral agility and co-ordination. Rameau broke new ground in using this sort of accompaniment in passages of dialogue (e.g. *Hippolyte et Aricie*, Act 4 scene iii). In his later operas, accompanied recitative is treated with growing flexibility and may indeed be used to add extraordinary intensity even to the briefest passages (ex.8).

**Ex.8** *Zoroastre* (1756 version), Act 3 scene viii

The vocal *airs* in Rameau's operas, like those of his contemporaries, are of four principal varieties: the dance songs and *ariettes* found exclusively in the divertissements, and the *airs de mouvement* and *monologues* of the main scenes. In most of his dance songs, Rameau adopts the traditional practice of 'parodying' (in this context, adapting words to) an existing dance. In a significant number, however, he reworks the material. Occasionally this reworking is so extensive that *air* and dance have wholly different musical forms (e.g. 'Pénétrez les humains' and the 'Air vif pour les Héros' in the prologue of *Le temple de la Gloire*).

Rameau's treatment of the *ariette* (the French used this diminutive for what, paradoxically, were their longest vocal items) underwent considerable development. In his first operas, these large-scale but essentially decorative da capo arias are not particularly numerous; moreover, vocal display is limited to long held notes and to occasional, fairly brief *vocalises* on certain standard words (*gloire*, *volez* etc). It was doubtless the expertise of singers like Marie Fel, Pierre Jélyotte and Sophie Arnould that encouraged the composer not only to include more *ariettes* in his later operas and revivals but also to increase the element of vocal display. The technical demands of an *ariette* like 'Un horizon serein' (*Les Boréades*, 1/iv), with its high tessitura and extended melismas (ex.9), would have been unthinkable 30 years earlier. Even so, the technique required in Rameau's music remained modest by contemporary Italian standards.

Quite different in character are the vocal set pieces employed outside the divertissements. Much the simplest are the *airs de mouvement* (sometimes known as *petits airs* or *airs tendres*) that are scattered through-

Ex.9 *Les Boréades*, Act 1 scene iv

et sou – le – – – – – – – – –

– – – – – – – ve les mers.

out the recitative. Rameau's treatment of these short airs – some only two or three bars long, most no more than two dozen – differs little from that of his predecessors. He is, however, inclined to make occasional use of orchestral rather than continuo accompaniment and to decorate the melodic line with appreciably more ornament (e.g. 'Que d'un objet aimé', *Les Boréades*, 3/ii).

By far the weightiest 'arias' are the large-scale *monologues* often situated at the beginnings of acts and employed exclusively for expressions of pathos. Rameau was naturally drawn to this type of air which, in the hands of composers such as Campra, Destouches and Montéclair, had already developed into a potent, highly-charged mode of expression. Although most of his *monologues* involve a da capo section, they have stylistically little in common with contemporary Italian da capo arias. The vocal lines, slow-moving, intense and almost entirely syllabic, have the character of heightened recitative. The opening ritornello introduces thematic ideas that are employed, often only loosely, in the subsequent accompaniments but not necessarily in the vocal line itself. Accompaniments tend to be very rich and sombre, as in 'Tristes apprêts' (*Castor et Pollux*, 1/iv)

271

or 'Lieux funestes' (*Dardanus*, 1744 version, 4/i), both of which have important lines for bassoons.

French opera in Rameau's day was as rich in ensembles and choruses as it had always been. In this, it contrasts strikingly with contemporary *opera seria* where such elements had become rare. Yet even by French standards, Rameau's first opera contains a high proportion of ensembles, several of them (e.g. the enharmonic Trio des Parques, *Hippolyte*, 3/iv) quite extensive. The opera includes a number of duets in which the characters express conflicting ideas in terse and vigorous counterpoint. To many Frenchmen, this sort of ensemble seemed wholly irrational; in response to criticism, therefore, Rameau shortened several of them during the first run of *Hippolyte* and thereafter composed fewer ensembles of this type. Duets in which the singers express the same sentiment remain an important ingredient. One of his late works, the 1756 version of *Zoroastre,* includes as many as eight, three of them admittedly very short. In these 'unanimous' duets, counterpoint is not wholly eliminated; it plays a very important part, for example, in 'Mânes plaintifs' (*Dardanus*, 1/iii). But more characteristic, especially in love duets, is a homorhythmic style in which parallel 3rds and 6ths predominate.

In their richness, variety and dramatic power, Rameau's choruses are comparable with those of the Handel oratorios and the Bach passions. They are deployed in the traditional French manner, either as important decorative components of the divertissements or as agents in the drama itself. It is in the latter role that the chorus is at its most powerful and expressive, whether in its reactions to dramatic events such as battles (*Castor*, 1754 version, 1/v), spectacular natural or supernatural phenomena (*Les fêtes de l'Hymen*, 1/vii) or, above all, to the deaths of protagonists (*Hippolyte*, 4/iii, iv; *Castor*, 1/i). Sometimes the distinction between divertissement and action choruses is blurred, as in those that occur during Theseus's trial by Pluto's court (*Hippolyte*, 2/iii, iv) or during Abramane's occult sacrifice (*Zoroastre*, 4/vi, vii). In the latter, the successive choruses build up to a climax of unprecedented ferocity as the forces of evil rouse themselves to vengeance.

Rameau normally maintained the traditional distinction between the *grand choeur*, or full four-part chorus in which the 'alto' part was sung by high tenors (*hautes-contre*), and the *petit choeur*, a semi-chorus consisting generally of three upper voice parts. Occasionally he would divide the *grand choeur* into as many as eight (e.g. 'Impétueux torrents', *Les fêtes de l'Hymen*, 1/vii). Here and elsewhere, he combines the chorus with independent lines for the principal singers. The chorus 'Quel bonheur, l'Enfer nous seconde' (*Zoroastre*, 4/vi) combines a three-part men's choir with lines for three furies and the allegorical figure of La Vengeance.

In his treatment of the orchestra, Rameau is generally more original than in his writing for voices, eloquent though that often is. Not only in the accompaniments to vocal pieces but also in the many purely instrumental movements, his eclectic approach and imaginative orchestration (the latter often misrepresented in the *Oeuvres complètes*) help create music of almost symphonic richness and variety. His introduction of instruments new to France (orchestral horns from about 1745, clarinets from 1749) is paralleled by his experimentation with instrumental techniques previously seldom used at the Opéra: pizzicato from 1744, glissando in 1745. With younger contemporaries such as Royer and Mondonville, he gradually developed a much more varied approach to the combining of wind and strings. In his later works he pioneered a style of orchestration less concerned with blend than with a 'counterpoint of timbres' – an approach to scoring in which superimposed layers are distinguished not only by instrumental timbre but also by their thematic material.

Orchestral virtuosity is at its greatest in the purely instrumental movements – the dances and various sorts of dramatic *symphonie*. Rameau's ballet music is second to none in its freshness and variety. Diderot was, of course, exaggerating when he claimed that before Rameau 'no-one had distinguished the delicate shades of expression that separate the tender from the voluptuous, the voluptuous from the impassioned, the impassioned from the lascivious'. But the composer's ability to capture a wider range of moods in his dance music, as elsewhere, is indeed one of his most remarkable gifts – the more remarkable given the limitations of form, phrase structure and rhythm imposed by contemporary choreography. Almost without exception he breathes new life into the standard patterns of menuet, gavotte, tambourin and the rest; at the same time, he vividly characterizes freer movements bearing such titles as 'Air tendre pour les Muses' or 'Air pour les guerriers'. No other Baroque dance music seems so clearly to suggest its own choreography. As the famous ballet-master Claude Gardel was modestly to admit: 'Rameau perceived what the dancers themselves were unaware of; we thus rightly regard him as our first master'.

Clear signs of Rameau's desire to integrate the instrumental movements can be seen in his development of the *ballet figuré* and dramatic entr'acte and in his re-thinking of the role of the overture. The *ballet figuré*, in which the dancers present a stylized action linked to that of the drama, may be found sporadically in the earlier 18th century and before; but it was not until Rameau – or rather his librettist Cahusac – championed the idea in their works of the 1740s that examples become plentiful. The dramatic entr'acte appears in the Rameau operas at about the same period. Traditionally, the entr'acte had almost always consisted of the repetition of an instrumental movement drawn almost at random from the act that had just ended. The 1744 version of *Dardanus*, however, includes a newly-composed *bruit de guerre* accompanying offstage action between Acts 4 and 5. An expanded version of this was used in 1754 between Acts 1 and 2 of *Castor*. Further specially composed entr'actes may be found in *Naïs*, *Acante et Céphise*, the 1756 version of *Zoroastre* and *Les Boréades*.

More significant is Rameau's transformation of the overture from an isolated introductory movement into one closely connected with the ensuing drama. Though briefly anticipated in *Castor*, the idea of

275

connecting the two did not gain ground until the mid-1740s. From that date, several of Rameau's overtures contain tone-paintings that clearly foreshadow the action (e.g. *Pigmalion, Zaïs, Zoroastre* and *Acante et Céphise*). Others are linked musically to a later scene (e.g. *Platée, La naissance d'Osiris* and *Les Paladins*). Some fall into both categories (e.g. *Les fêtes de Polymnie, Les surprises de l'Amour, Naïs* and *Les Boréades*). In all of these, Rameau anticipated Gluck by several decades. Rameau was also the first to diversify the form and style of the overture. Only those of his first two *tragédies* can truly be said to preserve the spirit of the Lullian French overture. Several of his later works adopt the general form – or even, in the case of *La princesse de Navarre*, the style – of the contemporary Italian overture with its two fast movements flanking a slower one.

In spite of such developments, it is remarkable how little Rameau's concept of opera seems to have changed when one views his output as a whole. *Hippolyte et Aricie* and *Les Boréades*, for instance, have much in common though separated by 30 years. The only major structural difference is the absence in the later work of the traditional prologue, considered redundant from the time of *Zoroastre* (1749) onwards. Yet even in his 60s and 70s, Rameau remained receptive to new musical fashions. His lofty and dignified idiom of the 1730s became noticeably influenced during the next two decades by the lighter German and Italian styles of the mid-18th century and softened by a proliferation of ornamental detail. The differences of style appear most acute from the

1750s onwards whenever new music was added to revivals of older operas.

A number of Rameau's works remained in the Opéra's repertory after the composer's death. Few, however, survived beyond 1770 and fewer still beyond the middle of that decade, when Gluck's operas took Paris by storm. Those that did survive were subjected to the same sort of reworking as the rest of the 'ancien répertoire'. There were those people, a small minority, who deplored what they saw as this corruption of taste. To Decroix, it even seemed a contributory cause of the Revolution.

CHAPTER THREE

# Theoretical writings

Rameau's writings show him as a true product of the Age of Reason. As a theorist he sought to reduce music to a science, and to derive universal harmonic principles from natural causes; as a musician he attempted to adapt these principles to the service of musical practice – notably, keyboard accompaniment and composition. His ideas continued to evolve and mature throughout his career; but they are based on several novel, fundamental concepts already proposed in his earliest and, in many ways, most influential and important work, the *Traité de l'harmonie*.

Rameau maintained that all music is founded on harmony, which arises from natural principles derived from the mathematical and physical bases of a vibrating body (*corps sonore*). Building on Zarlino's earlier work (adopting, in particular, the mathematical proofs of the *senario*), and using Descartes' empirical methodology, he argued the essential unity of harmony, represented in the fundamental sound (*son fondamental*).

Through an understanding of the physical nature of the fundamental sound, he developed the basic concepts that formed the central focus of his harmonic theories: harmonic generation (*génération harmonique*), harmonic inversion (*renversement*) and

278

the fundamental bass (*basse fondamentale*). He noted that each fundamental tone generates a sound that is naturally divisible into component parts, from which are derived the primary consonances in music, in order of relative perfection: octave, 5th and major 3rd. Their combination forms the perfect chord, the major triad. In the *Nouveau système* and later works, using results of the acoustical studies of Mersenne and especially Sauveur, Rameau determined that these intervals are naturally present (as partials) along with the fundamental in the sound produced by a vibrating body. To the primary consonances he added the minor 3rd, which he first obtained from the difference between the natural intervals of the 5th and the major 3rd. Later he offered alternative, though not conclusive, explanations for the derivation of minor. These included: a row of reciprocal tones inversely proportional to the overtone series (in *Génération*), thereby adopting Zarlino's theory of dualism, earlier rejected (in *Traité*); a theory of multiple generation, in which two fundamental sounds a minor 3rd apart are related as generators of a common tone, the third of a major triad being the fifth of its relative minor (in *Démonstration*); and the upper partials of a vibrating body, where the minor triad is formed by the ratios 10:12:15 (in *Code*).

Rameau considered the octave, the most perfect of the primary intervals, to be a replica (*réplique*) of the fundamental, which it represents regardless of position; from this followed the concept of harmonic inversion, applied to both intervals and chords. The primary consonances, through inversion, produce the

279

secondary: 4th, minor 6th and major 6th. Whether or not the fundamental sound is present in the bottom part of an interval or chord, it is understood as its generator tone and harmonic root. In music, a sequence of these roots is called the fundamental bass (distinct from the actual or thorough bass), which provides the foundation for Rameau's theories of harmonic succession.

Basic to harmonic progression in Rameau's system are two chord formations from which all other chords are derived: the perfect triad (*accord parfait*), major or minor, the source for consonance in music; and the 7th chord (*accord de la septième*), the source for dissonance. Normally, chords are not to exceed an octave in fundamental position, nor are they to be without a perfect 5th, an interval that Rameau regarded as the most important harmonic element in music. Chords lacking the 5th were considered incomplete, altered or inverted (including diminished and augmented triads, which he only later admitted to his system). Chords of the 9th or 11th were understood as formed by substitution (*accords par supposition*), where incomplete 7th chords were supplied with fundamental notes added a 3rd or 5th below the chord bass – notes which could not be inverted but determined the harmonic succession of the chord. Only later (in *Code*) did he classify the suspension as a type of *supposition*.

In discussing the construction of the 7th chord, Rameau projected a second theory of chord generation by 3rds: except for two major 3rds in succession, major and minor 3rds may be added to each other or to triads on different scale steps to form various species of 7th. Of these, the major triad with an added minor 3rd is considered the most perfect; it contains the fundamental harmonic dissonances from which all others derive: the major dissonance (diminished 5th) and the minor (minor 7th). The proper resolution of these intervals and, consequently, of this 7th chord to the perfect triad (both in root position) characterizes the perfect cadence (*cadence parfaite*), the most conclusive progression in music. Here the 7th chord, called *dominante tonique*, is found on a root a 5th above the perfect triad, called *tonique*; if the cadence involves inversion, it is considered imperfect (*imparfaite*). Other cadence types described by Rameau include: the irregular cadence (*cadence irrégulière*), where the tonic is followed by the dominant; the broken or deceptive cadence (*cadence rompuë*), where the dominant resolves to a triad on the sixth degree; and the interrupted cadence (*cadence interrompuë*), where the dominant resolves to another dominant a 3rd below. For Rameau, cadences provided the basis for harmonic progression in music – harmonic motion being regarded as a succession of cadences – as well as for the concepts of key (*ton*) and modulation (*modulation*). Root progression by 5ths is central to harmonic succession; that by 3rds engenders chromaticism and is useful in effecting key change.

The subdominant (*sous-dominante*) has a special place in Rameau's system, though he was never able completely to justify its importance on theoretical grounds. First named in the *Nouveau système*, it is explained through the perfection of the triple geomet-

# TRAITÉ
## DE
# L'HARMONIE
### Reduite à ſes Principes naturels;

*DIVISÉ EN QUATRE LIVRES.*

**LIVRE I.** Du rapport des Raiſons & Proportions Harmoniques.

**LIVRE II.** De la nature & de la proprieté des Accords;
Et de tout ce qui peut ſervir à rendre une
Muſique parfaite.

**LIVRE III.** Principes de Compoſition.

**LIVRE IV.** Principes d'Accompagnement.

*Par Monſieur RAMEAU, Organiſte de la Cathedrale
de Clermont en Auvergne.*

### DE L'IMPRIMERIE
De JEAN-BAPTISTE-CHRISTOPHE BALLARD, Seul
Imprimeur du Roy pour la Muſique. A Paris, ruë Saint Jean-
de-Beauvais, au Mont-Parnaſſe.

### M. DCC. XXII.
*AVEC PRIVILEGE DU ROY.*

*26. Title-page of Rameau's 'Traité de l'harmonie' (1722)*

ric progression, 1:3:9, where the tonic forms the central note of a sequence of 5ths flanked by two dominants, one above and one below. In the *Démonstration* Rameau altered his view of the subdominant and recognized its position as a product of musical experience rather than of nature; he reaffirmed that in later writings. The subdominant was assigned a singular role in harmonic progression. Rameau indicated that in cadences, as a rule, a perfect chord should appear only on the tonic; all other chords require a dissonance, normally the 7th. The dissonance assigned to the subdominant, however, was the added 6th, and there developed in his writings a specific theory of the derivation and use of this chord complex called *double-emploi*, which related to the double meaning of the chord depending on context: as subdominant with an added 6th, and as an inverted 7th chord on the second degree. Thus he justified the direct progression of subdominant to dominant within his harmonic system.

Throughout his writings Rameau continued to resort to 'the judgment of the ear' (*le jugement de l'oreille*) and to 'good taste' (*bon goût*) in seeking resolutions to problems insoluble through scientific or natural means, a recourse which provoked criticism. In his system he considered temperament a practical necessity, as a means of making possible modulation and motion by 5ths of fundamental sounds. Also, while maintaining that melody is derived from harmony, he stressed the need for adding ornamental dissonances (*notes d'ornement ou de goût*) to the harmonic notes of a melodic line in the interest of variety and taste.

283

Like many of his contemporaries, Rameau asserted that the primary aesthetic purpose of music was to express, to please the ear and to move the passions; he viewed harmony, however, as the fundamental source determining the essential character and coherence of musical expression. Late in his work (particularly in *Observations*, *Code* and *Origine des sciences*), he attempted to relate proportion in music to that in other disciplines, and sought to confirm the derivation of music from a universal, cosmic principle founded on nature and on unity (*le principle de tout est un*).

The influence of Rameau's theories was immediate and widespread. Based on study of both practical and theoretical writings on music and science that appeared in his own time and in the preceding century (principally French, Italian and Latin sources), his ideas underwent continuous re-evaluation and clarification throughout his works, and formed a broad base for the investigation and understanding of the nature of harmony for some 200 years. Rameau corresponded and debated with critics throughout Europe (notably Castel, Montéclair, Estève, Serre, Bollioud-Mermet, Mattheson, Euler, Martini, D'Alembert and Rousseau) on many issues raised in his works, bringing to a wide, international forum the testing of his concepts on practical and scientific grounds. He also sought approbation, successfully, from the French scientific academy, although he later broke with the Encylopédistes. Hardly a theorist from the period or from succeeding generations who wrote on harmony escaped the need to relate his work to

Rameau's, and the development of several national schools in music theory can be traced directly to his influence (notably in France, England and Germany). His ideas were points of departure for works by such significant theorists as Tartini, Marpurg, Fétis, Day, Hauptmann, Helmholtz, Oettingen, Riemann, d'Indy and Hindemith, and thereby occupy a crucial position in the development of harmonic thinking in Western music.

# WORKS

Editions: J.-P. Rameau: *Oeuvres complètes*, ed. C. Saint-Saëns, C. Malherbe and others (Paris, 1895–1924/R1968) [OC]
    J.-P. Rameau: *Pièces de clavecin*, ed. E. R. Jacobi (Kassel, 1958, rev.4/1972) [Jc]
    J.-P. Rameau: *Pièces de clavecin*, ed. K. Gilbert (Paris, 1979) [G]
    Rameau: *The Musical Works*, ed. N. Zaslaw and F. Lesure (in preparation) [Z]
Writings: J.-P. Rameau: *Complete Theoretical Writings*, ed. E. R. Jacobi (Rome, 1967–72) [Jw]
Numbers in the right-hand margins denote references in the text.

## DRAMATIC

All were performed at the Paris Opéra [L'Académie Royale de Musique] unless otherwise stated; information only given for 1st performances and principal revivals within Rameau's lifetime. The date of last complete or near-complete 18th-century performance at the Opéra is given in parentheses.

    * – wholly or largely autograph; † – contains autograph sections, passages, revisions and/or annotations

255–77

| Title (genre; no. of acts) | Libretto | Principal sources | Performance | Remarks | Edition | |
|---|---|---|---|---|---|---|
| Hippolyte et Aricie (tragédie en musique; prol, 5) | S.-J. Pellegrin | print: (Paris, c1733) [some copies with 'Changements conformes à la représentation'; some with revs made for 1742 revival; F-Pc, Pm, US Medford Tufts U., with MS revs; copy, †F-Po]; MSS: Dc, Pa, Pc, Pm [one with pr. title (Paris, 1742)], Po, V, GB-Cfm | 1 Oct 1733 / 11 Sept 1742, 25 Feb 1757 (28 June 1767) | major cuts and substitutions during first run | OC vi | 219, 220, 221, 227, 256, 257–9, 269 273, 276 |
| Samson (tragédie en musique; 5) | Voltaire | music lost; lib (Paris, 1745); MS libs: F-Pa, S-Sk and USSR Leningrad, Hermitage | unperf. | lib begun by Dec 1733; ov., chaconne, dances, Acts 3 and 5 rehearsed ?Oct 1734, subsequently abandoned; music said to have been re-used in Les Indes galantes (entrée Les Incas), Castor et Pollux, Les fêtes d'Hébé and Zoroastre; text (and probably music) of air 'Echo, voix errante' used in La princesse de Navarre and rev. of Les fêtes de Polymnie (1753) | lib in L. Moland, ed. *Voltaire: Oeuvres complètes*, iii (Paris, 1877–85) | 220, 256 |

| Title | Librettist | Sources | Date | Revisions/notes | Edition | Refs |
|---|---|---|---|---|---|---|
| Les Indes galantes [formerly Les victoires galantes] (opéra-ballet; prol, 2–4 entrées: Le turc généreux / Les Incas du Pérou / Les fleurs / Les sauvages) | L. Fuzelier | print: (Paris, c1736) [prol and 1st 3 entrées arr. as Quatre grands concerts; also contains new entrée Les sauvages]; MSS: *F-AG, Pa, Pc, Pn, Po* [one with pr. title (Paris, 1735)], *TLm, GB-Cfm,* | 23 Aug 1735 | prol, 2 entrées | OC vii | 215, 220, 221, 227, 232, 247, 256, 264 |
| | | | 28 Aug 1735 | 3rd entrée added; some rev. of prol and first 2 entrées | | |
| | | | 10 March 1736 | 4th entrée added | | |
| | | | 28 May 1743 | prol, various combinations of 3 or 4 entrées; from Feb 1744, prol and 2nd entrée perf. with other works | | |
| | | | 8 June 1751 | prol, entrées 1–3; from 3 Aug, Les sauvages replaced Le turc généreux; from 21 Sept, Les sauvages perf, with other works; from 24 Oct, prol, Les sauvages, Les Incas, Les fleurs | | |
| | | | 14 July 1761 | prol, entrées 1–3; from 18 Aug, Les sauvages replaced Le turc généreux; from 20 July 1762, prol and Les sauvages perf. with La guirlande | | |
| Castor et Pollux (tragédie en musique; prol, 5) | P.-J. Bernard | prints: (Paris, c1737) (Paris, c1754) [copy in *F-Pc* with MS revs]; MSS: *A, AG, AIXc,* Bibliothèque de Clermont-de-l'Oise, *Dc, Mc, NAc, Pa, Pn, Po, TLm, GB-Cfm, I-Baf, US-I* | (20 Sept 1761) 24 Oct 1737 | no prol, new Act 1, former Acts 1–5 reworked as Acts 2–5; some new music | OC viii | 219, 221, 233, 256, 257, 259, 260–1, 271–2, 273, 275 |
| | | | 8/11 June 1754 | minor rev. | | |
| Les fêtes d'Hébé, ou Les talents lyriques, (opéra-ballet; prol, 3 entrées: La poésie / La musique / La danse) | A. G. de Montdorge [?addns by Bernard, Pellegrin and A.-J. Le Riche de La Pouplinière] | prints: (Paris, c1739) [some copies with rev. 2nd entrée], (Paris, c1756 or later) [copies with rev. 2nd entrée, comprising either scenes i–iv or i–vi]; MSS: *F-AG, Pa, Pc, Pn* [one with pr. title (Paris, 1739)], *Po, GB-Cfm* | 21 May 1739 | from 23 June with rev. 2nd entrée | OC ix; edn. in Cyr (1975) | 220, 256 |
| | | | 27 July 1747 | minor revs; incl. 1 air by Le Vasseur | | |
| | | | 18 May 1756 | 1st entrée rev. | | |
| | | | 5 June 1764 | without prol; from 10 Jan 1765 prol reinstated | | |
| | | | (9 May 1765) | | | |

| Title (genre; no. of acts) | Libretto | Principal sources | Performance | Remarks | Edition | |
|---|---|---|---|---|---|---|
| Dardanus (tragédie en musique; prol, 5) | C.-A. Le Clerc de la Bruére | prints: (Paris, c1739), (Paris, c1744) [proof copy, †F-Po, copies in Po with MS revs]; MSS: AG, Pa, Pc, Pn [one with pr. title (Paris, 1739)], Po, TLm, GB-Cfm | 19 Nov 1739 / 23 April 1744 / 15 April 1760 / (29 March 1770) | cuts, addns and other changes (?collab. S.-J. Pellegrin) during 1st run / rev. as Nouvelle tragédie; major changes to plot, Acts 3–5 largely new music / without prol; further rev. | OC x | 219, 227, 256-7, 259-60, 275 |
| La princesse de Navarre (comédie-ballet; 3) | Voltaire | MSS: F-BO, Pc, Pn; lib (Paris, 1745) | Versailles, 23 Feb 1745 / Bordeaux, 26 Nov 1763 | for wedding of Dauphin with Maria Teresa of Spain; incl. spoken dialogue / with new prol by Voltaire | OC xi | 221, 228, 229, 232, 276 |
| Platée (comédie lyrique; prol: La naissance de la Comédie, 3) | J. Autreau adapted by A.-J. Le Valois d'Orville | print: (Paris, c1749) [proof copy, †Po]; MSS: Pa, Pn, Po | Versailles, 31 March 1745 / 9 Feb 1749 / 21 Feb 1754 / (28 March 1754) | for wedding of Dauphin with Maria Teresa of Spain / lib altered by Ballot de Sovot | OC xii | 221, 228, 256, 266, 276 |
| Les fêtes de Polymnie (opéra-ballet; prol: Le temple de mémoire, 3 entrées: La fable, L'histoire, La féerie | L. de Cahusac | print: (Paris, c1753) [proof copy, †Po]; MSS: Pa, Pn [one with pr. title (Paris, 1745)], †Po | 12 Oct 1745 / 21 Aug 1753 / (16 May 1754) | prol for victory of Fontenoy; cuts during 1st run / most cuts reinstated; some new music | OC xiii | 221, 228, 276 |
| Le temple de la Gloire (opéra-ballet; 5) | Voltaire | MSS: Pa, Pmeyer, †Pn, †Po, V, US-BE | Versailles, 27 Nov 1745 / 7 Dec 1745 / 19 April 1746 / (10 May 1746) | for victory of Fontenoy / rev. as prol (La caverne de l'Envie) and 3 entrées (Bélus, Bacchus, Trajan) | OC xiv | 228, 270, 282 |

| | | | | | | |
|---|---|---|---|---|---|---|
| Les fêtes de Ramire (acte de ballet; 1) | Voltaire (?rev. J.-J. Rousseau) | MS: *F.-V*; lib (Paris, 1745) | Versailles, 22 Dec 1745 | re-use of divertissements from La princesse de Navarre, linked by new lib and without spoken dialogue; copy in *F-V* contains at least one air (and ? some recit) by Rousseau, but not the ov. and other nos. he claims to have written | OC xi | |
| Les fêtes de l'Hymen et de l'Amour, ou Les dieux d'Egypte (opéra-ballet; prol, 3 entrées: Osiris Canope Aruéris ou Les Isies) | Cahusac | print: (Paris, *c*1748) [proof copy, *Po*, with addns, some†]; MSS: *AG*, *Pa*, *Pn* | Versailles, 15 March 1747 5 Nov 1748 9 July 1754 (9 July 1765) | for wedding of Dauphin with Maria-Josepha of Saxony without prol | OC xv | 263, 264, 273 |
| Zaïs (pastorale héroïque; prol, 4) | Cahusac | print: (Paris, *c*1748) [some copies with suppl. of addns; 2 copies, *Pc*, with MS addns; proof copy, †*Po*]; MSS: Compiègne, Bibliothèque municipale, *Pa, Pn* | 29 Feb 1748 19 May 1761 (22 March 1770) | without prol | OC xvi | 265, 276 |
| Pigmalion (acte de ballet; 1) | Ballot de Sovot, after A. Houdar de La Motte: *Le triomphe des arts* (entrée: La sculpture) | print: (Paris, *c*1748) [copy in *V*, annotated and corrected; MSS: *AG, BO, LYm, Pa, Pc, Pn*, †*Po* | 27 Aug 1748 9 March 1751 10 Aug 1760 31 March 1764 (22 March 1781) | perf. with other works perf. with other works perf. with other works perf. with other works | OC xvii/1 | 256, 263-4, 276 |
| Les surprises de l'Amour (opéra-ballet; prol: Le retour d'Astrée, 2 entrées: La lyre enchantée Adonis [from 1757, L'enlèvement d'Adonis]) | Bernard | first version: MSS: *Pn*, \**Pc* [prol only] later versions: prints: (Paris, *c*1755) [incl. L'enlèvement d'Adonis, La lyre enchantée and Anacréon; some copies incl. Les sibarites]: all entrées also issued separately (Paris, *c*1757); La lyre enchantée repr. (Paris, *c*1758) with changes; MSS: *Pn*, †*Po* | Versailles, 27 Nov 1748 31 May 1757 10 Oct 1758 (8 Feb 1759) | prol for Peace of Aix-la-Chapelle without prol, major rev. of entrées, with Anacréon (ii) as 3rd entrée; from 12 July, Les sibarites, (1753) replaced La lyre enchantée as 31 May 1757 but with rev. of La lyre enchantée and Anacréon (ii); from 7 Dec, Les sibarites replaced Anacréon | OC xvii/1 | 228, 276 |

| Title (genre; no. of acts) | Libretto | Principal sources | Performance | Remarks | Edition | |
|---|---|---|---|---|---|---|
| Naïs (pastorale héroïque; prol: 'L'accord des dieux', 3) | Cahusac | MSS: Lm, Pa, Pc, Pn, Po, US-Bp, Wc | 22 April 1749 | prol for Peace of Aix-la-Chapelle | OC xviii | 265, 275, 276 |
| | | | 7 Aug 1764 | P.-M. Berton claims to have made addns and revs | | |
| Zoroastre (tragédie en musique; 5) | Cahusac | print: (Paris, c1749) [annotated copies in F-Pa, Pc, Po, V]; MSS: Pa, Pc, Pn, Po, TLm, GB-Cfm | (3 Jan 1765) 5 Dec 1749 19 Jan 1756 | major rev. of plot; music of Acts 2, 3 and 5 largely new | ed. F. Gervais (Paris, 1964) | 221, 230, 233, 256, 259-60, 272, 273, 275, 276 |
| | | | (26 Jan 1770) | | | |
| Linus (tragédie en musique; 5) | Le Clerc de la Bruère | MSS: F-Pn [2 copies of vn 1 only, one †] | unperf. | rehearsed in or before 1752; most music lost, MS lib in Pn | — | 231, 256 |
| La guirlande, ou Les fleurs enchantées (acte de ballet; 1) | J.-F. Marmontel | print: (Paris: c1751) [†proof copy, and copy with addns and revs in Po]; MSS: AG, Pa, Pn | 21 Sept 1751 | with Les sauvages (from Les Indes galantes) and Les génies tutélaires (by F. Rebel and F. Francoeur) | ed. G. Beck (Paris, 1981) | |
| | | | 11 April 1752 | with Zelindor, roi des sylphes (by Rebel and Francoeur) and Pigmalion | | |
| | | | 20 July 1762 | with prol and Les sauvages (from Les Indes galantes) | | |
| Acante et Céphise, ou La sympathie (pastorale héroïque; 3) | Marmontel | print: (Paris, c1751) [copy in Pn with MS revs; proof copies, †Po]; MSS: Pa, Pc, Pn, †Po | (5 Sept 1763) 19 Nov 1751 | for birth of Duke of Burgundy | — | 265, 275, 276 |
| Daphnis et Eglé (pastorale héroïque; 1) | C. Collé | MSS: Pn, *Po | Fontainebleau, 30 Oct 1753 | — | — | 237 |
| Lysis et Délie (pastorale; 1) | Marmontel | music lost; lib (Paris, 1753) | unperf. | intended for perf. at Fontainebleau, 6 Nov 1753, but considered too similar to Daphnis et Eglé, abandoned | — | |

| Title | Librettist | Sources | Date, place | Remarks | Edition | References |
|---|---|---|---|---|---|---|
| Les sibarites (acte de ballet; 1) | Marmontel | print: (Paris, c1757); MSS: *Pn*, *Po* | Fontainebleau, 13 Nov 1753; 12 July 1757, 7 Dec 1758 (8 Feb 1759) | perf. with La coquette trompée (A. Dauvergne); entitled 'Sibaris' in some sources rev., added to revival of Les surprises de l'Amour | OC xvii/2 | 263 |
| La naissance d'Osiris, ou La fête Pamilie (acte de ballet; 1) | Cahusac | MSS: *Pc, Pn, *Po* | Fontainebleau, 12 Oct 1754 | for birth of Duke of Berry; with Les Incas du Pérou (from Les Indes galantes) and Pigmalion; at one stage entitled Les fêtes Pammilies; orig. intended as prol to (?projected) opéra-ballet Les beaux jours de l'Amour | — | 276 |
| Anacréon (i) (acte de ballet; 1) | Cahusac | MSS: †*Pc, Pn, Po* | Fontainebleau, 23 Oct 1754 | | — | |
| Anacréon (ii) (acte de ballet; 1) | Bernard | print: (Paris, c1757); MSS: *Pn, Po* | 31 May 1757 | added to revival of Les surprises de l'Amour as 3rd entrée | OC xvii/2 | |
| Les Paladins (comédie lyrique; 3) | anon. | MSS: *Pc, *Pn, †Po, GB-Cfm* | (2 May 1771) 12 Feb 1760 | lib attrib. D. de Monticourt by Beffara (1783–4) and in the Soleinne lib collection (*F-Pn*); attrib. P.-J. Bernard by Collé, who mentions C.-H. de Voisenon and de Tressan as possibilities | ed. in Wolf (1977); facs. (New York, 1986) | 233, 234, 266, 276 |
| Les Boréades (tragédie en musique; 5) | ?Cahusac | MSS: *F-Pc, †Pn, US-Bp* | (20 March 1760) unperf. | entitled Abaris in some sources; rehearsed Paris [25 April 1763]; Versailles [27 April 1763]; court perf. planned; lib attrib. Cahusac in Decroix [1776] and A. B. Teulières, continuator of Cathala-Coture: *Histoire politique, ecclésiastique et littéraire du Querci* (Montauban, 1785) | ed. in Térey-Smith (1971); facs. (Paris, 1982); *frags in Green, *Dijon 1983* | 233, 234, 256, 257, 262, 270, 271, 275, 276 |

| Title (genre; no. of acts) | Libretto | Principal sources | Performance | Remarks | Edition |
|---|---|---|---|---|---|
| Nélée et Myrthis (acte de ballet; 1) | anon. | MSS: *Pc, Pn | unperf. | autograph title: Mirthis; intended as one entrée in (?projected) opéra-ballet Les beaux jours de l'Amour. See La naissance d'Osiris. | OC xi |
| Zéphyre (acte de ballet; 1) | anon. | MSS: *Pc, Pn | unperf. | orig. entitled Les nymphes de Diane | OC xi |
| Io (acte de ballet; 1) | anon. | MSS: Pc, Pn | unperf. | all sources lack final divertissement | — |

Incidental music to plays by A. Piron (music by Rameau, possibly collab. others), all lost unless otherwise stated; plays pr. in *Oeuvres complettes d'Alexis Piron* (Paris, 1776): L'Endriague, opéra comique (3 acts), Foire St Germain, 8 Feb 1723; L'enrôlement d'Arlequin, opéra comique (1 act), Foire St Laurent, 3 Feb 1726; La P[ueclage], ou La rose, opéra comique (1 act), by July 1726, unperf., rev. as Le jardin de l'Hymen, ou La rose, Foire St Laurent, 5 March 1744, probably without Rameau's original music but with 1 air parodied from Hippolyte et Aricie; La robe de dissension, ou Le faûx prodige, opéra comique (2 acts), Foire St Laurent, 7 Sept 1726; Les courses de Tempé, pastorale (1 act), Comédie Française, 30 Aug 1734, extant vocal part of airs pr. in Sadler (1974) — 215, 253; 221

Doubtful: Le procureur dupe sans le savoir, opéra comique mêlé de vaudevilles (1 act), c1758, music lost; anon. lib (F-Pn) ?copied from a scoret found among Rameau's papers

### OTHER SECULAR VOCAL

Deux paysans (duet), S, B, bc, in Recueil d'airs sérieux et à boire de différents auteurs (Paris, 1707); facs. in Masson (1910)

Avec du vin (canon), S, S, T, in Recueil d'airs sérieux et à boire de différents auteurs (Paris, 1719); pubd in Traité de l'harmonie (1722); F. Robert, ed.: Airs sérieux et à boire à 2 et 3 voix (Paris, 1968); facs. in Jw i — 245

Ah! loin de rire (canon), S, A, T, B, pubd in Traité de l'harmonie (1722); F. Robert, ed.: Airs sérieux et à boire à 2 et 3 voix (Paris, 1968); facs. in Jw i

Reveillez-vous, dormeur sans fin (canon), S, S, S, S, S, pubd in Traité de l'harmonie (1722); facs. in Jw i

Mes chers amis, quittez vos rouges bords (canon), pr. in La Borde (1780); transcr. Schneider, RMFC (1985) — 245

Thétis (cantata), B, vn, bc, c1715–July 1718 (attrib. Bourgeois in F-Pn Vm⁷3613); OC iii — 211, 244

Aquilon et Orithie (cantata), B, vn, bc, c1715–19, rev. version pubd in Rameau: Cantates françoises à voix seule avec simphonie . . . livre premier (Paris, c1729–30); OC iii — 211

L'impatience (cantata), S, b viol, bc, c1715–22; OC iii — 211, 244

Les amants trahis (cantata), S, B, b viol, bc, by 1721; OC iii — 211, 244

Orphée (cantata), S, vn, b viol, bc, by 1 June 1721; OC iii — 211, 244

Le berger fidèle (cantata), S, 2 vn, bc, by 22 Nov 1728, pubd in Rameau: Cantates françoises à voix seule avec simphonie . . . livre premier (Paris, c1729–30); OC iii — 217, 243, 244

Cantate pour le jour de la [fête de] Saint Louis, S, tr, bc, ?c1745, *MS, Pc Rés.18061; facs. (Bias, France [1983]) — 243

Un Bourbon ouvre sa carrière (ariette), Haute-contre, 2 vn, bc, c1751, Pn Vm⁷3620 — 244

Médée (cantata), c1715–22; L'absence (cantata), c1715–22: both lost — 211

Misattrib: La musette (cantata) [by P. de La Garde]; Diane et Actéon (cantata) [by B. de Boismortier]: OC iii

Deuxième concert: La Laborde, G; La Boucon, air gracieux, g; L'agaçante, G; Premier menuet, G; 2e menuet, g

Troisième concert: La Lapoplinière, A; La timide, 1er rondeau gracieux, a; 2e rondeau gracieux, A; 1er tambourin, A; 2e tambourin en rondeau, a — 227

Quatrième concert: La pantomime, loure vive, B♭; L'indiscrette, B♭; La Rameau, B♭

Cinquième concert: Fugue, La Forqueray, d; La Cupis, d; La Marais, D — 251

Not by Rameau: 6 concerts, 3 vn, taille (va), bns, vc, db (MS, *Pn*, 1768); OC ii:

Premier–cinquième concerts: transcrs. of Pieces de clavecin en concerts (Paris, 1741)

Sixième concert: transcrs. of La poule; 1er menuet; 2e menuet; L'enharmonique; L'egiptienne: all from Nouvelles suites de pièces de clavecin (Paris, c1729–30)

## WRITINGS — 278–85

Edition: *Jean-Philippe Rameau: Complete Theoretical Writings*, ed. E. R. Jacobi (Rome, 1967–72) [Jw]

*Traité de l'harmonie réduite à ses principes naturels* (Paris, 1722; Eng. trans., 1737), Eng. trans. P. Gossett (New York, 1971); Jw i — 211, 213, 224, 278, 279, 282

'De la mechanique des doigts sur le clavessin', Pieces de clavessin (1724; pr. with Eng. and Ger. trans. in Jc; facs. in G)

*Nouveau système de musique théorique* (Paris, 1726; Eng. trans. in Chandler, 1975); Jw vi — 34, 214, 217, 224, 279, 281

'Remarques ... sur les différens genres de musique', Nouvelles suites de pieces de clavecin (c1729–30; pr. with Eng. and Ger. trans. in Jc; facs. in G)

'Examen de la conférence sur la musique', Mercure de France (Oct 1729); Jw vi

'Observations sur la méthode d'accompagnement pour le clavecin qui est en usage, et qu'on appelle échele ou règle de l'octave', Mercure de France (Feb 1730); Jw vi

'Plan abrégé d'une méthode nouvelle d'accompagnement pour le clavecin', Mercure de France (March 1730); Jw vi

'Réplique du premier musicien à la réponse du second', Mercure de France (June 1730); Jw vi

'Lettre de M. à M. sur la musique', Mercure de France (Sept 1731); Jw vi

*Dissertation sur les différentes méthodes d'accompagnement pour le clavecin, ou pour l'orgue* (Paris, 1732); Jw v — 214

'Lettre de M. Rameau au R. P. Castel, au sujet de quelques nouvelles réflexions sur la musique', Journal de Trévoux (July 1736); Jw vi

*Génération harmonique, ou Traité de musique théorique et pratique* (Paris, 1737; Eng. trans. in Hayes, 1968); Jw iii — 225–6, 279

'Remarques de M. Rameau sur l'extrait qu'on a donné de son livre intitulé "Génération harmonique" dans le Journal de Trévoux, décembre 1737', Le pour et contre, xiv (1738); Jw vi

*Mémoire où l'on expose les fondements du Système de musique théorique et pratique de M. Rameau* (1749), *MS, Paris, Institut de France; Jw vi

*Démonstration du principe de l'harmonie* [collab. D. Diderot] (Paris, 1750; Eng. trans. in Papakhian, 1973, and Briscoe, 1975); Jw iii — 231–2, 279, 283

*Nouvelles réflexions de M. Rameau sur sa 'Demonstration du principe de l'harmonie'* (Paris, 1752; Eng. trans. in Briscoe, 1975); Jw v

'Lettre de M. Rameau à l'auteur du Mercure', Mercure de France (May 1752); Jw vi

'Réflexions sur la manière de former la voix', Mercure de France (Oct 1752); Jw vi

'Extrait d'une réponse de M. Rameau à M. Euler sur l'identité des octaves', Mercure de France (Dec 1752); Jw iii

*Observations sur notre instinct pour la musique* (Paris, 1754); Jw iii — 34, 234, 235, 284

*Erreurs sur la musique dans l'Encyclopédie* (Paris, 1755); Jw v

*Suite des erreurs sur la musique dans l'Encyclopédie* (Paris, 1756); Jw v

*Prospectus, où l'on propose au public, par voye de souscription, un 'Code de musique pratique', composé de sept méthodes* [collab. F. Arnaud] (Paris, 1757); Jw iv

Réponse de M. Rameau à MM. les éditeurs de l'Encyclopédie sur leur dernier Avertissement (Paris, 1757); Jw v

Nouvelles réflexions sur le principe sonore (1758–9), MS, I-Bc; Jw vi

Code de musique pratique, ou Méthodes pour apprendre la musique … avec de nouvelles réflexions sur le principe sonore [collab. F. Arnaud] (Paris, 1760); Jw iv — 34, 234, 279, 280, 284

Lettre à M. d'Alembert sur ses opinions en musique (Paris, 1760); Jw iv

'Réponse de M. Rameau à la lettre de M. d'Alembert', Mercure de France (April 1761); Jw v

'Source où, vraisemblablement, on a dû puiser la première idée des proportions', Mercure de France (April 1761); Jw v

'Origine des modes et du tempérament'. Mercure de France (June 1761); Jw v

'Suite de la Réponse', Mercure de France (July 1761); Jw v

Origine des sciences, suivie d'une controverse sur le même sujet (Paris, 1762); Jw iv — 284

'Lettre de M*** à M. D**** sur un ouvrage intitulé "l'Origine des sciences"', Mercure de France (April 1762, i); Jw vi

'Seconde lettre de M*** à M*** ou Extrait d'une controverse entre le Géomètre & l'Artiste sur "l'Origine des sciences"', Mercure de France (April 1762, ii); Jw vi

'Observations de M. Rameau sur son ouvrage intitulé, "Origine des sciences"', Mercure de France (June 1762); Jw vi

'Conclusions sur l'origine des sciences', Journal encyclopédique (July 1762); pr. in Lescat, Dijon 1983

'Lettre aux Philosophes', Journal de Trévoux (Aug 1762); Jw vi

Vérités également ignorées et intéressantes tirées du sein de la nature (c1764); MSS: *F-Pn, inc.; S-Smf (rev. version of Vérités interessantes [after Sept 1763]); both ed. in Schneider, 'Rameau: Les vérités' (1985) — 234

MSS attrib. Rameau: L'art de la basse fondamentale par Rameau. Manuscrit en partie inédit (d'après d'Alembert) (between 1737 and 1750), Paris, Institut de France; Leçons de musique (? between 1737 and 1750), CH-Gpu [also attrib. J.-J. Rousseau]

?Lost: Traité de la composition des canons en musique (see Schneider, RMFC, 1985)

For Rameau's letters relating to music theory, see Jw v, vi (indexed in vi, p.lxxi) and Miller (1985); other letters pr. in Mercure de France, May 1752, March 1765, June 1765; Ducharger (1761); Decroix (1776); Brenet (1902/3); La Laurencie (1907); Tiersot (1935); Girdlestone (1957, rev.2/1969); Jacobi (1963); Jw vi

# BIBLIOGRAPHY

### GENERAL

*Walther ML*

J. C. Nemeitz: *Séjour de Paris* (Leiden, 1727)

M. S. de Valhebert: *L'agenda du voyageur, ou Le calendrier des fêtes* (Paris, 1727, 1732, 1736)

T. Rémond de Saint-Mard: *Réflexions sur l'Opéra* (The Hague, 1741/*R*1972)

L. Bollioud-Mermet: *De la corruption du goust dans la musique françoise* (Lyons, 1746/*R*1978)

P.-L. D'Aquin de Château-Lyon: *Lettres sur les hommes célèbres . . . sous le règne de Louis XV* (Paris and Amsterdam, 1752, ii rev. 1753 as *Siècle littéraire de Louis XV, ou Lettres sur les hommes célèbres*)

A. J. Labbet de Morambert and A. Léris, eds.: *Sentiment d'un harmoniphile sur différens ouvrages de musique* (Paris, 1756/*R*1972)

M.-P.-G. de Chabanon: *Eloge de M. Rameau* (Paris, 1764)

'Essai d'Eloge historique de feu M. Rameau', *Mercure de France* (Oct 1764, no.1)

H. Maret: *Eloge historique de M. Rameau* (Dijon, 1766)

C. Palissot de Montenoy: 'Rameau', *La nécrologe des hommes célèbres de France*, i (Paris, 1767)

J.-J. Rousseau: *Dictionnaire de musique* (Paris, 1768/*R*1969)

J.-J.-M. Decroix: *L'ami des arts, ou Justification de plusieurs grands hommes* (Amsterdam and Paris, 1776)

A. P. C. Favart, ed.: *Mémoires et correspondance littéraires, dramatiques et anecdotiques de C. S. Favart* (Paris, 1808/*R*1970)

J.-J.-M. Decroix: 'Rameau', *Biographie universelle, ancienne et moderne*, ed. L. G. Michaud, xxxvii (Paris, 1824), 28

E.-.J.-F. Barbier: *Chronique de la régence et du règne de Louis XV* (Paris, 1857)

C. Collé: *Journal et mémoires . . . sur les hommes de lettres, les ouvrages dramatiques et les événements les plus mémorables du règne de Louis XV, 1748–1772*, ed. H. Bonhomme (Paris, 1868)

M. Tourneux, ed.: *Correspondance littéraire, philosophique et critique par Grimm, Diderot, Raynal, Meister, etc* (Paris, 1877–82)

S. H. Dubuisson: *Mémoires secrets du XVIIIe siècle: lettres du Commissaire Dubuisson au Marquis de Caumont, 1735–1741*, ed. A. Rouxel (Paris, 1882)

J. le Rond d'Alembert: *Oeuvres et correspondance inédites*, ed. C. Henry (Paris, 1887/*R*1967)

E. Boysse, ed.: *L'administration des menus: journal de Papillon de la Ferté . . . (1756–80)* (Paris, 1887)

# Bibliography

M. Brenet: 'La jeunesse de Rameau', *RMI*, ix (1902), 658–93, 860; x (1903), 62, 185

H. Quittard: 'Les années de jeunesse de J.-P. Rameau', *RHCM*, ii (1902), 61, 100, 152, 208

J.-G. Prod'homme: 'La musique à Paris, de 1753 à 1757, d'après un manuscrit de la Bibliothèque de Munich', *SIMG*, vi (1904–5), 568

L. de La Laurencie: 'Quelques documents sur Jean-Philippe Rameau et sa famille', *BSIM*, iii (1907), 541–614

——: *Rameau: biographie critique* (Paris, 1908, 2/1926)

L. Laloy: *Rameau* (Paris, 1908)

L. de La Laurencie: 'Rameau, son gendre et ses descendants', *BSIM*, vii (1911), 12

P.-M. Masson: 'Lullistes et Ramistes, 1733–1752', *L'année musicale*, i (1911), 187

G. Cucuel: *La Pouplinière et la musique de chambre au XVIIIe siècle* (Paris, 1913/R1971)

J. Tiersot: *Lettres de musiciens écrites en français du XVe au XXe siècle, i: 1480 à 1830* (Paris, 1924)

G. Migot: *Jean-Philippe Rameau et le génie de la musique française* (Paris, 1930)

L. Vallas: *Un siècle de musique et de théâtre à Lyon, 1688–1789* (Lyons, 1932/R1971)

P.-M. Masson: 'Une lettre inédite de Rameau', *Mélanges de musicologie offerts à M. Lionel de La Laurencie* (Paris, 1933), 201

J. Tiersot: 'Lettres inédites de Rameau', *ReM*, xvi (1935), 15

P.-M. Masson: 'Une polémique musicale de Claude Rameau en faveur de son frère (1752)', *RdM*, xviii (1937), 39

J. Gardien: 'A propos d'"une polémique musicale de Claude Rameau en faveur de son frère (1752)"', *RdM*, xix (1938), 16

J. Gaudefroy-Demombynes: *Les jugements allemands sur la musique française au XVIIIe siècle* (Paris, 1941)

J. Gardien: *L'orgue et les organistes en Bourgogne et en Franche-Comté au XVIIIe siècle* (Paris, 1943)

——: *Jean-Philippe Rameau* (Paris, 1949)

L. Welter: 'Quelques précisions sur le second séjour de Rameau à Clermont, en qualité d'organiste', *Bulletin historique et scientifique de l'Auvergne*, lxxi (1951), 62

H. Charlier: *Jean-Philippe Rameau* (Lyons, 1955)

C. Girdlestone: *Jean-Philippe Rameau: his Life and Work* (London, 1957, rev. 2/1969)

J. Malignon: *Rameau* (Paris, 1960)

G. de Froidcourt, ed.: *La correspondance générale de Grétry, augmentée de nombreux documents* (Brussels, 1962)

V. Fedorov: 'Les années d'apprentissage de Rameau', *Chigiana*, xxi (1964), 19

*Jean-Philippe Rameau, 1683–1764* (Paris, 1964) [exhibition catalogue pubd by Bibliothèque Nationale, Paris]

R. A. Leigh, ed.: *J.-J. Rousseau: Correspondance complète* (Geneva, 1965–84)

L. Boulay: '"Lettres de Monsieur Clément": références musicales (1748–1750)', *RMFC*, vi (1966), 227

G. Snyders: *Le goût musical en France aux XVIIe et XVIIIe siècles* (Paris, 1968)

T. Besterman, ed.: *Voltaire: Correspondence and Related Documents* (Geneva, 1968–77)

H. Giroux: 'Autour de Jean-Philippe Rameau', *Mémoires de l'académie des sciences, arts et belles-lettres de Dijon*, cxvii (1969), 87

M. Barthélemy: 'L'actualité musicale dans les publications périodiques de Pierre-François Guyot Desfontaines (1735–1746)', *RMFC*, x (1970), 107

N. Dufourcq: *La musique à la cour de Louis XIV et de Louis XV, d'après les mémoires de Sources et Luynes (1681–1758)* (Paris, 1970)

——: '"Nouvelles de la cour et de la ville" (1734–1738) publiées par le comte E. Barthélemy, Paris, 1879: extraits concernant la vie musicale collationnés', *RMFC*, x (1970), 101

M. Benoit: *Musiques de cour: chapelle, chambre, écurie, recueil de documents, 1661–1733* (Paris, 1971)

——: *Versailles et les musiciens du roi: étude institutionnelle et sociale, 1661–1733* (Paris, 1971)

R. Machard: 'Les musiciens en France au temps de Jean-Philippe Rameau d'après les actes du secrétariat de la Maison du Roi', *RMFC*, xi (1971), 7–117

C. Marandet: 'Notes pour servir à l'histoire des orgues et des organistes en Auvergne', *Bulletin historique et scientifique de l'Auvergne*, lxxxv (1971), 81

J. Renwick, ed.: *J. F. Marmontel: Mémoires* (Clermont-Ferrand, 1972)

C. B. Paul: 'Rameau, d'Indy and French Nationalism', *MQ*, lviii (1972), 46

B. Gérard: 'La musique dans les églises de la cité aux XVIIe et XVIIIe siècles, d'après les registres paroissiaux (1611–1733)', *RMFC*, xvi (1976), 153

E. Giuliani: 'Le public de l'Opéra de Paris de 1750 à 1760: mesure et définition', *IRASM*, viii (1977), 159

G. Sadler: 'A Letter from Claude-François Rameau to J. J. M. Decroix', *ML*, lix (1978), 139

# Bibliography

L. Rosow: 'Lallemand and Durand: Two Eighteenth-century Music Copyists at the Paris Opéra', *JAMS*, xxxiii (1980), 142

G. Cowart: *The Origins of Modern Criticism: French and Italian Music 1600–1750* (Ann Arbor, 1981)

G. von Proschwitz, ed.: *Alexis Piron, epistolier: choix de ses lettres* (Gothenburg, 1982)

M.-T. Bouquet-Boyer: 'Rameau et l'esprit de famille', *Jean-Philippe Rameau: Dijon 1983*

A. de Brosses: 'Rameau jugé par deux Bourguignons: le Président de Brosses et Loppin de Gemeaux', *Jean-Philippe Rameau: Dijon 1983*

C. Kintzler: *Jean-Philippe Rameau: splendeur et naufrage de l'esthétique du plaisir à l'age classique* (Paris, 1983)

J. de La Gorce, ed.: *Jean-Philippe Rameau: Dijon 1983*

L. Libin: 'A rediscovered portrayal of Rameau and *Castor et Pollux*', *Early Music*, xi (1983), 510

D. Pistone: 'Rameau à Paris au XIXe siècle', *Jean-Philippe Rameau: Dijon 1983*

R. Savage: 'Rameau's American Dancers', *Early Music*, xi (1983), 441

N. Zaslaw: 'Rameau's Operatic Apprenticeship: the First Fifty Years', *Jean-Philippe Rameau: Dijon 1983*

H. Schneider: 'Rameau et sa famille: nouveaux documents', *RMFC*, xxiii (1985), 94–130

### WORKS: GENERAL

P. Papillon: *Bibliothèque des auteurs de Bourgogne*, ed. P. L. Joly (Dijon, 1742)

F. W. Marpurg: *Der Critische Musicus an der Spree* (Berlin, 1749–50)

E. Lebeau: 'J. J. M. Decroix et sa collection Rameau', *Mélanges d'histoire et d'esthétique musicales offerts à Paul-Marie Masson*, ii (Paris, 1955), 81

C. M. Girdlestone: 'Rameau's Self-borrowings', *ML*, xxxix (1958), 52

J. R. Anthony: *French Baroque Music from Beaujoyeulx to Rameau* (London, 1973, rev. 2/1978, rev. Fr. trans., 1981 as *La musique en France à l'époque baroque*)

C. Massip: 'Rameau et l'édition de ses oeuvres: bref aperçu historique et méthodologique', *Jean-Philippe Rameau: Dijon 1983*

H. Schneider: 'Rameau et la tradition lulliste', *Jean-Philippe Rameau: Dijon 1983*

R. P. Wolf: 'An Eighteenth-Century *Oeuvres complètes* of Rameau', *Jean-Philippe Rameau: Dijon 1983*

N. Zaslaw: 'The New Rameau Edition', *MT*, cxxiv (1983), 28

Rameau

DRAMATIC WORKS

F. and C. Parfaict: *Histoire de l'Académie royale de musique depuis son établissement jusqu'à présent* (MS, 1741, *F-Pn* nouv. acq. fr.6532) [1835 copy with annotations by Beffara, *Pn* fr.12.355]

——: *Mémoires pour servir à l'histoire des spectacles de la Foire, par un acteur forain* (Paris, 1743)

J.-B. Durey de Noinville: *Histoire du Théâtre de l'Académie royale de musique en France* (Paris, 1753, rev. 2/1757/*R*1972)

L. de Cahusac: *La danse ancienne et moderne, ou Traité historique de la danse* (The Hague, 1754/*R*1971)

A. de Léris: *Dictionnaire portatif des théâtres* (Paris, 1754, 2/1763)

*Mémoires pour servir à l'histoire de l'Académie royale de musique vulgairement l'Opéra depuis son établissement en 1669 jusqu'en l'année 1758* (MS Amelot, *F-Po* Rés.516)

L.-C. Lavallière: *Ballets, opéra, et autres ouvrages lyriques, par ordre chronologique depuis leur origine* (Paris, 1760/*R*1967)

J. G. Noverre: *Lettres sur la danse, et sur les ballets* (Lyons and Stuttgart, 1760/*R*1967, 2/1783; Eng. trans., 1930/*R*1966, rev. 2/1951)

L.-F. Beffara: *Dictionnaire de l'Académie royale de musique* (autograph MS, 1783–4, *F-Po* Rés. 602)

E. Dacier: 'L'Opéra au XVIIIe siècle: les premières représentations du "Dardanus" de Rameau, Novembre-Décembre 1739', *La revue musicale*, iii (1903), 163

R. Rolland: 'Un vaudeville de Rameau', *Mercure musical*, i (1905), 19

G. Cucuel: 'La question des clarinettes dans l'instrumentation du XVIIIe siècle', *ZIMG*, xii (1910–11), 280

L. de La Laurencie: 'Rameau et les clarinettes', *BSIM*, ix (1913), 27

J.-G. Prod'homme: 'Notes d'archives concernant l'emploi des clarinettes en 1763', *RdM*, i/5 (1919), 192

P.-M. Masson: 'Le "ballet heroïque" ', *ReM*, ix/8 (1928), 132

——: *L'opéra de Rameau* (Paris, 1930/*R*1972)

A. Gastoué: 'Les notes inédites du marquis de Paulmy sur les oeuvres lyriques françaises (1655–1775)', *RdM*, xxii/1 (1943), 1

C. D. Brenner: *A Bibliographical List of Plays in the French Language, 1700–1789* (Berkeley, 1947/*R*1979 with Foreword and index by M. A. Keller and N. Zaslaw)

H. Leclerc: ' "Les Indes galantes" (1735–1952): les sources de l'opéra-ballet, l'exotisme orientalisant, les conditions matérielles du spectacle, fortune des "Indes galantes" ', *Revue d'histoire du théâtre*, v (1953), 259

P.-M. Masson: 'Les deux versions du "Dardanus" de Rameau', *AcM*, xxvi (1954), 36

# Bibliography

E. G. Ahnell: *The Concept of Tonality in the Operas of Jean-Philippe Rameau* (diss., U. of Illinois, 1957)

D. J. Grout: 'The *Opéra comique* and the *Théâtre italien* from 1715 to 1762', *Miscelanéa en homenaje a Monseñor Higinio Anglés* (Barcelona, 1958–61), i, 369

M. Whaples: *Exoticism in Dramatic Music, 1660–1800* (diss., Indiana State U., 1958)

N. Demuth: *French Opera: its Development to the Revolution* (Horsham, Sussex, 1963)

J. R. Anthony: 'The French Opéra-ballet in the Early 18th Century: Problems of Definition and Classification', *JAMS*, xviii (1965), 197

C. R. Barnes: *The 'Théâtre de la Foire' (Paris, 1697–1762): its Music and Composers* (diss., U. of Southern California, 1965)

C. Cudworth: 'Richard, Viscount Fitzwilliam, and the French Baroque Music in the Fitzwilliam Museum, Cambridge', *FAM*, xiii (1966), 27

C. Girdlestone: 'Voltaire, Rameau and "Samson" ', *RMFC*, vi (1966), 133

J. Malignon: 'Zoroastre et Sarastro', *RMFC*, vi (1966), 145

R. L. de Voyer de Paulmy, Marquis d'Argenson: 'Notices sur les oeuvres de théâtre', *Studies on Voltaire and the Eighteenth Century*, xlii-xliii, ed. H. Lagrave (1966)

H. C. Wolff: 'Rameaus "Les Indes galantes" als musik-ethnologische Quelle', *Jahrbuch für musikalische Volks- und Völkerkunde*, iii (1967), 105

G. Seefried: *Die 'Airs de danse' in den Bühnenwerken von Jean-Philippe Rameau* (Wiesbaden, 1969)

W. H. Kaehler: *The Operatic Repertoire of Madame de Pompadour's Théâtre des petits cabinets (1747–1753)* (diss., U. of Michigan, 1971)

M. Térey-Smith: *Jean-Philippe Rameau: 'Abaris ou Les Boréades'. a Critical Edition* (diss., U. of Rochester, Eastman School of Music, 1971)

C. Girdlestone: *La tragédie en musique (1673–1750) considerée comme genre littéraire* (Geneva, 1972)

H. Lagrave: *Le théâtre et le public à Paris de 1715 à 1750* (Paris, 1972)

G. E. Barksdale: *The Chorus in French Baroque Opera* (diss., U. of Utah, 1973)

[D. Diderot, attrib.]: 'Réponse à l'auteur de la "Lettre sur les opéras de Phaéton et d'Hippolyte", 1743', *Studies on Voltaire and the Eighteenth Century*, cxix, ed. J. T. de Booy (1974), 341–96

301

G. Sadler: 'Rameau, Piron and the Parisian Fair Theatres', *Soundings*, iv (1974), 13

R. Cotte: *La musique maçonnique et ses musiciens* (thesis, U. of Paris IV, 1975)

M. Cyr: *Rameau's 'Les fêtes d'Hébé'* (diss., U. of California, Berkeley, 1975)

G. Sadler: 'Rameau's last opera: *Abaris, ou Les Boréades*', *MT*, cxvi (1975), 327

R. P. Wolf: *Jean-Philippe Rameau's comédie lyrique 'Les Paladins' (1760): a Critical Edition and Study* (diss., Yale U., 1977)

M. Cyr: 'Rameau e Traetta', *NRMI*, xii (1978), 166

H. C. Wolff: 'Voltaire und die Oper', *Mf*, xxx (1978), 257

T. Green: 'La genèse d'une ariette de Rameau', *Les sources en musicologie: Orléans La Source 1979*, 151

G. Sadler: 'Rameau's "Zoroastre": the 1756 Reworking', *MT*, cxx (1979), 301

R. S. Ridgway: 'Voltaire's Operas', *Studies on Voltaire and the Eighteenth Century*, clxxxix (1980), 119–51

G. Sadler: '*Naïs*, Rameau's "Opéra pour la paix" ', *MT*, cxxi (1980), 431

P. F. Rice: *The Fontainebleau Operas of Jean-Philippe Rameau: a Critical Study* (diss., U. of Victoria, Canada, 1981)

G. Sadler: 'Rameau and the Orchestra', *PRMA*, cviii (1981–2), 47

T. Green: ' "Chants d'allégresse": le travail contrapuntique de Rameau', *IMSCR, xiii: Strasbourg 1982*

N. Anderson: 'Rameau's *Platée*: Burlesque or Grotesque?' *Early Music*, xi (1983), 505

S. Bouissou: ' "Les Boréades" de J.-Ph. Rameau: un passé retrouvé', *RdM*, lxix (1983), 157

M.-F. Christout: 'Quelques interprètes de la danse dans l'Opéra de Rameau', *Jean-Philippe Rameau: Dijon 1983*

R. Fajon: 'Le préramisme dans le répertoire de l'Opéra', *Jean-Philippe Rameau: Dijon 1983*

T. Green: 'Les fragments d'opéras dans la partition autographe de Zéphyre', *Jean-Philippe Rameau: Dijon 1983*

N. Lecomte: 'Les divertissements exotiques dans les opéras de Rameau', *Jean-Philippe Rameau: Dijon 1983*

B. Lespinard: 'De l'adaptation des airs de danse aux situations dramatiques dans les opéras de Rameau', *Jean-Philippe Rameau: Dijon 1983*

C. Massip and R. P. Wolf: 'Rameau Catalogue Project', *French Baroque Music: a Newsletter*, no.1 (1983), 6; no.2 (1984), 2

F. Moreau: 'Les poètes de Rameau', *Jean-Philippe Rameau: Dijon 1983*

M. Noiray: '*Hippolyte et Aricie* et *Castor et Pollux* à l'Opéra-

# Bibliography

comique', *Jean-Philippe Rameau: Dijon 1983*

L. Rosow: 'French Baroque Recitative as an expression of tragic declamation', *Early Music*, xi (1983), 468

G. Sadler: 'Rameau, Pellegrin and the Opéra: the Revisions of "Hippolyte et Aricie" during its First Season', *MT*, cxxiv (1983), 533

——: 'The Paris Opéra Dancers in Rameau's Day: a Little-known Inventory of 1738', *Jean-Philippe Rameau: Dijon 1983*

L. Sawkins: 'New Sources for Rameau's *Pigmalion* and other works', *Early Music*, xi (1983), 490

R. P. Wolf: 'Rameau's *Les Paladins*: from Autograph to Production', *Early Music*, xi (1983), 497

——: 'Jean-Philippe Rameau: *Les Paladins*: Prospectus for an edition', *French Baroque Music: a Newsletter*, no.1 (1983), 11

S. Bouissou: '*Les surprises de l'Amour* de Jean-Philippe Rameau: Rapport pour un projet d'édition', *French Baroque Music: a Newsletter*, no.2 (1984), 8

G. Sadler: *The Operas of Jean-Philippe Rameau* (in preparation)

### OTHER WORKS

P.-M. Masson: 'Deux chansons bachiques de Rameau', *BSIM*, vi (1910), 298

L. de La Laurencie: *L'école française de violon de Lully à Viotti* (Paris, 1922–4/*R*1971)

K. Dale: 'The Keyboard Music of Rameau', *MMR*, lxxvi (1946), 127

Z. Klitenic: *The Clavecin Works of Jean-Philippe Rameau* (diss., U. of Pennsylvania, 1955)

D. Fuller: *Eighteenth-century French Harpsichord Music* (diss., Harvard U., 1965)

——: 'Accompanied Keyboard Music', *MQ*, lx (1974), 222

D. Tunley: *The Eighteenth-century French Cantata* (London, 1974)

M. Cyr: ' "Inclina Domine": a Marian Motet wrongly attributed to Rameau', *ML*, lviii (1977), 318

——: 'A New Rameau Cantata', *MT*, cxx (1979), 907

D. Ferran: 'La technique de clavier en France entre 1650 et 1750', *Orgues méridionales*, vi–vii (1979), 33

K. Gilbert, ed.: preface to *J.-P. Rameau: Pièces de clavecin* (Paris, 1979)

G. Sadler: 'Rameau's Harpischord Transcriptions from "Les Indes galantes" ', *Early Music*, vii (1979), 18

J. A. Sadie: *The Bass Viol in French Baroque Chamber Music* (Ann Arbor, 1980)

M. Cyr: 'Towards a Chronology of Rameau's Cantatas', *MT*, cxxiv (1983), 539

J. Duron: 'Le grand motet: Rameau face à ses contemporains', *Jean-Philippe Rameau: Dijon 1983*

D. Fuller: 'Les petits marteaux de M. Rameau', *Early Music*, xi (1983), 516

J. R. Mongrédien, ed.: *Catalogue thématique des sources du grand motet français (1663–1792)* (Munich, 1984)

PERFORMING PRACTICE AND MISE EN SCENE

A. Tessier: 'Les habits d'opéra au XVIIIe siècle: Louis Boquet, dessinateur et inspecteur général des Menus Plaisirs', *Revue de l'art*, xlix (1926), 15, 89, 173

A. M. Nagler: 'Maschinen und Maschinisten der Rameau-Ära', *Maske und Kothurn*, ii (1957), 128

A. Boll: 'L'oeuvre théâtrale de Rameau: sa mise en scène', *ReM* (1964), no.260, p.13

F. Lesure: *L'opéra classique français: XVIIe et XVIIIe siècles* (Geneva, 1972)

A. M. Nagler: 'J. N. Servandonis und F. Bouchers Wirken an der Pariser Oper', *Bühnenformen-Bühnenräume-Bühnendekorationen . . .: Herbert A. Frenzel zum 65. Geburtstag* (Berlin, 1974), 64

N. Zaslaw: 'The Enigma of the Haute-Contre', *MT*, cxv (1974), 939

M. Cyr: 'On Performing 18th-century "Haute-contre" Roles', *MT*, cxviii (1977), 291

R. P. Wolf: 'Metrical Relationships in French Recitative of the Seventeenth and Eighteenth Centuries', *RMFC*, xviii (1978), 29

M. Cyr: 'Eighteenth-century French and Italian Singing: Rameau's Writing for the Voice', *ML*, lxi (1980), 318

G. Sadler: 'The Role of the Keyboard Continuo in French Opera, 1673–1776', *Early Music*, viii (1980), 148

M. Cyr: ' "Basses" and "Basse continue" in the Orchestra of the Paris Opéra, 1700–1764', *Early Music*, x (1982), 155

T. G. Boucher: 'Rameau et les théâtres de la Cour (1745–1764)', *Jean-Philippe Rameau: Dijon 1983*

M. Cyr: 'Performing Rameau's cantatas', *Early Music*, xi (1983), 480

J. de La Gorce: 'Scénographie des opéras de Rameau représentés à Paris du vivant du compositeur', *Rameau: le coloris instrumental* (Paris, 1983), 53 [exhibition catalogue, Musée instrumental, Conservatoire national supérieur de musique]

——: 'Twenty Set Models for the Paris Opéra in the time of Rameau', *Early Music*, xi (1983), 429

——: 'Décors et machines à l'Opéra de Paris au temps de Rameau: inventaire (1748)', *RMFC*, xxi (1983), 145

N. McGegan and G. Spagnoli: 'Singing Style at the Opéra in the Rameau Period', *Jean-Philippe Rameau: Dijon 1983*

## Bibliography

S. Milliot: 'Rameau et l'orchestre de l'Académie royale de musique, d'après les exemplaires des répétitions de ses opéras', *Jean-Philippe Rameau: Dijon 1983*

G. Sadler: 'Rameau's Singers and Players at the Paris Opéra: a little-known Inventory of 1738', *Early Music*, xi (1983), 453

L. Sawkins: 'Nouvelles sources inédites de trois oeuvres de Rameau: leur signification pour l'instrumentation et l'interpretation du chant', *Jean-Philippe Rameau: Dijon 1983*

N. Zaslaw: 'At the Paris Opéra in 1747', *Early Music*, xi (1983), 515

### THEORY

*BurneyH*

C. Batteux: *Les beaux-arts réduit à un même principe* (Paris, 1746/*R*1970, 3/1773/*R*1971)

C.-E. Briseux: *Traité du beau essentiel dans les arts . . . avec un traité des proportions harmoniques* (Paris, 1752)

P. Estève: *Nouvelle découverte du principe de l'harmonie, avec un examen de ce que M. Rameau a publié sous le titre de Démonstration de ce principe* (Paris, 1751, 2/1752)

J. le R. D'Alembert: *Elémens de musique théorique et pratique, suivant les principes de M. Rameau* (Paris, 1752/*R*1966, 2/1762, 3/1772; Ger. trans. by F. W. Marpurg as *Systematische Einleitung in die musikalische Setzkunst*, 1757)

J.-A. Serre: *Essais sur les principes de l'harmonie* (Paris, 1753/*R*1967)

J.-L. de Béthisy: *Exposition de la théorie et de la pratique de la musique, suivant les nouvelles découvertes* (Paris, 1754, rev. 2/1764/*R*1972)

F. W. Marpurg: *Historisch-kritische Beyträge zur Aufnahme der Musik* (Berlin, 1754–78/*R*1970)

Ducharger: *Réflexions sur divers ouvrages de M. Rameau* (Rennes, 1761)

J.-A. Serre: *Observations sur les principes de l'harmonie* (Geneva, 1763/*R* 1967) [Ger. trans. and commentary by J. A. Hiller: *Wöchentliche Nachrichten* (Leipzig, 1767)]

P.-J. Roussier: *Traité des accords, et de leur succession selon le système de la basse-fondamentale* (Paris, 1764/*R*1972)

J. A. Scheibe: *Über die musikalische Composition*, i (Leipzig, 1773) [no other parts pubd]

F. W. Marpurg: *Versuch über die musikalische Temperatur, nebst einem Anhang über den Rameau- und Kirnbergerschen Grundbass* (Breslau, 1776/*R*)

J.-B. de La Borde: *Essai sur la musique ancienne et moderne* (Paris, 1780/*R*1972)

W. Jones: *A Treatise on the Art of Music* (Colchester, 1784, 2/1827)

M. P. King: *A General Treatise on Music* (London, 1800, rev. 2/1801)

F.-J. Fétis: *Esquisse de l'histoire de l'harmonie* (Paris, 1840)

H. Goldschmidt: *Die Musikästhetik des 18. Jahrhunderts* (Zurich and Leipzig, 1915), 107

M. Shirlaw: *The Theory of Harmony ... with an Examination of the Chief Systems of Harmony from Rameau to the Present Day* (London, 1917, Illinois, 2/1955)

J. Tiersot: 'Lettres inédites de Rameau', *ReM*, xvi (1935), 15

A. R. Oliver: *The Encyclopedists as Critics of Music* (New York, 1947)

J. Thomas: 'Diderot, les Encyclopédistes et le grand Rameau', *Revue de synthèse*, xxviii (1951), 46

A. Schaeffner: 'L'orgue de barbarie de Rameau', *Mélanges d'histoire et d'esthétique musicales offerts à Paul-Marie Masson* (Paris, 1955), 135

E. R. Jacobi: *Die Entwicklung der Musiktheorie in England nach der Zeit von Jean-Philippe Rameau* (Strasbourg, 1957, 2/1971)

——: 'Harmonic Theory in England after the Time of Rameau', *JMT*, i (1957), 126

R. Suaudeau: *Le premier système harmonique, dit clermontois, de Jean-Philippe Rameau* (Clermont-Ferrand, 1958)

J. Doolittle: 'A Would-be "Philosophe": Jean-Philippe Rameau', *Publications of the Modern Language Association of America*, lxxiv (1959), 233

J. Ferris: 'The Evolution of Rameau's Harmonic Theories', *JMT*, iii (1959), 231

M. Shirlaw: 'The Science of Harmony: the Harmonic Generation of Chords', *JMT*, iv (1960), 1

M. M. Keane: *The Theoretical Writings of Jean-Philippe Rameau* (diss., Catholic U. of America, Washington, DC, 1961)

E. R. Jacobi: 'Nouvelles lettres inédites de Jean-Philippe Rameau', *RMFC*, iii (1963), 145

H. Pischner: *Die Harmonielehre Jean-Philippe Rameaus, ihre historischen Voraussetzungen und ihre Auswirkungen im französischen, italienischen und deutschen musiktheoretischen Schrifttum des 18. Jahrhunderts: ein Beitrag zur Geschichte des musikalischen Denkens* (Leipzig, 1963)

J. Chailley: 'Rameau et la théorie musicale', *ReM* (1964), no.260, pp.65–96

E. Leipp: 'Critique des fondements de la théorie de Jean-Philippe Rameau', *ReM* (1964), no.260, p.97

A. Machabey: 'Jean-Philippe Rameau et le tempérament égal ("Nouveau système de musique théorique", 1726)', *ReM* (1964), no.260, p.113

306

# Bibliography

L. Gossman: 'Time and History in Rousseau', *Studies on Voltaire and the Eighteenth Century*, xxx, ed. T. Besterman (1964), 311

E. R. Jacobi: 'Rameau and Padre Martini: New Letters and Documents', *MQ*, l (1964), 452

——: ' "Vérités intéressantes": le dernier manuscrit de Jean-Philippe Rameau', *RdM*, l (1964), 76–109

J. W. Krehbiel: *Harmonic Principles of Jean-Philippe Rameau and his Contemporaries* (diss., Indiana U., 1964)

M.-G. Moreau: 'Jean-Philippe Rameau et la pédagogie', *ReM* (1964), no.260, p.47

R. A. Leigh: 'Rousseau et Rameau', *Correspondance de Jean-Jacques Rousseau*, ii (Geneva, 1965), 338

C. B. Paul: *Rameau's Musical Theories and the Age of Reason* (diss., U. of California, Berkeley, 1966)

D. Hayes: *Rameau's Theory of Harmonic Generation: an Annotated Translation and Commentary of 'Génération harmonique' by Jean-Philippe Rameau* (diss., Stanford U., 1968)

B. L. Green: *The Harmonic Series from Mersenne to Rameau: an Historical Study of Circumstances leading to its Recognition and Application to Music* (diss., Ohio State U., 1969)

C. B. Paul: 'Jean-Philippe Rameau (1683–1764), the Musician as "Philosophe" ', *Proceedings of the American Philosophical Society*, cxiv (1970), 140

P. Gossett: Preface to *Jean-Philippe Rameau: Treatise on Harmony* (New York, 1971)

C. B. Paul: 'Music and Ideology: Rameau, Rousseau and 1789', *Journal of the History of Ideas*, xxxii (1971), 395

B. Billeter: 'Der Naturbegriff bei Jean-Philippe Rameau: aus Anlass der soeben erschienenen Gesamtausgabe der theoretischen Schriften', *Neue Zürcher Zeitung*, cxciv (1973), 51

A. R. Papakhian: *Jean-Philippe Rameau's 'Démonstration du principe de l'harmonie' (1750) and Pierre Estève's 'Nouvelle découverte du principe de l'harmonie' (1752): a Translation* (diss., Western Michigan U., Kalamazoo, 1973)

E. C. Verba: 'The Development of Rameau's Thoughts on Modulation and Chromatics', *JAMS*, xxvi (1973), 69

D. Hayes: 'Rameau's "Nouvelle Méthode" ', *JAMS*, xxvii (1974), 61

R. Wokler: 'Rameau, Rousseau, and the "Essai sur l'origine des langues" ', *Studies on Voltaire and the Eighteenth Century*, cxvii, ed. T. Besterman (1974), 179

R. L. Briscoe: *Rameau's 'Démonstration du principe de l'harmonie' and 'Nouvelles réflexions de M. Rameau sur sa démonstration du principe de l'harmonie': an Annotated Translation of Two Treatises by Jean-Philippe Rameau* (diss., Indiana U., 1975)

B. G. Chandler: *Rameau's 'Nouveau système de musique théorique': an Annotated Translation with Commentary* (diss., Indiana U., 1975)

S. Baud-Bovy: 'Rameau, Voltaire et Rousseau', *Revue musicale suisse*, cxvi (1976), 152

C. P. Grant: *Kirnberger versus Rameau: Toward a New Approach to Comparative Theory* (diss., U. of Cincinnati, 1976)

——: 'The Real Relationship between Kirnberger's and Rameau's Concept of the Fundamental Bass', *JMT*, xxi (1977), 324

D. Lewin: 'Two Interesting Passages in Rameau's "Traité de l'harmonie" ', *In Theory Only*, iv/3 (1978), 3

E. C. Verba: 'Rameau's Views on Modulation and their Background in French Theory', *JAMS*, xxxi (1978), 467

A. Cohen and L. E. Miller: *Music in the Paris Academy of Sciences, 1666–1793* (Detroit, 1979)

E. C. Verba: *A Hierarchic Interpretation of the Theories and Music of Jean-Philippe Rameau* (diss., U. of Chicago, 1979)

J. W. Bernard: 'The Principle and the Elements: Rameau's Controversy with D'Alembert', *JMT*, xxiv (1980), 37

G. H. Anderson: *Musical Terminology in J.-P. Rameau's 'Traité de l'harmonie': a Study and Glossary based on an Index* (diss., U. of Iowa, 1981)

W. E. Caplin: *Theories of Harmonic-Metric Relationships from Rameau to Riemann* (diss., U. of Chicago, 1981)

C. Kintzler: 'Rameau et Voltaire: les enjeux théoriques d'une collaboration orageuse', *RdM*, lxvii (1981), 139

C. Berger: 'Ein "Tableau" des "Principe de l'harmonie": *Pygmalion* von Jean-Philippe Rameau', *Jean-Philippe Rameau: Dijon 1983*

J. Chailley: 'Pour une lecture critique du premier chapitre de la *Génération harmonique*', *Jean-Philippe Rameau: Dijon 1983*

A.-M. Chouillet: 'Présupposés, contours et prolongements de la polémique autour des écrits théoriques de Jean-Philippe Rameau', *Jean-Philippe Rameau: Dijon 1983*

M.-E. Duchez: 'Connaissance scientifique et représentation de la musique: valeur épistémologique de la théorie ramiste de la basse fondamentale', *Jean-Philippe Rameau: Dijon 1983*

C. Kintzler: 'Rameau: le sujet de la science et le sujet de l'art à l'âge classique', *Jean-Philippe Rameau: Dijon 1983*

P. Lescat: '*Conclusions sur l'origine des sciences*, un texte méconnu de Jean-Philippe Rameau', *Jean-Philippe Rameau: Dijon 1983*

L. E. Miller: 'Rameau and the Royal Society of London: "New" Letters and Documents', *ML*, lxvi (1985), 19

H. Schneider: *Jean-Philippe Rameau, 'Les vérités intéressantes': kommentierte Konkordanzedition* (Wiesbaden, 1985)

# Index

# Index

# Index

# Index